PASOLD PUBLICATIONS

General Editor: K. G. PONTING

VOLUME 1

A PRACTICAL TREATISE ON DYING

By William Partridge

Originally published in 1823

This edition edited by K. G. Ponting (1973)

VOLUME 2

EMPLOYER AND EMPLOYED

Ford, Ayrton & Co. Ltd, Silk Spinners

By Elizabeth R. and John H. P. Pafford

VOLUME 3

THE WEST RIDING WOOL TEXTILE INDUSTRY

A Catalogue of Business Records from the Seventeenth to the Twentieth Century

By Patricia Hudson

VOLUME 4

THE WEST RIDING WOOL TEXTILE INDUSTRY 1770–1835

A Study of Fixed Capital Formation

By D. T. Jenkins

VOLUME 5

WILTSHIRE AND SOMERSET WOOLLEN MILLS

By K. H. Rogers

VOLUME 6

THE INDUSTRIALIZATION OF A CENTRAL EUROPEAN CITY

Brno and the Fine Woollen Industry in the 18th Century

By Herman Freudenberger

The Industrialization of a Central European City

Brno and the Fine Woollen Industry in the 18th Century

By Herman Freudenberger

PASOLD RESEARCH FUND LTD
Edington, Wiltshire
1977

ISBN 0 903859 07 6

PRINTED IN ENGLAND BY W. S. MANEY AND SON LTD HUDSON ROAD LEEDS LS9 7DL

TO

PAULETTE

CONTENTS

PREFACE

Few portions of a book give an author more pleasure to write than the preface, which provides him with a rare opportunity to acknowledge some of the debts accumulated in the formation of his ideas. For me this task has been saddened as a result of the recent death of Professor Otakar Odlozilik under whose auspices this study began many years ago in its original form as a dissertation toward the Ph.D. degree at Columbia University. While not specializing in economic history, Odlozilik imparted to me a sympathetic understanding of the history of the Habsburg Monarchy and a profound respect for the historical method of research. His death in the summer of 1973 has robbed the historical community of a modest and courageous scholar.

No debt is more pleasant to acknowledge than that which I owe to Professor David S. Landes from whom I learned the basic concepts of economic history. At a time when he himself was over-burdened with numerous obligations he gave generously of his time and energy to help me prepare an acceptable dissertation. Even though this activity occurred many years ago, it is always amazing to me how many ideas that were formed then still adhere in an almost pristine fashion.

In my further development I was fortunate indeed to encounter the ideas and concepts of Dr Fritz Redlich whose friendship and continuing intellectual stimulation I have enjoyed now for well over a decade. It was in collaboration with him that one of the concepts on which this study depends was worked out. The idea of the protofactory as an institutional form preceding the more sophisticated structure of the modern factory had its inception in discussions that culminated in a joint-article on the subject.[1] He has always been a sympathetic and constructive as well as a severely honest critic of my efforts.

From all three scholars and friends I have gained greatly. The study is, however, dedicated to my wife, who has suffered the trials and tribulations so common in the marital relationships within the scholarly community that their repetition borders on triteness. She has tried, I fear with only indifferent success, to induce me to use the English language so that communication becomes clear and succinct.

[1] H. Freudenberger and F. Redlich, 'The Industrial Development of Europe: Reality, Symbols, Images,' *Kyklos*, XVII (1964), 372–403.

Many others have contributed to this effort. In particular my good friends Professors Emmet Larkin and Solomon Wank have aided in the formulation of ideas and their articulation. Professor Radomir Luza has gone well beyond the obligation of friendship and subjected the entire manuscript to a thorough, critical reading. Lastly in this incomplete listing of my intellectual creditors there is Professor Gerhard Mensch, who has found in this case-study of an enterprise that resulted in the industrialization of a city a source for a reconceptualization of historical processes, an exercise that has proved of mutual benefit.

My collection of the source material began in 1953 in Vienna while on a Fulbright grant and the present study was completed twenty years later in the same city and under the same auspices. My earlier stay was made immeasurably pleasant by the kindness of Univ.-Prof. Dr Erna Patzelt in whose seminar for cultural and economic history at the University of Vienna I spent many pleasant hours and under whose direction I learned a deeper appreciation of Austrian history.

The raw material for the study is located in the Austrian and Czechoslovak state archives. To the officials of these archives I owe an unpayable debt. Above all, it was in the Hofkammerarchiv, which during much of the period of my research was under the direction of Hofrat Univ.-Prof. Dr Hanns Leo Mikoletzky, that I found a warm and co-operative reception. Similarly, my gratitude for the help I have received from the State Archives and the Municipal Archives in Brno is very great.

The study was aided financially by grants from the Fulbright Program, the American Philosophical Society, and Institute for International Education, the Inter-University Committee on Travel Grants, the ACLS-SSRC Joint Committee on East European Studies, the Graduate School of Business Administration of Harvard University and Tulane University Council on Research.

The Pasold Research Fund has kindly undertaken the publication of this study. I am deeply grateful to Mr Kenneth Ponting, the Fund's Research Director, for helping to make the publication possible as well as for his thorough reading of the manuscript. At the same time I wish to thank Mr Negley Harte for his painstaking editorial effort in order to strengthen both the stylistic and substantive elements of the book. Lastly, I wish to express my gratitude to Mrs Theresa Bonvillain for having typed several versions of this study.

ABBREVIATIONS

fl.	— Gulden
HKA	— Hofkammerarchiv
I.Ö.	— Innerösterreich
kr.	— Kreutzer
N.Ö.	— Niederösterreich
SAB	— státní archiv v Brné
SUA	— státní ústřední archiv

NOTE ON TERMINOLOGY AND MEASURES

Several terms that are used quite frequently throughout this study deserve some explanation. They may seem somewhat strange. In general, they conform with usage in Central Europe and are direct translations from the German of the eighteenth century. One of these terms is 'Hereditary Lands' (*Erbländer*), employed by eighteenth-century Habsburg officials to include Bohemia, Moravia, Silesia, and the Austrian lands, though strictly speaking, only the Austrian lands fall into this category. Another phrase to be found frequently in the ensuing pages is 'fine cloth' (*feines Tuch*) — a woollen cloth made of finely spun yarn and using Segovia wool or wool of equivalent quality. The word 'corporation' is here used as a general term for various organizations that usually possessed a government charter entitling them to prescribed privileges and rights and allowing them, like medieval corporations, to claim an autonomous position. Craft guilds, chartered merchant groups, town municipalities, and the Jewish communities of Bohemia and of Moravia are examples of corporate bodies in the semi-medieval environment of the Habsburg Monarchy.

Concerning the names of towns, the following rule is observed: the present-day spelling of the names as indicated in a geographical gazetteer is adopted wherever possible, but the name as found in the documents is appended in parenthesis when the name is first used.

The following weights and measures were used. The money values are the standard ones of the second half of the eighteenth century.

(a) MONEY

1 fl.	=	60 kr. (Kreutzer) or 1/2 Reichsthaler
1 kr. (Kreutzer)	=	4 Pfennig
1 fl. (Liège)	=	20 Stüber or sous
1 sou (Liège)	=	1.5 kr. (Austrian)
1 Reichsthaler	=	120 Gröschel or 90 Kreutzer in Breslau

(b) CLOTH

1 Brabant ell	=	about 69 cm. or 9/10 Viennese ell
1 Schmitz	=	4 ells
1 Stern Kött	=	1 skein of warp
1 Wiener Fuss	=	31.602 cm.
1 Strähn	=	1 skein

(c) DISTANCE

1 Austrian sq. mile	=	22.238 English sq. miles
1 German/Austrian mile	=	ca. 7.5 km. or 4.7 English miles
1 Post (Post Charte)	=	2 German miles = 15 km.
1 Klafter	=	6 Fuss = 189.612 cm.

SYNOPTIC TABLE OF THE HISTORY OF THE BRNO FINE-CLOTH FACTORY

Year	Leading Personalities; Management	Number of Looms	Labour Force
1751 (Kladruby)	Toussaint, representing Emperor; Bailoux	10 (Maximum during period)	*c.* 200 (Maximum during period)
1764 (Brno)	Moravian Loan Bank (Dobruška, Heller, Hönig, et al.)	3	
1766		5	68
1767	Köffiller; Delimont, Superintendent	12	
1768	Köffiller and Brno cloth merchants, Pachner, Steyrer, Stimmer, Weber, and Progini; Pachner, Managing Director	18	
1769	Delimont dismissed; Jean Hermann, new superintendent	24	
1770	Stimmer, Weber & Progini left firm on a/c personal bankruptcy		
1772	Seitter, 'associate' & managing director; Garttner, new partner	36	
1773		33 large 7 small	721
1777	Pachner & Stimmer no longer with firm on a/c 'financial inability'; Garttner probably left, too.	32 large in good condition	686
1780	Schweickhart, new partner	45	756
1781		61 large 7 small	1,000
1785	Marvancy, new partner		
1788		101 large 18 small	2,000
1789	Bankruptcy of firm; Köffiller & Schweickhart the sole remaining partners		

THE SUCCESSIVE SYSTEMS OF ORGANIZATION OF THE FINE-CLOTH FACTORY

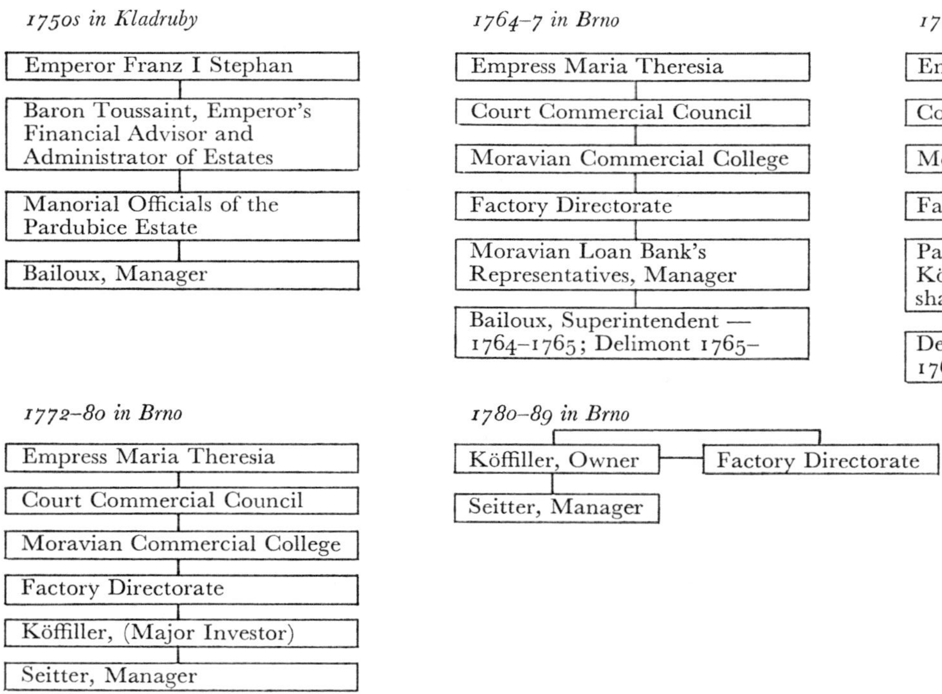

Chapter I

INTRODUCTION

Brno (Brünn) today is Czechoslovakia's second largest city and one of its most important industrial centres. With a long tradition dating back to the fourteenth century as a commercial entrepot and a political meeting place for the princes and nobility of Moravia, Brno began its rise to industrial prominence in the middle of the eighteenth century. At the beginning at least this rise was accomplished with the massive support of the central government of the Habsburg Monarchy, which at the time was primarily concerned with the external security of the country following the disastrous War of the Austrian Succession in the 1740s. To acquire the necessary resources for this purpose and to provide a sounder foundation for the great power pretensions of the Monarchy the country had to be made more prosperous. In the view of Maria Theresia, the ruler, commerce and industry provided the only means to make her lands prosperous.[1]

Brno's Achievement

One of the major beneficiaries of this policy turned out to be the city of Brno and its environs. An important reason for this accomplishment was that the ground had been well prepared in Brno over a period of about a century for this type of modernization effort. Specific events occurred that when pieced together in retrospect reflect a continuing interest in or at least a tolerance for social change in that city. Viewed through the prism of an oustanding event from which can be directly traced the forward momentum of the Brno region, the previous hundred years can be seen as a gestation period in which outside influences successfully intermingled with local movements to provide the foundations of a new era.

The outstanding event was the establishment of the so-called Brno Fine-Cloth Factory in 1764. It proved to be the main stem from which the textile industry grew. If one wished to draw a 'family tree' for Brno's industry, one would find that the original enterprise was beginning to produce shoots in the 1770s, most of them too weak to

[1] Karl Pribram, *Geschichte der österreichischen Gewerbepolitik von 1740 bis 1860* (Leipzig, 1907), 26.

survive but in the 1780s some did become powerful enough to grow their own branches. A horizontal expansion took place with all the new industrialists having been trained in the original firm or in one of its offsprings. All the new enterprises were founded by outsiders drawn to Brno from Germany proper by the first woollen mill. In the 1790s backward, vertical, and further horizontal proliferation linkages began to build up, businesses that were also to a large extent operated by immigrant Germans. In this way the manufacture of textile machinery and eventually other types of machines became well-established so that in the middle of the nineteenth century, firms in Brno began to produce machines for the developing sugar-beet industry. Some Britishers had by 1850 also selected Brno as their place of manufacture with the Manchester-trained Thomas Bracegirdle operating a machine shop that employed between 300 and 350 workers and included 70 lathes.[1]

These developments can be traced back to the woollen enterprise founded in 1764. Its fate will serve as the primary focus of this study. Since it was the creation of a Cameralistically or Mercantilistically inspired government policy, the role of the state figures strongly in the ensuing narrative.[2] Such Mercantilistic enterprises have often been compared to hothouse flowers that could not survive without the protection of the state.[3] Although the Brno firm may be considered another case-study supporting this hypothesis, it can also serve as a fine example of the success of Mercantilistic effort since it had spawned an entire industry by the time of its own destruction.

To demonstrate this point the evolution of Brno's industry from the 1780s to about 1820 will be sketched at the end of this study. The calamitous events of the French Revolution and the Napoleonic wars, had by then run their course. Some of the economic concomitants of these events such as the Continental System had beneficial effects on Brno's industry, while others like some of the periods of war during which Austria faced Napoleon had detrimental results. Among the worst experiences were the so-called Austrian state-bankruptcies of 1811 and 1816 and the flood of cheap English textiles after the Napoleonic wars. Brno had successfully weathered

[1] [Anonymous], *Die hundertjährige Geschichte der Ersten Brünner Maschinen-Fabriks-Gesellschaft* (Leipzig, 1921), 73. [Anonymous], *Bericht der Handels- und Gewerbekammer in Brünn . . . im Jahre 1851* (Brünn, 1854), 129.

[2] Cameralism was the central European version of Mercantilism. The words will be used interchangeably for the most part in this study.

[3] Joseph Koulischer, 'La grande industrie aux XVIIe et XVIIIe siécles: France, Allemagne, Russie', *Annales d'Historie Economique et Sociale*, III (1931), 11–46.

all these problems, although many of the old firms were forced to close their doors by the end of this period. New enterprisers took over from the old and helped to carry forward the momentum that made Brno the largest producer in the Austrian Empire of woollen textiles by value in 1841. In that year nearly 58,000,000 fl. of woollen goods were produced in the entire Monarchy and Brno was responsible for over 13,000,000 fl. Its nearest competitors were the old woollen centres Liberec (Reichenberg) in northern Bohemia with 7,000,000 fl. and Jihlava (Iglau), the Moravian centre with 5,000,000 fl.[1] Only eighty years before these two cities were the best known woollen centres in the Monarchy and Brno was not even deserving of any mention in an enumeration of wool manufacturing places for informational purposes within the central government in Vienna.[2]

The Gestation Period in Brno

Brno's success in the economic arena may well have been among the indirect and certainly incidental results of its valiant, sixteen-week resistance to the onslaught of Swedish troops in 1645. This action, which blunted the Swedish drive toward further penetration into the Habsburg Monarchy and possibly toward Vienna itself, raised the city in the esteem of Emperor Ferdinand III (reigned 1637–59) well above that of other cities, which in general enjoyed the ruler's displeasure.[3] As far as he was concerned all towns were disagreeable because they had been hotbeds of Protestantism and rebellion. Brno, like other royal towns, had lost many of its most active citizens in the re-Catholization drive known as the Counter-Reformation, and was saddled with large fines for rebellion and with debts incurred for this and other war-connected reasons. Although in this way severely weakened in its capability to recover, the city benefited from the more benevolent attitude of the monarch, who reduced the city's punishment and also helped it by having an increasing number of government offices located there. The number of government officials, of resident noblemen with their

[1] Johann Slokar, *Geschichte der österreichischen Industrie und ihrer Förderung unter Kaiser Franz I.* (Wien, 1914), 338, 357. Jaroslav Joza, *Z minulosti textilního prumyslu v libereckem kraji* (From the History of the textile industry in the Liberec district) (Liberec, 1958), 108.

[2] HKA, red no. 891, f 64, 'Verzeichniss derjenigen Örter in den deutschen Erbländern, wo beträchtliche Tücher-Manufakturen sind . . .' (29 places were mentioned).

[3] *František Šujan, Dějepis Brna* (History of Brno) (Brno, 1902), 225. Also, Gregor Wolny, *Die Markgrafschaft Mähren*, 6 vols. (Brünn, 1835–1842), II, part I, 104 ff.

retinues and of persons coming to Brno to transact business with state agencies thus became greater during the remainder of the seventeenth and the eighteenth centuries. Economically, this conglomeration of persons with tastes for more sophisticated consumption goods could create an important regional demand for manufactured goods that at first might have to be satisfied by imports but that one day could serve, as it had elsewhere, as a catalyst for the growth of regional industry.[1] It meant, moreover, that ideas were more likely to penetrate from the outside.

One of the specific forms through which new ideas entered Brno was through the person of Paul Ignaz Morgenthaler, who settled there in 1654 following a felicitous marriage with a wealthy young widow and who became part of the local patriciate.[2] This condition and the continuing fine rapport that he enjoyed with the regional nobility as a result of having been in the entourage of a wealthy aristocrat helped him to rise to high positions in the city, including that of municipal judge and in the late 1660s royal judge, positions that carried more administrative than judicial responsibilities.[3]

Morgenthaler's interest in economic affairs preceded his employ in the noble household but it was probably strongly aided by the four years of travels that he spent in association with the son of the aristocratic family during his grand tour of Europe.[4] He had supposedly published some material on economic matters as early as 1649 in which he seemed to be strongly influenced by Barthelemy de Laffemas, the minister of finance under the French king Henry

[1] For the importance of widening demand see, D. E. C. Eversley, 'The Home Market and Economic Growth in England 1750–1780', in E. L. Jones and G. E. Mingay, eds., *Land, Labour and Population in the Industrial Revolution* (London, 1967), 206–59; E. W. Gilboy, 'Demand as a Factor in the Industrial Revolution, *Facts and Factors in Economic History: Essay presented to E. F. Gay* (Cambridge, Mass., 1932); John Kennedy, 'Observations on the Rise and Progress of the Cotton Trade in Great Britain', *Memoirs of the Literary and Philosophical Society of Manchester* 2nd series, III (1819), 116 ff. According to Kennedy 'about the year 1750 . . . the manufactory (of cotton) was carried on to an extent sufficient to supply a limited home consumption . . . when a stagnation . . . in the demand for cotton fabrics . . . took place, it was natural that the manufacturer, rather than be out of employment, endeavoured to find a market for his goods in other countries. And from this principle arose a foreign trade . . . '.

[2] Vladimír Burian, 'První moravský merkantilista Pavel Hynek Morgentaller', (The first Moravian Mercantilist Paul Henry Morgenthaler), *Brno v minulosti a dnes*, III (1962), 72–80.

[3] Cf. Alfons Huber and Alfons Dopsch, *Oesterreichische Reichsgeschichte* (Wien, 1901), 187.

[4] Vladimír Voldán, 'Cesta hofmistra Morgentallera jižní a západní Evropou' (Travels of Hofmeister Morgenthaler in southern and western Europe), *Brno v minulosti a dnes*, IX (1970), 104–15.

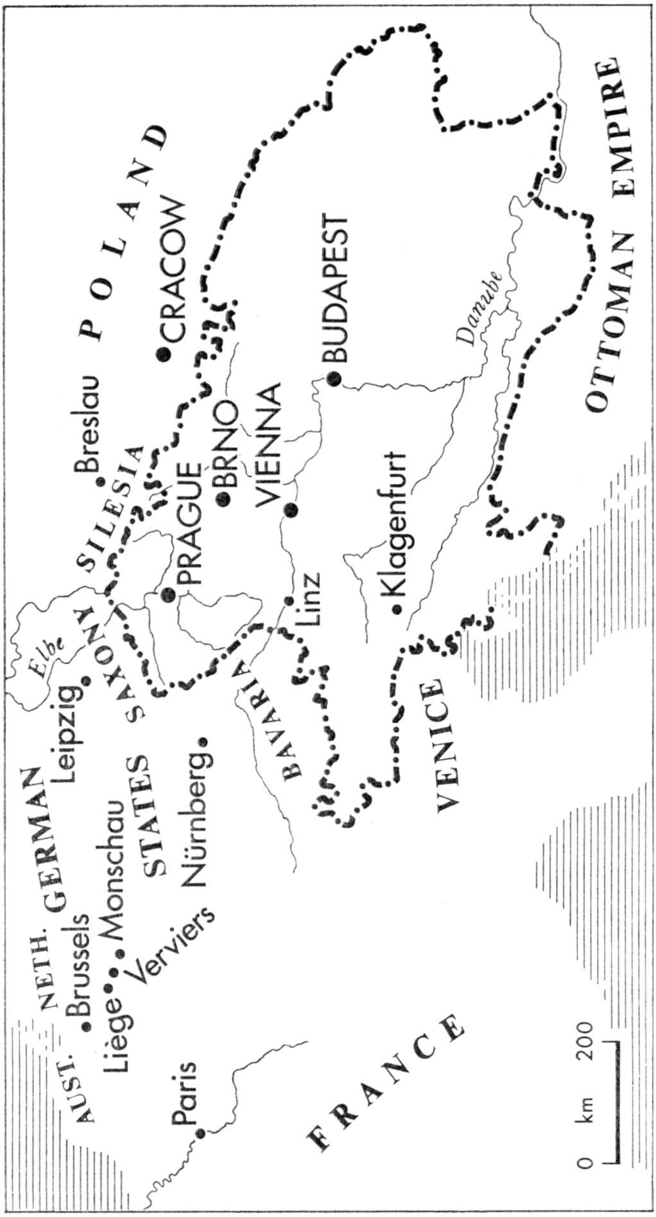

The Habsbury Monarchy in the mid-eighteenth century

IV. Although his name does not appear in the conventional literature on Cameralism, he seems to fit well into that category. A short summary of his ideas includes a number of observations which are remarkable less for their uniqueness than the fact that they were propounded by a person in a provincial capital a number of years before the celebrated book on the sources of national wealth by Thomas Mun in England was published in 1666 and also before the well-known Cameralist Johann Joachim Becher made his appearance in Vienna. Morgenthaler felt that a powerful state required a large treasury which could be filled best by a well-employed population that was increasing in numbers. Money being for the state what nerves were for the man, the ruler should promote the welfare of his people for only in this way could he maximize his revenues. He should furthermore have an incorruptible bureaucracy and a system of taxation that did not drive people out of the country. Governments must of course interfere in the economy so that the drain of money ceases and so that the available resources could be used more efficiently. Fallow land should be brought under cultivation; prisoners, beggars and loafers should be put to work and those goods should be manufactured at home for which money leaves the country. After his arrival in Brno, Morgenthaler submitted proposal along these lines to the Emperor but nothing came of them.

Interestingly, there was yet another Mercantilist in Brno at this time. Fabian Sebastian Malivsky von Maliv, a lawyer, recommended to the Moravian Estates in 1663 that they recruit 100,000 to 150,000 craftsmen and have them settle in the country.[1] Unfortunately, Malivsky's proposals suffered the same fate as Morgenthaler's. Although both proposals were ignored, it is still remarkable that they were composed at all in this provincial city with little in the way of a cultural life. Morgenthaler's and Malivsky's presence and their activities indicate, however, that the city was tolerant of unusual views. Consequently, Brno presents a picture of less stagnation than other cities of the time, including even Prague which was further to the west and hence presumably more open to the intellectual currents coming from Dresden and Leipzig and the rest of western Europe.

The two Mercantilists might, of course, represent no more than an odd accident of history. It is true that no other persons of such unusual economic interest came to Brno in the following century. On the other hand, further efforts to encourage economic progress

[1] Burian, 'První moravský merkantilista', 86 ff.

emanating from Brno are to be found without exceedingly great difficulty, indicating at least that Morgenthaler and Malivsky were not merely transient phenomena, but were among the first identifiable instances of a long process of gestation leading to Brno's future success.

Even though Malivsky made a proposal that approached the fantastic he also tried his own hand at manufacturing. In 1660 he began a fine-cloth factory in the town of Ivančice (Eibenschitz), a property of Prince Liechtenstein. Unfortunately, the project fell victim to the Turkish incursions of the time. Undaunted, Malivsky founded yet another fine-cloth enterprise, of which even less is known. There is no evidence available, however, on how he financed his two attempted enterprises, whether he employed his own funds, those of the manorial lord, or was supported by a government agency. Whatever the facts may have been with his own enterprises, Malivsky clearly expected the government to be instrumental in inducing general economic development. Along with many other writers and government officials, he most likely viewed such action on the part of the government as in its own fiscal interest if nothing else. The direct causal relationship between poor people and a poor king was well known; and the Habsburg monarchs needed no one to inform them that they were poor.

Government Participation in the Gestation Process in the Seventeenth Century

The indigenous efforts in Brno toward change, although vital in preparing the ground for modernization and industrialization later, were overshadowed by the moves at the centre of the empire. A ponderous mass of poorly organized territories, the Habsburg Monarchy was in need of a sharp improvement in its economic and political system if it was to fulfill the 'Great Power' task that it seemed destined to assume. Whatever the definition of royal poverty might have been, the monarch required additional revenues and although not averse to appealing to alchemists to solve his problems, he also made more sensible inquiries. Actually, one of the persons brought to the court of Emperor Leopold I (reigned 1658–1705) for this purpose combined alchemy with his other more profound interests. This man was Johann Joachim Becher, a typical seventeenth-century universal genius, who included among his activities the practice of medicine.[1] A mercurial individual, he

[1] Herbert Hassinger, *Johann Joachim Becher (1635–1682)* (Wien, 1951), 8–16.

came to Vienna in the 1660s with numerous plans for the economic development of the Monarchy. Even though few of his plans had the desired results at the time, they proved to be influential over the following century.

Possibly as an indirect result of Becher's suggestions but for very pragmatic reasons as well, the Emperor requested in the early 1680s recommendations and analyses from his officials in various parts of the Monarchy concerning the amelioration of the chaotic state of fiscal affairs. Among the officials who submitted memorandums were two who resided in Brno and whose blunt statements could certainly not have endeared themselves to many persons in power.[1] They held a greedy nobility chiefly responsible for the Monarchy's fiscal ills, a nobility that was aided and abetted by a usurious Jewry and an exploiting church, all of whom together kept the peasants impoverished and impeded legitimate commerce. Because of their own strong fiscal orientation, the officials in effect proposed remedies that were little more than tinkering with the antiquated system of taxation. Nevertheless, the emanation of such analyses and advice from Brno speaks well for the climate of opinion there.

Before any meaningful reforms were able to be inaugurated, there intervened the Turkish war and the abortive siege of Vienna in 1683. This traumatic experience became the catalyst for a famous, patriotic tract that was published the following year. With the ringing title *Österreich über alles; wann es nur will* (Austria overall, when it only desired to) Philipp W. von Hörnigk, Becher's brother-in-law, tried to rouse the Habsburg Monarchy to undertake the necessary radical changes in its political economy that would prevent future threats of this kind and permit the country to occupy its rightful place in the world. Although Hörnigk's book was not a work of great originality it was highly influential throughout the eighteenth century, leading the editor of its 1784 edition to assert that Austria's great progress was largely owing to this work.[2]

In the late 1690s, during an all too brief interval between wars, fresh efforts were organized to improve the economic and financial condition of the Monarchy. Despite the earlier analyses and recommendations, Emperor Leopold I again gave orders in 1698

[1] Alfred Fischel, 'Zur Finanzgeschichte Mährens Reformvorschläge unter Kaiser Leopold I', *Zeitschrift des deutschen Vereines für Geschichte Mährens und Schlesiens*, xxv (1923), 44–77.

[2] Heinrich Gerstenberg, 'Philipp Wilhelm von Hörnigk', *Jahrbücher für Nationalökonomie und Statistik*, CXXXIII (1930), 813. Benedikt Franz Hermann, *Herrn Johann von Hornek's Bemerkungen über die österreichische Staatsökonomie* (St Petersburg, 1784), Preface.

for an examination of the causes for the government's and the Monarchy's poverty and requested proposals for improvement.[1] The Bohemian and Moravian officials once again bent to their task. It is significant that all the reports dispatched from Brno — from the governor of Moravia, the captain of the Brno district, and from the municipal council of the city, a body composed of burghers — had a progressive, Mercantilistic character.[2] Again, however, as indeed twenty years earlier, these well-meant efforts were aborted by war. Desperately in need of money and painfully aware of its basic economic problems, the Habsburg Monarchy began nevertheless a long dynastic struggle to win the throne left vacant by the death of the last of the Habsburg house in Spain. The nature of the response from the officials in Brno, however, is further evidence of a strong strain toward progressiveness in economic thinking.

In 1681 the responding officials had pleaded for the improvement of the lot of the peasantry and suggested that measures should be instituted to curb the excesses of the nobility. Similarly the memorandums in response to the Emperor's requests in 1698 emphasized the importance of increasing the general well-being of the people, as a result of which the Habsburg treasury would be enriched. Money should circulate at a greater velocity and this could best be accomplished by placing it in the hands of the population rather than allowing it to be concentrated among a few rich persons.[3] This was of course a very pragmatic attitude. The wealthier the people at large were the greater would be the flow of funds from taxation, tolls and tariff duties into the treasury of the central government, a general position that many Mercantilist writers in England and elsewhere supported.[4]

Increasing the Momentum for Economic Development

War, indecision, and corruption at the court of Emperor Leopold I had frustrated the seemingly good intentions of the

[1] Alfred Francis Pribram, *Das böhmische Commerzcollegium und seine Thätigkeit* (Prag, 1898), 13; Josef Nožicka, 'K hospodařské politice Brna koncem 17. stoletì', (On the Economic Policy of Brno Toward the End of the 17th Century), *Brno v minulosti a dnes*, II (1961), 171.

[2] Nožicka, 'K hospodařske politice', 173–5.

[3] Ibid., 171 f.

[4] Cf. J. J. Becher, *Politische Discurs*, 2nd Edn. (Frankfurt, 1673), 442; Charles Wilson, 'The Other Face of Mercantilism', *Royal Historical Society Transactions*, 5th Series, IX (1959), 91, 98; A. W. Coats, 'Changing Attitudes to Labour in the Mid-Eighteenth Century, *Economic History Review*, 2nd Series, XI (1959), 36; Sebastien le Prestre Vauban, *Project de dîme royale*, ed. E. Coornaert (Paris, 1933) XXXVII, 7.

monarch and some of his advisers. His two sons who became, successively, rulers of the large and extended territories of the Habsburg dynasty attacked the economic problems with greater intensity and pushed at least the so-called Hereditary Lands — Bohemia, Moravia, Silesia, Lower Austria, Upper Austria and Inner Austria — in the direction of greater development. Joseph I, whose reign from 1705 to 1711 was not only short but completely dominated by the War of the Spanish Succession, was able nevertheless to increase the modernization impulses by forming economic investigating commissions which continued in existence and whose proposals served as the basis for the economic policies of his brother Karl VI (reigned 1713–40). Following the peace of Utrecht and Rastatt in 1713/14, which ended this last great dynastic war, constructive economic activity was again undertaken and Moravia and in particular Brno were among the intended beneficiaries.

For Moravia and other parts of the Monarchy there were instituted so-called commercial councils (*Commerzcollegien*). Their task was to analyse the economy in each area and to propose measures for development. The Moravian council did not exhibit any noteworthy activity, unfortunately. Another agency created at this time was similarly ineffective. The so-called *Bankal-Collegium* whose goal was to assist the government financially and to create stable monetary conditions hardly had a chance to operate at all, being inhibited in its efforts in Moravia especially as a result of terrible epidemics and famines then raging in that area.[1] Other means to develop industry and trade were also explored. Projects were begun to make a number of rivers more navigable and to connect them with the Danube by means of a canal. Karl VI also pushed for an overland route to connect various towns in his realms with the Adriatic Sea through the ports Trieste and Rijeka (Fiume), which were declared free ports in 1719. He began the construction of a road that was to lead from the Adriatic over the Semmering Pass to Vienna and from there by way of Brno to Breslau, the Silesian entrepot. The portion from Vienna to Breslau was actually started in 1727 and the portion of the road to Brno was completed in 1740, the year of the death of Karl VI. Among his major plans the Emperor wanted to make Turkey more accessible to Habsburg

[1] Wilhelm Schramm, 'Mähren unter Karl VI', *Oesterreichisch-Ungarische Revue*, (1889), 243.

trade, toward which end he prevailed upon the Sublime Porte to agree to include in the peace treaty of Passarowitz (1718) a trade agreement favourable to Habsburg merchants and manufacturers.[1]

All these efforts might be classed under the heading of the creation of overhead social capital to allow the individual initiative of the private sector in the economy to unfold itself strongly. The Emperor was, however, aware that the low calibre of Habsburg commercial institutions would make exploitation of the new opportunities very difficult. He therefore caused a large trading company, the Oriental Company, to be formed and invested it with far-reaching privileges as well as large sums of money from his own treasury. In numerous other respects Emperor Karl actively supported projects for the economic growth of his lands. Frequently, however, he found his hopes frustrated by his own inability at organization and control, by conflicts with his pretensions in the field of international diplomacy and war and by the secular obstruction of the *status quo* in society. Nevertheless, his efforts stand testimony to the continuing and increasing interest on the part of the rulers in economic growth.

Early Industrial Enterprises

Partly as a result of the industrial policies of the Habsburg rulers from about 1660 to 1740, a number of enterprises were formed. It is especially the textile manufacturing firms that are pertinent in the present context, since they represented a part of the general fund of information on which the Brno Fine-Cloth Factory and its immediate predecessor had to depend. This is not the place to list all nor to evaluate how their experiences contributed to the establishment at Brno. They ranged from a silk mill established on a nobleman's estate by Becher in the 1660s, a woollen fabrics firm organized by a burgher of Linz (Upper Austria) and eventually taken over by the Oriental Company, a nobleman's woollen cloth factory in

[1] For details see, among others, *Handlungseinverständniss zwischen dem kais. königl. Hofe und der ottomanischen Pforte . . . 24 Hornung, 1784* (Wien, 1785), 17. Franz Martin Mayer, 'Zur Geschichte der österreichische Handelspolitik unter Kaiser Karl VI', *Mitteilungen des Institutes für österreichische Geschichte*, XVIII (1882), 129–45; Franz Martin Mayer, *Die Anfänge des Handels und der Industrie in Oesterreich und die orientalische Companie*, (Innsbruck, 1882); Josef Dullinger, 'Die Handelskompagnien Oesterreiches nach dem Oriente und nach Ostindien in der ersten Hälfte des 18. Jahrhunderts', *Zeitschrift für Sozial- und Wirtschaftsgeschichte*, VII (1900), 44–83.

Horní Litvínov (Oberleutensdorf) in western Bohemia and finally a woollen cloth and stocking factory on an estate not far from Brno.[1]

The factory, established in 1701 on the Slavkov (Austerlitz) estate, a property of Count Andreas Dominik Kaunitz, the grandfather of the famous minister and diplomatist, is primarily of interest because of its possible effect on the climate of opinion in Brno. Manufacturing woollen-cloth and stockings, it remained in existence for about a dozen years, although never very successful. Brno was its nearest market and at one point a merchant from that city was contemplating partnership with Count Kaunitz.[2] The manager of the industrial enterprise at Slavkov, a man who seems to have been as incompetent as he was unpleasant, appears to have subverted the proposed arrangement. Much of the output was sold in Vienna where subsequently another merchant who was the principal purchaser of these goods also went through an abortive attempt to enter into partnership with the Moravian nobleman.[3] Soon thereafter the aristocratic owner made a lease agreement with a penniless Italian merchant — an obvious error. Finally, a group of Swiss merchants took over the enterprise for a time.[4] Many of the workers were Swiss and had been recruited at Kaunitz's expense.

How much of this enterprise was known in Brno is almost impossible to determine at this time. Since, however, a merchant from that city was known to have had close connexions with the Slavkov enterprise, some knowledge of its experience might have circulated. Knowledgeable persons could have learned that the central government and the ruler were interested in promoting industrialization. Furthermore, they would have discovered that noblemen like Kaunitz who had travelled widely abroad had been impressed with the industrial and commercial prosperity of places like Holland and England and that they were willing to invest their own resources in

[1] For more extensive discussion see, Arnošt Klíma, *Manufakturní období v Čechách*, (The Manufactory Period in Bohemia) (Praha, 1955). A. F. Pribram, *Commerz-collegium*; Christian d'Elvert, *Zur Cultur-Geschichte Mährens und Oest. Schlesiens* (Brünn, 1870); František Mainuš, *Vlnařství a bavlnařství na Moravě a ve Sleszku v XVIII. století* (The Woollen and Cotton Industry in Moravia and Silesia in the 18th century) (Brno, 1960); Viktor Hofmann, 'Beiträge zur neueren Wirtschaftsgeschichte. Erster Teil. Die Wollenzeug Fabrik zu Linz an der Donau.' *Archiv für österreichische Geschichte*, CX (1926), 415–712; Herman Freudenberger, *The Waldstein Woolen Mill; Noble Entrepreneurship in Eighteenth-Century Bohemia* (Boston, 1963).

[2] Jindřich Šebánek, 'Textilní podniky moravských Kouniců' (The textile enterprises of the Moravian Kaunitzes), *Časopis Matice Moravské*, LV (1931), 159–60.

[3] Ibid., 442–4.

[4] Ibid., LVI (1932), 101–48.

order to introduce the basis for a similar prosperity at home. Brno's citizens, on the other hand, would also have become aware of the difficulties that would confront anyone who wished to introduce innovations. The Slavkov experience could have provided encouragement for those Brno citizens who were dissatisfied with the lack of entrepreneurship but it could also have contributed further corroborating evidence for those burghers who resisted change.

More than likely there were many influential persons in Brno who shared with citizens of towns elsewhere in the Monarchy and in Europe as a whole a hostility toward capitalistic, concentrated workshops. The prevailing structure of industry strongly favoured the small production unit in which a master worked with a few journeymen, apprentices and helpers on the basis of rules laid down by the guild to which he belonged. Following the regulations definite limits were placed on the amount that each unit could produce per year, the number of looms and workers and the technology that could be employed. Since it was the policy of the central government from the late seventeenth century to increase industrial output especially of goods that were being imported, this institutional structure was considered harmful. Vested interests organized in guilds and municipalities were hostile to change of any sort and above all to technological innovation. The government policy-makers considered the abolition of guilds at one time with the probably mistaken expectation that the individual masters would act more reasonably once they could follow their own self-interest completely. This was too radical a step for the Habsburg society of the time. Consequently, more modest measures were adopted. One of these was the legal designation 'factory' (*Fabrik*) in the early eighteenth century for larger productive enterprises especially chartered by the government and protected against the interference of municipalities and guilds.[1] These factories were not subject to any limitations concerning their output, their employment of workers or their methods of manufacturing. Despite government protection, they did not, however, enjoy a good reputation among the population. During the entire century people looked upon them as akin to penitentiaries and workhouses in which persons were forced to work for some penal purpose or another. Guilds and municipalities were forbidden to discriminate against present or former workers of factories. The numerous cases

[1] Slokar, *Geschichte*, 1.

in which the government had to step in to assure such persons fair treatment testify to the continued prejudice that they faced.

Fortunately, in Brno there was no dominant guild like in Jihlava, a royal town not far to the west which the clothmakers had dominated for several centuries.[1] That the obstructive features of the guild spirit did not exist to so great degree as elsewhere, must certainly have been a factor in making Brno more willing to adopt innovations. Moreover, persons like Morgenthaler, Malivsky and the government officials reporting to Vienna represent at least some evidence that there was a certain amount of dissatisfaction with the goal-achievements in Brno, to use the terminology of the sociologists.[2] The experience of the estate factory of Count Kaunitz may have added to the tension that was presumably building up between the old and the new social system, a requirement for social change to come about.

Social Factors Favouring and Obstructing Innovation

It is important but extremely difficult to identify the factors that favoured innovations and those that obstructed them. On the basis of circumstantial evidence one is, however, able to speculate. That critics were respected members of Brno society, as was the case with Morgenthaler, and Malivsky, speaks for a high level of tolerance for different opinions. Foreigners among the burghers of the city might also point in a similar direction. A superficial analysis of the persons admitted to the rights of a burgher between 1675 and 1715, to use two arbitrary dates, reveals that about 15 of a sample of nearly 200 names had Italian origin, about the same number came from Bavaria and over 25 from other parts of Germany.[3] The appearance of a number of Italian names among the merchants testifies either to the presence of a foreign colony or at least a group of people whose ethnic background connected them with well-known commercial and industrial traditions. The Italian along with the native merchants were members of a Commercial Brotherhood (*Handelsbruderschaft*) founded in 1701.[4]

[1] For further details on Jihlava see, Christian d'Elvert, *Geschichte und Beschreibung der (königlichen Kreis-und) Bergstadt Iglau in Mähren* (Brünn, 1850); Franz Ruby, *Das Iglauer Handwerk* (Brünn, 1887); Karl Werner, *Urkundliche Geschichte der Iglauer Tuchmacher-Zunft* (Leipzig, 1861).

[2] Neil J. Smelser, *Social Change in the Industrial Revolution* (Chicago, 1959), 15.

[3] J. Dosoudil, 'Die Brünner Bürgeraufnahmen 1559–1845', *Zeitschrift des deutschen Vereines für Geschichte Mährens und Schlesiens*, XXXI–XXXIX (1929–1937).

[4] Bertold Bretholz, *Brünn, Geschichte und Kultur* (Brünn, 1938), 240 f.

The presence of the foreign element could be considered a factor indicating a tolerance for change. On the other hand, the Brotherhood with its implication of exclusivity could be considered a retarding factor especially if entry was difficult. On this matter, the evidence is inconclusive. Since the membership was reduced from the original twenty-six in 1701 to twenty-one in 1756, one might conclude that the *Brotherhood* was restrictive.[1] The opposite tendency is, however, indicated by the fact that Michael Köffiller, whose son was to be very important in the management and control of the Fine-Cloth Factory, became head of the Brotherhood soon after he had migrated to Brno from Carinthia in 1730. Besides becoming head of the corporation, he also became the richest burgher of the city with connexions throughout Europe. Exactly how important the role of the Brotherhood was is not easily ascertainable. The fact that no Czech names appeared on its rolls may not be very significant, since a considerable number of such names were to be found among the burghers.

There were of course no Jews enrolled in the Brotherhood. As a matter of fact, they were formally excluded from living within the city since 1454 when the friar Capistrano led an anti-Jewish crusade throughout central Europe. Nevertheless Jews played a role of some importance in the city's economic affairs. They were allowed to visit the markets held in Brno and a number of them definitely lived in a suburb outside the walls. Some may actually have lived within the walls of the town in houses owned by noblemen, who were not subject to the municipal jurisdiction in such matters. Most rich aristocrats had Jews attached to them, the so-called *Hausjuden*. These were frequently intermediaries, buying and selling goods, investing and borrowing money for their protectors. In addition, on noble estates Jews acted as innkeepers, leather tanners, potash producers and brandy distillers. They fulfilled many function that produced income for the lord of the manor. Eventually, when Jews were given greater freedom of action, they contributed to Brno and the Monarchy as financiers and factory owners.

The presence of outsiders such as Italians, Jews and new migrants in Brno could suggest a certain openness of society. This condition was further accentuated by the contingents of government officials in the Moravian capital as well as the fairly large number of clergymen and of nobles. The nobility had been drawn to the city from the time of the establishment there of the high court of Moravia in

[1] Ibid.

the middle of the seventeenth century. Along with nobles, clergymen, and bureaucrats came much building activity which continued until the early decades of the following century,[1] leading one to presume a considerable amount of economic activity.

The building activity of the nobility and clergy gave Brno's economy a potentially volatile character, which was increased by the consumption habits of the aristocrats. For one thing, few noblemen resided permanently in Brno, nor, for that matter, in any other one place. Very probably there were periods, such as when the Diet of the Moravian Estates met, that a large number of nobles was present; at other times their houses were merely inhabited by a skeleton staff of servants. This practice would have to have a destabilizing effect on the town's economy, with irregular alternating spurts of high activity and lethargy. While it would be unrealistic to expect the nobles and their families to purchase most of their articles of clothing and other luxury goods in the provincial capital, the local merchants would nevertheless have to stock an inventory somewhat more costly and possibly larger than in other towns of similar size. We can draw the conclusion that the local merchant community carried higher risks but at the same time had a better chance of realizing larger returns from their sales of goods and services.

Against these potential benefits the burghers of Brno also faced many detrimental aspects. To build the town houses of the nobility many humbler homes within the narrow confines of the walls had to give way. The leaders of the municipality in the late seventeenth century requested an extension of their walls in the direction of the Spielberg, a fortress on a hill overlooking the town, but were denied permission supposedly for military reasons.[2] Worse than pushing their way into the small town, as far as the burghers were concerned, was the successful claim of the nobles and prelates to be freed of most of the exactions that the town placed on its inhabitants.[3] This must have been a painful situation since in the middle of the seventeenth century around 80 to 90 houses out of a total of about 450 in Brno belonged to privileged persons, that is, nobles, clergy and others not subject to the laws and ordinances of the city.[4]

[1] Bretholz, *Brünn*, 238.
[2] Burian, 'Prvni moravsky merkantilista', 75.
[3] Christian d'Elvert, *Beiträge zur Geschichte der k. Städte Mährens, insbesondere der k. Landeshauptstadt Brünn* (Brünn, 1860), 76.
[4] Nožička, 'Hospodařske politice', 176–7.

Geographical Endowments

What were some of the other endowments of the Brno area to make it a good location for industrial progress? Since the progress of industrialization began in Brno with the woollen industry, was there a particularly large supply of wool? Was the water in Brno especially beneficient as means of wool washing and/or dyeing or were there swift streams that could be easily harnessed to drive the water wheels of industrial plants? Were weather conditions particularly advantageous, possibly in terms of high average humidity which can be an aid in carding and spinning or was the year-round temperature more moderate than elsewhere? That Brno possessed few of these particular locational advantages seems indicated by the fact that its name did not appear in a list compiled in 1761 of nearly thirty places in the Austrian and Bohemian areas in which woollen cloth was being produced.[1]

Although there may not have existed many locational advantages specific to the wool industry, Brno possessed other benefits. Geographically, it was associated with the Danube region and was not very far distant from Vienna.[2] It was on the traditional route from Vienna to Breslau and it was for that reason that Karl VI built a road. Moreover, Hungary and Poland were in reasonable proximity, as one of chief woollen manufacturers of Brno pointed out.[3] Thus, the city was in a good position to take advantage of a market for its finished goods. He also mentioned that wool was easy to be procured from estates in the vicinity. Eventually, Brno's industrialization was also materially aided by the sizeable coal and iron seams within its larger area. Lastly, it enjoyed a high degree of land utilization, there being little land that could not be usefully exploited.

Mid-Eighteenth-Century Conditions

By the middle of the eighteenth century a number of innovational factors had combined with the given conditions to provide a basis for Brno's industrialization. Many of the innovational factors had outside origins, with the policies of the central government under Empress Maria Theresia (reigned 1740–80) being of critical importance. For the Habsburg Monarchy as a whole and for the

[1] HKA, red. no. 891, f. 64, 'Verzeichniss derjenigen, Örter in den deutschen Erbländer, wo beträchtliche Tuch-Manufacturen sind . . . '.
[2] Wolny, *Markgrafschaft Mähren*, Vol. II, Part I, xvi, xxii.
[3] HKA, red no. 882, f. 395–401. The writer was Wilhelm Mundy, see pp. 159 ff

Brno region in particular a gestation period had run its course and a time of major social change was at hand.

As far as economic matters were concerned, the Habsburg government was mainly concentrating its efforts in those dominions of the Hereditary Lands which were left after King Frederick II of Prussia had annexed Silesia, previously one of the most productive areas both in terms of tax revenue and general wealth.[1] A large standing army for the defence of the Monarchy and plans for a war of reconquest were unquestionably the main motives for the forceful economic policy that was now inaugurated. Generals and other leaders of the government demanded economic progress as a primary means for the resources that large armies required.

In 1743, shortly after the end of her first war, Maria Theresia, whose schooling in things economic was certainly extremely deficient, expressed her amazement that so little 'care [had been] taken in the promotion of commerce and manufacturing which [were] after all, the only means by which the [Habsburg] lands [could] be made prosperous . . .'.[2] To accomplish her purpose, the Empress, although privately very conservative, decided to place all the powers of her government behind the effort of economic change.[3] That she was able to discern this basic problem with such relative ease may have been due to her native abilities, for all reports on her education agree that she was woefully unprepared in all subjects of statecraft. Some historians insist that her father, Karl VI, deliberately kept her uneducated, presumably because he hoped for a male heir until the end of his life. His own interest in economic and political affairs was great and his accomplishments, despite the continuing adverse opinion of generations of historians, were many.

If not from her father, Maria Theresia may have acquired the correct impulses in economic and political affairs from her consort, Franz Stephan of Lorraine, whose effect on financial and economic policy until his death in 1765 was unquestionably considerable.[4] The Emperor's influence on his wife is difficult to measure, however, possibly owing to his own wish for anonymity. Whatever the case

[1] Friedrich Walter, *Die Österreichische Zentralverwaltung*. II. Abteilung, Vol I, half Vo. I. (Wien, 1938), 255; Christian d'Elvert, *Zur Österreichischen Finanzgeschichte mit besonderer Rücksicht auf die böhmischen Länder* (Brünn, 1886), 531.

[2] K. Pribram, *Geschichte*, 26.

[3] Otto Hintze, 'Der österreichische und der preussische Beamtenstaat in 17. und 18. Jahrhundert', *Staat und Verfassung* (Göttingen, 1962), 331.

[4] Hanns Leo Mikoletzky, 'Franz Stephan von Lothringen als Wirtschaftspolitiker', *Mitteilungen des österreichischen Staatsarchivs*, XIII (1960), 231–57. See also Fred Hennings, *Und sitzet zur linken Hand*, (Wien, 1961), 291.

might have been concerning the enigmatic relationship of Franz Stephan and Maria Theresia relative to the governing of the Monarchy, there is clear archival evidence that the textile mill here being discussed came into existence under his auspices. During the first decade and a half of its existence the factory was located in Kladruby (Kladrub), a village belonging to the Pardubice (Pardubitz) estate which was under the control of the Emperor. That the woollen mill was located there was due to his direct intervention; beyond that one cannot tell how much personal control he exercised. In this instance, as in many others, he worked through other persons, this time through his personal financial adviser and chief administrator of the Imperial estates, Baron Toussaint, who had come with him from Lorraine. Presumably Toussaint's orders represented his master's wishes, in which case Franz Stephan's management left much to be desired. After fourteen years of failure the factory was moved to Brno. The Emperor seems to have continued to interest himself in its fate, if one wishes to believe the statement of the firm's officers when they were complaining in 1776 about their troubles. They had become shareholders at the urgings of Franz Stephan.[1]

Undoubtedly the Emperor was somewhat of a dilettante and probably entered upon his industrial exploits with a light heart. He was more than a fashionable worldling, however; he was also a perceptive financial expert, well known for his dealings in various economic undertakings.[2] Franz Stephan must therefore also be appraised on the basis of a good businessman, that is an individual who invested for profit and planned his activities at least partly with profit maximization in mind. Such a conclusion is supported by some of his other industrial activities. He had a profitable cotton enterprise on his Šaštín (Sassin) estate, one that in 1754 was sold to a group of Viennese businessmen, and an earthenware enterprise on a neighbouring estate Holič (Hollitsch) belonging to him.[3] Beyond that he had investments in a Trieste development company. All this indicates that his interest in woollen textiles was probably based on solid economic considerations, that is, he

[1] HKA, red no. 894, f. 637–76.

[2] Leopold von Ranke, 'Aus den Papieren des Grosskanzler Fürst. Maria Theresia, ihr Staat und ihr Hof in Jahre 1755', *Historisch-politische Zeitschrift*, II (1833–1836), 667–740.

[3] Anton Špiesz, *Manufakturne obdobie na Slovensku 1725–1835* (Bratislava, 1961), 32. Hanns Leo Mikoletzky, 'Holics und Sassin, die beiden Mustergüter des Kaisers Franz I. Stephan', *Mitteilungen des österreichischen Staatsarchivs*, XIV (1961), 190–212.

expected an advantage to accrue to him. Lastly, he was after all a most important public personage with a sense of obligation for the common welfare of the Monarchy. All evidence points to a strong Mercantilist bias according to which the government should always be prepared to intervene in the national economic life to achieve prescribed goals.

If Emperor Franz I Stephan acted in an ambiguous way, as the 'greatest industrialist' according to a sarcastic remark made by the Prussian king,[1] and at the same time as a member of the government deeply concerned with economic development, he represented the anachronistic condition of the Habsburg Monarchy. To a large extent the monarch and the state were still viewed as identical, and the monarchy and its people still the property of the ruler. This is not to say that the ruler could act arbitrarily and was not subject to numerous traditional constraints. More than anything else autocratic rule in the eighteenth century suffered in its exercise from the lack of available governmental tools and techniques. It was, as Sir John Hicks has written, in the 'middle phase', of which deficiency of tax revenues was a distinguishing characteristic.[2] Centralized direction and control of a people's activities were moreover made difficult by the inability to collect the necessary information and to make rational use of available data. There was nevertheless a clear awareness whether in England or in Austria that the deliberate policies of a government required a wide network of information. What persons like Sir William Petty and Gregory King represented in England, J. J. Becher and Wilhelm von Schröder, another seventeenth-century Cameralist in Vienna, both of whom had lived in London, meant for Central Europe. 'Political Arithmetic' seemed necessary before English, Austrian and other governments in Europe could free themselves from the chains of medieval personal political relationships and elevate the state to a rational impersonal and egalitarian mechanism that could marshal the resources of a people in the interest of an aggressive national ego.

Agencies of Economic Development

To aid the process of formulating and enforcing a policy for the more rapid growth of the political economy of the Habsburg Monarchy, a centralized agency was formed in 1746. Known as the Court Commercial Council (*Hofkommerzienrat*) it worked

[1] Ranke, 'Aus den Papieren'.
[2] John Hicks, *A Theory of Economic History* (London, 1969), 62–3, 82–3.

through a more or less well-organized system of commercial councils, the *Commerzien-Concesse*.[1] The council in Vienna and the Moravian Council in Brno were inextricably involved in the relocation of the woollen mill that is the focus of this study in Brno and its progress there during its first decade. Formally abolished in 1776, this system was the primary carrier of the Mercantilistic policy of the central government. As one of its nineteenth-century critics, himself a high official in the government and closely concerned with economic policy, remarked, it was hampered by over-bureaucratization.[2] It was hampered in its operations by its lack of clear identity within the governmental structure in Vienna. It would of course be too much to expect a smooth-functioning government bureaucracy during this 'middle phase' of its development. Nevertheless, it was clearly to the credit of the economic planning and policy agencies of the Habsburg Monarchy during the 1750s, 1760s and 1770s to have increased the momentum of industrialization.

Among other things, these agencies were responsible for one of the first examples of co-ordinated planning, that is of assembling pertinent data and determining useful targets for accomplishing industrial growth on a year by year basis. These operational plans (*Operationpläne*) were of course crude in the extreme by modern standards. They reported specific actions such as the founding of a new industry and the suggested recruitment of particular skills. In this manner the limited resources at the government's command for development purposes could be expended in a rational manner. During the 1750s for example, the central agency had between 130,000 to 560,000 fl. at its disposal and expended between 41,000 and 355,000 fl. A good part of the expenditure comprised salaries which in 1763 may have amounted to 70,000 fl.[3] The regional commercial councils for the most part had their own sources of revenue and expended monies independently of the Vienna headquarters. Because of the overlapping nature of the bureaucracy, it is difficult to give a definite overall view of their activities.[4]

Economic Policy

Money, however important, was not nearly as crucial as personnel in this effort to promote industrialization. The first president of the

[1] Walter, *Die österreichische Zentralverwaltung*, 344–5.
[2] Anton von Kraus-Elislago, *Autobiographie* (Wien, 1849).
[3] HKA, red no. 47, f. 101, 106, 131, 140, 170, 177, 204, 208, 213.
[4] HKA, red no. 40, ff. 142–5.

centralized body was one of the most able of Habsburg officials, Count Philipp Kinsky, who accepted the presidency in 1746 and continued in that capacity until his death in 1749. Disliked but respected by Maria Theresia, this appointment very likely represented a demotion for Kinsky who had served as Supreme Chancellor of the Bohemian Chancellory in Vienna before 1746, in which post he had been a stout defender of Bohemia's position in the monarchy. He was, however, well qualified for his new post as chief economic planner, having previously served under Karl VI both as a member of a commission for tariff reform and the Bohemian Commercial Council.[1] His successor in the post was another Bohemian aristocrat, Count Rudolph Chotek. During his tenure of office, which lasted until 1762 when he was promoted to a higher position, an increasingly rigid Mercantilistic policy predominated. He was well-acquainted with and impressed by the economic accomplishments of western European countries and seems to have had a fairly flexible outlook on economic matters.[2] During this period of what might be described as frenzied Mercantilism, the works of J. H. G. von Justi on political economy were also very influential. He, too, did not favour rigid direction of the economy by the state. The government in his opinion should step in then when the private economy was unable to carry out its task. Moreover, he preferred support for small enterprises rather than the large firms that were usually called forth by government action.[3] Although the government officials adopted the same general principles, pragmatism forced them to honour them more in the breach than in practice. As Chotek wrote in one document in reference to the Kladruby woollen mill shortly before it was transferred to Brno, there was not enough of the entrepreneurial spirit nor the required forces in the private economy to make the system of private enterprise work.[4] Josef von Sonnenfels, a professor of political economy and a highly influential government official during the last decades of the eighteenth century, was also a proponent of a decentralized economy in which small, private enterprise would carry on the bulk

[1] Ottocar Weber, 'Der Zolltarif für Böhmen vom Jahre 1737', *Mitteilungen des Vereins für Geschichte der Deutschen in Böhmen*, XXXI (1892), 367 n.

[2] Walter, *Die österreichische Zentralverwaltung*, 253. Chotek has been frequently characterized as a tool of Emperor Franz I Stephan.

[3] J. H. G. von Justi, *Staaswirtschaft oder systematische Abhandlung aller Ökonomischen und Camerawissenschaften die zur Regierung eines Landes erfordert sind*, 2 vols (Leipzig, 1758).

[4] HKA, red no. 891, f. 34–41, April 1761.

of economic activity.[1] Probably the strongest adherent to decisive state control of the economy was Hofrat Bernard von Degelmann, permanent secretary of the Court Commercial Council and probably its dominant spirit during the 1750s and 1760s.[2]

Part of this policy was the creation of a strong protective tariff and more basic, of a large area served by a single tariff instead of the destructive system which allowed various portions of the Monarchy to impose import, export and transit duties on goods emanating from or destined for other jurisdictions. In this way goods traded between Bohemia and Upper Austria, for example, were treated almost like those of complete foreigners. A hesitative attempt had first been made toward this goal earlier in the century when Emperor Karl VI failed to bring all the lands of the Bohemian crown together into one tariff area and instead settled for a tariff in 1737 that encompassed only Bohemia proper.[3] The merchants of Breslau were the main obstacle. They required a special status for their goods, which were primarily traded between western and eastern Europe. Breslau, as an entrepot, did not fit into a scheme that had as its purpose the cutting-off of imports and the protection and growth of domestic commerce and industry. Even after the Habsburg officials of the mid-eighteenth century no longer had to consider the commercial interests of the Silesian merchants, who were now subject to the less tender mercies of a Hohenzollern king, it still took over twenty years of negotiation and compromise before a unified tariff for the Hereditary Lands, with the exception of Tyrol, was created. Unfortunately, the tariff which was enacted in 1775 still did not free the entrepreneurial forces in the Habsburg Monarchy. There were obvious drawbacks to the 1775 tariff and its slightly modified successor in 1784, the most important of which was that it did not allow for an unrestricted flow of goods between the various component parts.[4]

The protective tariffs of 1775 and 1784 were instituted so that the economy of the Hereditary Lands could unfold without fear of

[1] Josef von Sonnenfels, *Grundsätze der Polizey, Handlung — und Finanzwissenschaft*, 3 vols (Wien, 1770–72).

[2] Konrad Schünemann, 'Die Wirtschaftspolitik Josephs II in der Zeit seiner Mitregentenschaft', *Mitteilungen des Institutes für österreichische Geschichte* XLVII (1933), 22.

[3] Ottocar Weber, 'Zolltarif', 374; Siegfried Tschierschky, *Die Wirtschaftpolitik des schlesischen Kommerzkollegs 1716–1740* (Gotha, 1902), 101.

[4] Adolf Beer, 'Die Zollpolitik und die Schaffung eines einheitlichen Zollgebietes unter Maria Theresia', *Mitteilungen des Institutes für österreichische Geschichte* XIV (1893), 237–326.

foreign competition and with the assurance of a large internal market unhampered by numerous tolls and tariffs. Another government policy having the purpose of permitting the private economy to operate without undue obstructions dealt with the Habsburg guild system. Ever since the late seventeenth century, when the government began to take measures toward economic development, the guilds had been a painful thorn in the side of this policy. Total destruction of the guilds was considered but not carried out for fear of creating even worse economic problems. The guilds stood not only in the way of economic growth, but they also represented a medieval anachronism in their stubborn insistence that their traditional prerogatives could not be touched by the royal government. During the 1720s and 1730s they had to face some direct and some oblique attacks which prepared the way for the major assault against them in the 1750s. The government of Karl VI, while anxious to promote economic growth, was often more concerned with the immediate need for revenues. For example, a decree offering protection to craftsmen unable to enter the guilds of Vienna, was primarily a fiscal measure.[1] Although it was not very successful as a money-raising measure, the decree provided an opportunity for nearly 5,000 masters who were not members of any guild to carry on their business openly. In the process, government officials discovered that nearly half of the craftsmen in Vienna and suburbs did not belong to guilds.

The introduction of the permits for Vienna's unorganized craftsmen proved to be an important contribution to a freer economic environment for the entire Monarchy. With the enactment of general laws in the 1730s relating to the incorporation of guilds, the breach in the restrictive system of commerce and industry was still further widened.[2] As in many other moves of this type, the 1750s proved to be critically important. During that decade a legal distinction between crafts servicing local needs (*Polizey-Gewerbe*) and those whose market went beyond local needs (*Commercial-Gewerbe*) was created.[3] The commercial crafts were made free of production limitations and permitted to work as the market demanded.

[1] Karl Pribram, 'Die Einführung der Schutzdekrete unter Karl VI. in Wien', *Schmollers Jahrbuch*, XXX (1906), 885.

[2] General Zunft-Artikulen für die Zünften deren Königl. Böhmischen Erb-Landen de Anno 1739. See also W. Gustav Kopetz, *Allgemeine österreichische Gewerbs-Gesetz Kunde*, 2 vols. (Wien, 1829, 1830), I, iv, 15.

[3] K. Pribram, *Geschichte*, 363; See also Hans Rizzi, 'Das österreichische Gewerbe im Zeitalter des Merkantilismus', *Zeitschrift für Volkswirtschaft, Sozialpolitik und Verwaltung*, XII (1903), 92 f.

Summary

The industrialization policy of the mid eighteenth-century Habsburg Monarchy was based on practical principles and thus fitted in well with the reforming activities of Maria Theresia's most influential minister, Count Friedrich Wilhelm Haugwitz. Industrialization, no less than changes in the administrative structure of the government, was to provide the Monarchy with the means for war. To a large extent this was to be brought about by improving the tax base. To accomplish this, Haugwitz was anxious to force his fellow nobles into contributing a more equitable share, especially since they had been for decades virtually freed from direct taxation. But he was also convinced that a prosperous population as a whole would improve the financial picture. While considerations of military defence were paramount with Haugwitz and other government officials we may do them an injustice if we believe they had no other interests. They, like the theorists from whom they derived their models, were very likely also concerned about promoting the general welfare (*Glückseligkeit*) which Justi and Becher, among others, never tired of preaching.[1] Then as now, it was possibly simpler to bring about desirable social change by appealing to the gods of war than those of peace.

It had taken roughly a century to bring these ideas to fruition. During the gestation period for the Habsburg Monarchy in general a somewhat parallel phenomenon had taken place in Brno, the capital of Moravia, one of the so-called Hereditary Lands of the House of Austria. Brno was not uniquely equipped to be a show-place for the Mercantilistic policy of the central government. However, thanks to its natural and internal social endowments it had the ingredients for a large forward spurt in its industrial strength, so that in the nineteenth century it could be referred to as the Manchester of the Habsburg Monarchy.

[1] Cf. Friedrich Walter, 'Die ideellen Grundlagen der österreichischen Staatsreform von 1749', *Zeitschrift für öffentliches Recht*, XVII (1937), 200; Justi, *Staatswirtschaft*, I, xx, 35, 66; Louise Sommer, *Die österreichischen Kameralisten*, 2 vols (Wien, 1920, 1925), I, 17–28.

CHAPTER II

THE RURAL FACTORY

'To make her lands more prosperous' meant to Maria Theresia and her government, among other things, the prevention of harmful leakages abroad of money for the purchase of manufactured goods. Approximately 1,000,000 fl. was being spent annually on imported fine-woollen cloths in the middle of the eighteenth century, according to information that the Empress received from her officials.[1] In the Habsburg Monarchy itself considerable quantities of woollen textiles were produced each year, with the conspicuous exception of the finer qualities. Clothmakers guilds forbade their manufacture, possibly in silent recognition that the required skills were not available and the merchants who procured the product abroad were more than satisfied with the situation as it stood. The merchants received long credit from their suppliers and their customers were used to the products they provided. Government officials anxious to improve the economic condition of the Monarchy, however, believed that clothmakers could be taught improved methods and that merchants could easily shift their allegiance to domestic suppliers. The introduction into the Monarchy of a fine-cloth manufacturing capability was therefore a fit subject for attention.

First Steps to Industrialization

Since a large portion of imported fine cloth was manufactured at Verviers, a part of the Bishopric of Liège (in modern Belgium), it was only logical that skilled workers who could train the clothworkers of the Habsburg Monarchy should be recruited there. By good fortune some official apparently knew of a native of Verviers who was an employee in an establishment of a Viennese merchant. Consequently, Count Philipp Kinsky, in his capacity as president of the Bank Administration (*Bankal-Administration*) in 1748, commissioned Guillaume Joseph Bailoux, 38 years of age and the son of a recog-

[1] HKA, red no. 893, f. 845 ff.; Hörnigk in his *Österreich über alles, wann es nur will* (Leipzig, 1707), 117 estimated at the end of the seventeenth century that more than 7,000,000 fl. of various types of woollen textiles were being imported each year.

nized family of weavers in Verviers, to undertake this task.[1] It is somewhat curious that Kinsky did not use his position as head of the Court Commercial Council, the agency designated to effect the economic development of the Habsburg Monarchy.[2] It may have been that the economic planning body was devoid of the necessary funds and that the Bank Administration was more affluent. To be sure, no large sums of money were involved. Only the travelling expenses of the artisans whom Bailoux recruited in Verviers were being defrayed. On arrival in the Habsburg Monarchy the Belgians were dispatched under Bailoux's leadership to Jihlava, the well-known Moravian cloth-making centre. There they were to act as one body and the local clothmakers' guild was to finance their work.[3]

Foreign Weavers and Proud Guilds

If it was the purpose of the government officials to wipe out the deficit resulting from the importation of the fine woollens, this step proved to be both hesitant and clumsy. They dumped forty Netherland craftsmen without any ceremony in Jihlava, where half of the 450 members of the clothmakers' guild were out of work.[4] Moreover, the native masters insisted that they were fully as capable as the foreigners to manufacture high quality cloth. Their statutes forbade the production of webs of the large number of threads required for fine cloth. Despite the distress of their members, the leaders of the guild made no effort to change the regulations so that the demand for fine cloth could be met. Such an action would seem reasonable in the face of the threat to their existence represented by the Verviers craftsmen. What seemed to have provoked them most was that they had to finance the operations of the foreign artisans. By March 1749, they had reportedly devoted over 3,000 fl. from the guild's treasury for this purpose.[5] The Netherlanders could then have been in Jihlava for only a few months.

[1] Pierre Lebrun, *L'industrie de la laine à Verviers* (Paris, 1948), 413–14. Bailoux had apparently come to Vienna in 1746. (HKA, red no 73, Bundle 'N', 30 ex Junio 1789). This datum was contained in a plea by his niece to be allowed to return to her native land and to receive travel money for the purpose.

[2] HKA, red no. 891, f. 34–41, Wien, 6 April 1961, '. . . Kinsky Qua Ministerial Banco Deputations Praesident . . .'.

[3] HKA, red no. 891, f. 34–41, Wien, 6 April 1961: 'Kinsky . . . damals sich berühret haben, eine derley Manufactur und zwar nebst der annoch subsistirenden Tuch Gewerbschaft in Iglau anzulegen . . .' HKA, red no. 2, 24 März, 1749, Leop. Jos. Hantl, Municipal Councilman of Jihlava complained that the foreign workers cost the guild a considerable amount.

[4] HKA, red no. 2, 24. März, 1749, Leop. Jos. Hantl . . .

[5] Ibid.

It may be too much to expect the Habsburg officials to realize that the foreign workers might upset a rather delicately balanced social equilibrium in which the various relationships between individual persons and groups had been carefully established. Severe discontent could result in xenophobic rage. For several centuries Jihlava's weavers had been collected in a nominally democratic guild, numbering at one time 700 members, in which some members were more equal than others. Even though it was a practice strictly forbidden in the guild statutes, the richer masters did in fact employ their poorer fellows. Also outside the statutory regulations and undermining the feeling of independence was the fact that cloth merchants acted as putters-out to the local weavers.[1] Each master was supposed to procure his own raw materials which he had to weave according to the regulations of the guild and then to offer the finished product at the assigned market places and times where merchants were permitted to make their purchases. Since the guild was unable to protect the poorer weavers from exploitation either from within or without, there existed tensions that could only be exacerbated by the intrusion of outsiders. The act of suddenly depositing some two scores of strangers was the final insult: what self-respecting master could admit that he was not totally familiar with the mystery of his craft!

Success under such conditions would have been difficult to achieve in the best of circumstances. The refinement of fine-cloth making in England several decades earlier seems to have been the subject of similar problems there. In 1688, according to the well-known nineteenth-century writer Andrew Ure, fifty Walloons came to England and with royal encouragement began the working and dyeing of fine cloths from Spanish wool alone. 'Arts unknown to this nation before and indeed declared to be impossible . . . The backwardness of England in this important branch of trade has been accounted for as . . . owing to the municipal laws of England and its usages toward strangers.'[2] Considerable doubt exists as to the accuracy of his statement relative to the English fine woollen industry. Nevertheless, what he says is apposite for the Austrian position. Miss Mann in her recent book on the West of England cloth industry records the settlement of Dutch specialists who brought improved methods for the manufacture of fine cloth to

[1] For further details, see Ruby, *Iglauer Handwerk*; Werner, *Iglauer Tuchmacher-Zunft*.

[2] Andrew Ure, *The Philosophy of Manufactures* (London, 1835), 136.

England, but she discovered no particular difficulties with which they might have been confronted by local clothmakers.[1] The Belgian fine-cloth makers in Jihlava however faced problems. Matters were made considerably worse by Bailoux, the leader of the band, who was by all reports an obnoxious and arrogant man.

When the Jihlava guildsmen complained about their unwelcome guests, the Empress Maria Theresia quickly decided to resettle them in less antagonistic surroundings.[2] Encouraged by the information that the Netherlanders had produced fairly good cloth from native wool, she decided to turn the further disposition of the Belgians over to her consort, Emperor Franz I Stephan.[3] Very likely this swift decision, coming after the Belgian clothmakers had been in Jihlava for only a brief period, was partially conditioned by the earlier experience in neighbouring Bohemia, where efforts to introduce fine-cloth making had also run into stubborn opposition by guildsmen.[4] The refusal of the Bohemian and Moravian guilds to advance what seemed to favour their own self-interest proved to be a phenomenon that has bedevilled generations of economic developers in other contexts.

Far from an Urban Environment

Following the abortive attempt at the retraining of urban masters in Jihlava, the experiment was moved to a former hunting castle in the village of Kladruby, famous for its stud farms. There under the presumably direct control and protection of the Emperor himself it was free to develop into a model enterprise which could be emulated by others. Instead of having to deal with stubborn guild masters who referred constantly to their contractual rights as contained in their charters, the Emperor would have to cope with merely his dependent peasants. Not legally free, as were the Jihlava masters, the serf-peasants were nevertheless not chattels; passive resistance was part of their defence against unwelcome innovation. The officials of the manor were nevertheless able to exert direct pressures on the potential labour force. In Jihlava on the other hand, the enterprise had to depend for its success on more voluntary compliance to the orders of the central government.

[1] J. de L. Mann, *The Cloth Industry in the West of England from 1640 to 1880* (London, 1971), 11–14.
[2] HKA, red no. 891, f. 1–3, 10 April 1749.
[3] HKA, red no. 891, f. 6, Wien.
[4] A. F. Pribram, *Commerzcollegium*, 212–13: 231–7.

The move to the countryside had the benefit of protection against the opposition of guildsmen, but it incurred other liabilities. The potential manpower was composed of peasants whose primary occupation was working the land. To be sure, they knew how to spin and weave, these being fairly ubiquitous skills. Peasants everywhere in Europe spun and wove for their own consumption and in addition worked for traders who periodically collected the yarn or the unfinished cloth.[1] They were involved to some extent in the industrial market mechanism. Frequently such work was part of the manorial obligation of the peasants. In skill they were without question far behind the urban craftsmen, but to the potential factory master this could have been a blessing in disguise. At least he did not have to contend with the hostility of the masters like those in Jihlava. They had resented deeply efforts from outside to have them change their methods of production, because, as they averred they knew the skills fully as well as the foreign craftsmen and rejected them as contrary to the ordinances of their guild. Possibly because of the minimal nature of the changes, the guild-masters were

Bohemia and Moravia in the mid-eighteenth century

[1] Cf. Lujo Bretano, 'Über den grundherrlichen Charakter des hausindustriellen Leinengewerbes in Schlesien', *Zeitschrift für Social-und Wirtschaftsgeschichte*, 1, (1893), 318–340; E. Tarle, *L'industrie dans les campagnes en France à la fin de l'ancien régime* (Paris, 1910), 16.

especially resistant since their pride was touched to the quick. The peasant-weavers on the other hand, had little reason to exhibit such pride; if they were receptive to a change from agricultural to industrial labour, they had less to unlearn. They were, moreover, subject to the orders of their manorial lord while the Jihlava masters insisted on their freedom and independence.

If in a perverse way the introduction of a new technology might be easier with the untutored peasants of the Bohemian manor than with the accomplished masters of Jihlava, there would be a number of externalities that could prove to be major problems. Over the centuries during which the cloth industry had existed in Jihlava, a social division of labour had evolved which made life go relatively smoothly. No one needed to think twice where to procure his wool nor where to sell his cloth. Everyone knew the markets and the merchants and was ready to walk to the oblong, somewhat steeply sloping market place in order to sell or to buy as necessary. There was also a common fullery, a dyehouse and tentering frames, all owned by the guild. Masters had to purchase materials from the guild with the strong likelihood that they would be forced to pay monopoly prices. Unhappy as they might be about these and other exactions, they nevertheless had the services available. In a rigidly circumscribed society they were well aware of the fact that their leaders — the supposed equals when all the masters sat down to their weekly *Morgensprache*, the forenoon drinking and discussion meeting which every member of the guild was required to attend — were in fact better off by virtue of various special rules. They were permitted to produce more cloths each year and employ more journeymen and apprentices. However dissatisfied with this unequal society the ordinary guild master might have been, he knew his niche and unquestionably gained some social benefit from this fact.[1]

Among the other beneficial externalities that the Belgian cloth-makers would miss in their little Bohemian village were the various craftsmen who normally serviced the textile manufacturers of Jihlava. The cabinet-maker and the smith as well as the butcher, the baker and the candlestick-maker were all mostly urban craftsmen. In addition, Jihlava, lying on an old trade route that led from Vienna to Prague, clearly had locational advantages. Kladruby, on the other hand was in a little, inaccessible corner of a huge estate. Lastly, there was also a government machinery that

[1] Mainuš, Vlnařství, 57–81; d'Elvert, *Iglau*; Werner, *Iglauer Tuchmacher-Zunft*; Ruby, *Iglauer Handwerk*.

fitted the particular requirements of free artisans. Even though the patrician leaders of the town like the leaders of the guild were often in conflict with the rank and file members, they still symbolized the free status of the craftsmen and their supposed right of self-determination.

In Kladruby, the Netherlanders found few of the social and political perquisites to which they were accustomed either in Verviers or in the Moravian town, Jihlava. All of the externalities which were almost a natural component of towns had to be created, except that in the new setting they had to be largely internalized. There were no merchants who put out raw materials and organized the sale of the finished goods, nor were there markets at which raw wool and finished woollens were offered for sale, where buyer and seller met. Nor were there easy connecting links to other markets such as Leipzig, Breslau, or Linz. And where, in Jihlava, the guild owned a tentering area and a fulling mill, in Kladruby the centrally-organized workshop had to provide this fixed capital itself. It would be too much to say that these factors determined the size of the enterprise. Nevertheless, the minimum capacity of a fullery or a dyehouse surely could be expected to be one of the controlling elements on the number of looms, for example, that would be operated. Severe underutilization of equipment with fairly high fixed costs would increase the average cost of a unit of the finished goods considerably. Entrepreneurs would be induced therefore to lower average unit costs by taking advantage of economies of scale.[1] Such problems did not need to trouble the master-weaver in a town like Jihlava where an equilibrium condition had evolved over time so that the various facilities for the production of woollen cloth matched the needs for their use.

These were of course the problems of management and did not concern the craftsmen employed in the enterprise. More difficult for them would be the rural and manorial setting in which they were now placed. They were free; and all their neighbours were peasants, ubiquitous and degraded. The Belgian workers represented a concentrated workforce under the explicit direction of a manager whose orders came directly from the Emperor's agent, the manager of all the imperial estates, the same person who supervised the officialdom of the estate itself. This could hardly fit well with the manorial officials, whose control over the inhabitants had hitherto

[1] Cf. Hicks, *Theory of Economic History*, 142; Edith Penrose, *The Theory of the Growth of the Firm*, (Oxford, 1959).

been unchallenged. Having escaped from the jealousy of their nominal Moravian peers in Jihlava, the clothmakers from Verviers thus had come into another hostile and in many ways more difficult environment in Kladruby.

The problems that vexed the industrial undertaking in a rural setting could have been predicted on the basis of the experience of the well-known textile works in Horní Litvinov (Oberleutensdorf) and the less well-known textile works of the Counts Kaunitz at Slavkov. A brief survey of the social and administrative relationships on manorial estates makes it clear that the unpleasant tensions that arose between the officials of the Pardubice manor, of which Kladruby was a part, and the factory's manager should not have come as a complete surprise.

Pardubice was a large and rich estate in the eastern part of Bohemia. According to an official estimate in 1756, it was worth 2,710,000 fl., the highest valuation of any Bohemian estate at the time. This estate had a population of between 40,000 and 50,000 persons.[1] To be sure, the net income derived from rents in 1764 was only somewhat over 55,000 fl. whereas another imperial estate Zbiroh (Zbirow) yielded twice that sum. This difference may be partly explained by income from the large iron works that existed at Zbiroh on the one hand, and on the other hand, some extraordinary expenditures at Pardubice, as mentioned but not explained on a note that accompanied the resumé of incomes of the Bohemian imperial estates.[2]

Kladruby was a little village of less than 400 souls, on the right bank of the Elbe river. It was tucked away in the westernmost corner of the estate, one of 157 places and towns that were responsible to the chief administrator in the castle in the town of Pardubice some twenty kilometres and a four-hour trip away. The estate itself formed nearly one-fifth of the total area of the Chrudim jurisdictional district and in the 1833 census held somewhat more than one-sixth of its population. The topography of the Pardubice was almost level throughout. It was poor in soil but rich in fish ponds and forests. The Elbe river, which was not navigable at this point,

[1] Pardubice was an estate (*Herrschaft*) and like most of the estates in Bohemia and Moravia exercised the rights of an *Obrigkeit* over the population. These jurisdictional rights are most closely akin to manorial rights elsewhere in the Middle Ages. M. E., 'Verzeichniss der Herrschaften und Güter in Böhmen nach dem Werthe derselben', *Archiv der Geschichte und Statistik von Böhmen*, Joseph von Riegger, ed., (Dresden, 1792–1795), II, 372–4; J. G. Sommer, *Das Königreich Böhmen*, v, Chrudimer Kreis (Prag, 1837), 44. In 1833 its population was 55,000.

[2] Haus-Hof-und Staatsarchiv, Poschakten, J. S., Karton No. 8, f. 82.

was useful mainly for the floating of lumber. In the early nineteenth century and presumably earlier as well, most of the forest land and almost all the fish ponds, which had been artificially created several centuries before, belonged to the owner of the estate. On the other hand, ninety per cent of the arable land was in the hands of peasants, a number of whom had immigrated from Prussian Silesia and formed several new villages in 1778–80. As the other inhabitants of the Chrudim district, the peasants of the Pardubice estate were undoubtedly primarily engaged in cultivating the soil and raising cattle for their own sustenance. Besides that they must have comprised a good number of the 20,000 part-time flax and hemp spinners in the district who in the industrial census of 1966 were responsible for a production of 220,000 fl. or more than half of the entire industrial production reported for the district.[1] If it was this type of industrial activity that attracted the woollen-cloth plant to Kladruby, then it came there under the mistaken illusion of building on a ready-made supply of skilled labour. That the peasants were not a willing supply of labour became clear when the administrator of imperial estates in Vienna had to issue a direct order to provide the factory with spinners and spoolers at the very start of its existence. It is not completely clear however whether the workers were reluctant to come to the factory or whether they were held back by antagonistic manorial officials.

The Administration of a Manorial Estate

Pardubice being a large manorial estate whose owner was an absentee, a substantial bureaucracy was required for its administration. At the apex of the hierarchy, as on other large estates in Bohemia, there sat the estate manager or chief steward (*Oberamtamann*), who represented the owner both in his capacity as a public authority (*Obrigkeit*) and as the private landowner. His importance is exemplified by the large sum of 4,000 fl. that he had to deposit to assure his honest conduct while in office, a sum four times as large as that required of the official with the next highest bond. As could be expected he also received the largest salary but his 700 fl. was only twice that of the *Burggraf*, the second in command on the estate, whose bond of 800 fl. was only one-fifth as great as that of his superior. The *Burggraf's* cash salary of 369 fl. per year was higher

[1] HKA, red no. 794, f. 680–92, 'General Landes-Aufnahm und Manufacturs Tabella des Königreichs Böheim pro Anno 1776'.

than that of several other officials such as the collector of rents (*Rentmeister*), the official in charge of the orphan's funds (*Waysenschreiber*) and the tax collector (*Contributionsschreiber*) each of whom deposited 1,000 fl. in bond.[1] All of them added to their salaries through the receipt of various fees and unquestionably through illegal requisitions. On the imperial manors the officials were probably more capable, if not more honest, and may have been somewhat better paid than on other estates where both by virtue of their low income and the constant pressure to extract high revenues for their lords, they were cast in the role of the peasants' oppressors.[2] Their employers, absentee lords, enjoyed life in sumptuous town houses in Prague, where their great mansions with their formal Baroque gardens are still very much in evidence, or at Court in Vienna. They usually concerned themselves little with the welfare of their subjects, an observation that should not, however, obscure the fact that some Bohemian and Moravian aristocrats were well aware of the meaning of *noblesse oblige* and took their responsibilities as family head and protector of their servile subjects very seriously.[3] Circumstantial evidence suggests that the Emperor as the *Obrigkeit* at Pardubice saw to it that the population on his manors was decently treated.

In the Habsburg Monarchy, the *Obrigkeit* continued to carry out its quasi-governmental functions until the relevant officials were formally assimilated into the governmental apparatus in 1848.[4] Thus, although the lord of the manor — who in the case of Pardubice was the Emperor — was responsible for the adjudication of disputes, the enforcement of government decrees and the collection of taxes, it was actually the chief steward who dealt with these routine matters. To the peasant he was the enforcing authority; the state was far off. While this institutional arrangement might remove much of the stigma from the central government for the numerous harsh exactions to which the peasant was subject, it also prevented the peasants, who after all comprised the vast bulk of the total

[1] SUA, Zbiroh, Gehalts-Tabella 1746 für sämmtliche Wirtschafts-und Schichtsbeamten auf den böhmischen Cameral Herrschaften.

[2] Werner Stark, 'Die Abhänigkeitsverhältnisse der gutsherrlichen Bauern Böhmens im 17. und 18. Jahrhundert', *Jahrbücher für Nationalökonomie und Statistik*, CLXIV (1952), 274–8.

[3] Cf. Christoph Thienen-Adlerflycht, *Graf Leo Thun im Vormärz*, (Graz-Köln, 1967); Freudenberger, *The Waldstein Woolen-Mill*.

[4] Alois Brusatti, 'Die Stellung der herrschaftlichen Beamten in Österreich in der Zeit von 1780 bis 1848', *Vierteljahrschrift für Sozial-und Wirtschaftsgeschichte*, XLV (1958), 505–516.

population, from having any particular loyalty to the country and the monarch. Not only did this condition obstruct the process of modern nation-building, but it had other potentially deleterious effects. If the centralization of government activities was a desirable step in the progress of modern man, the parochial and patrimonial condition of the Habsburg people must be considered harmful. A non-centralized government could, of course, have proved in the end more beneficial to society and there was at least a fairly strong basis for this type of evolution in Bohemia and Moravia.

In the 1750s when the woollen-cloth factory was located in Kladruby, the chief steward of the Pardubice estate was not directly responsible to the Emperor, the lord of the estate, but instead to Baron François Joseph von Toussaint.[1] Since at least 1737, Toussaint was the responsible official for all of the Emperor's estates which besides the Bohemian imperial estates included several in other parts of the Monarchy privately owned by Franz Stephan. In the historical literature on the subject, Toussaint often becomes one of the proxies for the Emperor in the latter's financial and economic operations. Also often cast in this role by historians are, among others, Count Rudolph Chotek, the head of the Court Commercial Council between 1749 and 1761, and Count Johann Ludwig von Harbuval und Chamaré, both of whom acted frequently in their own name but supposedly for the Emperor.[2] At any rate, in the dealings with the Kladruby woollen-cloth works, the name Toussaint was prominent and determining but it must remain moot how much autonomy of action he exercised. More often than not Toussaint's directives did not go to the chief steward but instead went directly to the second in command on the manor, Dr Oppelt, very likely a holder of a degree in jurisprudence, the *Burggraf*, and the person in charge of the lord's economic interest.

The main actors in the Kladruby woollen mill were then Baron Toussaint, in overall charge of the Emperor's manors, the *Burggraf* of Pardubice, and Guillaume Joseph Bailoux, the manager of the enterprise. Bailoux deserves further discussion if only because he represents a type of person often met in the conscious and organized transmission of techniques and technology. Even more important he was the potential entrepreneur on whose skill depended the success of the venture.

[1] Mikoletzky, 'Franz Stephan', 251 ff.
[2] Ibid.

The Belgian Manager

Troublesome and complaining, persons like Bailoux seem often to be the necessary failures that provide part of the manure for the tree of economic revolution — to alter and adjust for our purposes the famous dictum of Thomas Jefferson concerning the tree of liberty. Bailoux was born in 1710, the son of a manufacturer and merchant of woollen cloth. In a 1722 list of clothiers his family, then headed by his widowed mother, had an output that ranked it among the lower fifty percent.[1] Assuming that his mother continued to operate the business, Bailoux would have grown up within the environment of a middle-sized workshop and would presumably have imbibed the traditions and methods of a self-respecting master of the town. Whether this background was sufficient to prepare him for the management of a manufacturing enterprise employing over one hundred workers is questionable.

Was he simply an adventurer who wanted to make a great career for himself? Did the plan for the recruitment of workers in Verviers originate with him or was he sought out by government officials who had selected the fine-cloth industry for development? To follow Bailoux in his tale as he expounded it in letters to the Empress more than a decade later, he was an audacious entrepreneur who was constantly frustrated by unsympathetic officials. Count Chotek, head of the Court Commercial Council, on the other hand insisted that he was a brazen and worthless fellow. To Maria Theresia, he was an artist and an industrious worker whose foibles should be forgiven. Bailoux was not unique; there were many others of his type at this period, persons who offered their knowledge and who made extravagent claims for their ability to carry out great innovations. They remind one of the careers of gamblers whose methods often verge on the criminal. Bailoux in fact was incarcerated for fraud but was released by order of the Empress. Very likely, as in many other instances, her intuition was sound. Often it does require eccentric personalities to effect innovations. But with such persons also goes a substantial risk that the supposed innovator was a fraud, who in the words of Joseph II many years later, was expert mainly in extracting funds out of the pockets of public officials.[2] By the 1780s when Joseph made these remarks the Monarchy was already the beneficiary of a momentum that provided it eventually with a

[1] Lebrun, *Verviers*, 413–14. I wish also to thank M. Lebrun for information on Bailoux's parentage and the date and place of his birth.

[2] K. Pribram, *Geschichte*, 396–400.

modest industrial revolution. He could afford to be scornful of the efforts of his predecessor whose 'mistakes' helped the Habsburg Monarchy to enjoy a significant upward trend in its economy. The fine-woollen cloth industry that Bailoux aided in establishing made a considerable contribution to this process, although he disappointed the hopes of those who saw in him a potential entrepreneur. He was, however, one of the more knowledgeable persons available and was therefore a logical choice to aid in the search for a new location, when the foreign workers in Jihlava had to be moved to another location in 1749.

Re-Location

The Belgian master was joined in his task by Commercial Councillor (*Kommerzienrat*) Reinhard von Westerhold, who presumably headed the two-man team. Westerhold was a member of the Bohemian Commercial Council, a body that he had joined only the year previous. He himself was shortly to become an industrialist on his own account. To him goes the credit, for example, of having founded the first protofactories, i.e., larger, centralized workshops, within the area of today's Prague.[1]

Westerhold's career is instructive, not only in order to learn more about a man whose influence proved important at a vital stage of the enterprise that is being examined here. It also demonstrates one method by which the Habsburg Monarchy went about the task of industrialization. Born in the Westphalian town of Recklinghausen, he first appears in the Habsburg records when he was appointed a permanent secretary (*Assessor*) to the Bohemian Commercial Council in 1748, having served previously as governor (*Hofmeister*) to the children of Count Thun.[2] This may hardly seem the sort of employment in which one would find a person who was an expert in woollen manufacture and who was to become an important government official for economic matters and an industrialist. On the other hand, his background in this respect at least is reminiscent of Morgenthaler's a century before in Brno.

On the basis of the extant records, it is difficult to evaluate Westerhold's expertise in industrial and economic matters. He was successful as a government official if his increased responsibilities are a key, and he was beyond that an entrepreneur. Beside his post

[1] J. Janáček, 'Westerholdovská zahrada', (*Westerhold's garden*), *Časopis Společnosti Přatel Starožitnosti*, LXII (1954), 179.
[2] SUA, SM C-66-1, f. 186.

as a permanent secretary in the Bohemian Commercial Council for which he received 400 fl. per year,[1] he became 'factory inspector' for Prague in 1756 with a 300 fl. salary, inspector of fustians produced in the area (*Barchent Inspektor*) in 1760 for 200 fl. and finally the head of a lace factory established by the wife of one of his deceased colleagues on the Commercial Council for 200 fl.[2] As an entrepreneur he established three different industrial enterprises in his 'garden' and in each case he was able to have government agencies favour him with interest-free loans and monopoly privileges. Two months after he purchased the 'garden' for 5,500 fl., he received an interest-free loan of 6,000 fl., to be repaid in ten years, 'so that he could do something useful' in the textile industry.[3] This loan came from the Bank Deputation, which had previously been instrumental in recruiting skilled workers under Bailoux's direction. Six months later Westerhold was honoured with another loan of 6,000 fl., for the same purpose. This time the commercial authorities, of which he was a member, were the lenders. With these sums he began a fustian factory in 1749. In the following year, he established a leather tannery and for this purpose borrowed a total of 11,700 fl., without interest from the royal pawn office (*K. K. Pfand und Leihamt*). He also founded a factory for the drawing of copper wire (*Leonische Fabrik*) to be brocaded with silver and gold.[4] Before he died in 1769, he seemed to have become interested in yet another enterprise. He promised to deposit 1,000 fl. to the credit of a foreign velvet manufacturer, one Anton Bonoanni. When he died, he left an estate whose assets were inadequate to cover his debts.[5]

Westerhold, the resourceful, venturesome man from Westphalia, and Bailoux, the Verviers master dyer and clothmaker, were the team that devoted a three-week period in June 1749 to finding a desirable place for the Verviers workers who were being harried in Jihlava. After having visited the Bohemian imperial estates of Brandys (Brandeis), Kolín (Kolin), Poděbrady (Podiebrad) and Pardubice, they decided that the village of Kladruby at the Western point of the Pardubice estate, would prove to be the most suitable.[6]

[1] HKA, red no. 40, f. 147.

[2] SUA, CG Elenchen, 1756–A–3, 1760–A–Z, 1761–A–12.

[3] Janaček 'Zahrada', 179: '... damit ich im stand gesetzt werden möchte in der Woll, Spinn-und Zeugmacherei dem Commerzio was nützliches beizubringen.'

[4] HKA, red no. 911, 26 May 1752.

[5] Ibid., no. 41, 22 May 1769; no. 42, 12 Jan. 1769.

[6] SUA, CG 1731–54, A–2–1749 *c.* 419, 10 April 1749; 31 May 1749; 27 Juni 1749.

The report that Westerhold gave to the Bohemian Commercial Council at its sitting on 27 June 1749 is worthwhile rendering in detail here for the full flavour of the recommendations. Having determined that at the other sites a fulling mill could not be erected, the two experts decided upon the garden of a former stud-farm in Kladruby because of the availability of sufficient quantities of good water and the existence of useful buildings that could easily and cheaply be put into shape. Altogether some 7,000 fl., might be needed for construction purposes. The dye works could be located in the kitchen of a former hunting castle; a stream in which the wool and cloths could be also rinsed, flowed immediately past it. Moreover, there would be no problem in directing the flow of the water to the dye vats by way of a wooden channel. On the main floor of the castle, there were large rooms that could be used for storage. The ten rooms on its second storey could serve as work space. In one wing of the building the press could be located and workers could live in the other wing. Two empty houses and several barracks in the vicinity could also serve as living quarters for the foreign workers. The fulling mill could either be placed on the stream or near the water-driven mill of a neighbouring village. There was little question, Westerhold concluded, that Kladruby was the most convenient place in Bohemia for a woollen cloth factory especially since numerous spinners were already working on their own account in neighbouring villages and estates and wool could be procured without much trouble from the imperial estates, and from several other places not far away.

Westerhold recommended that a sum of 23,000 to 30,000 fl. be set aside. To make the work in Kladruby more attractive for the workers from Verviers, Westerhold proposed that they should be offered free living quarters and some material such as wood. This was the report that Councillor Westerhold submitted to his colleagues on the Bohemian Commercial Council, assuring them at the same time that a great benefit would result from this large-scale enterprise which seemed to him to be assured of large and profitable market.[1]

Entrepreneurial Function

Since Maria Theresia had entrusted her consort with the further disposition of the Belgian craftsmen and, moreover, since Pardubice,

[1] SUA, CG 1731–54, A–7–1749 Referat über die Tuch Fabrique in Cladrup, 27 Juni 1749.

of which he was the manorial lord, was destined to be the location for their industrial activity, it is difficult to understand why Westerhold offered his detailed recommendations for the approval of the members of the Bohemian Commercial Council. Bailoux, on the other hand, incorporated his proposals in a memorandum several months later to the head of the central administration of the imperial estates in Vienna.[1] Without giving specifics, he asked for a sum of 17,046 fl. As entrepreneur he also requested various privileges such as having free lodging for his family as well as for the families of his workers, exemption from all tax payments for a twenty-year period, among other things.

What the decisions were in the light of these proposals cannot be determined for lack of specific evidence. Some inferences as to the size and source of the investment can be made from memorandums that flowed as a result of the disastrous condition of the woollen mill in Kladruby at the end of its existence there. In one of these there appear some indications of the capital that the estate invested in this venture. Hoping to have the surplus of wool from its sheep worked into cloth, the estate provided the factory with a capital of 10,000 fl. initially, this being apparently the value of the refurbished buildings that were to serve for working space and dwellings.[2] This sum was of course only one-third of that suggested by Westerhold and nearly 50 per cent less than Bailoux's more modest request. To gain a more accurate understanding of the manor's investment in this industrial venture, one ought to add the wood and possibly even the foodstuffs that were made available either free or at low cost to the workers and the plant. Since Bailoux had no funds of his own and since he most probably drew all of the salary assigned to him, his investment in the firm can be considered to have been nil. Moreover, there is no evidence that any other private person shared in the ownership of this enterprise while it was located in Kladruby. In addition to its initial investment, the estate also made numerous cash advances, as indicated by scattered records after 1753.[3] Amounts from 200 fl. to over 9,000 fl. appear in these highly incomplete records, but it is impossible to make any precise estimate of the total amounts. These monies were used for wage payments and probably for the purchase of dyes and other goods that could

[1] SUA, ČDKM v Pardubice, 18 de Fevrier 1750.

[2] HKA, red no. 891, f. 106–15, 31 Dec. 1761, 'Allerunterthänigster Vortrag des . . . Commercien Directori.'

[3] SUA, ČDKM v Pardubice, f. 1–81.

not be furnished directly by the estate. When the factory was moved to Brno in January 1764, it still owed the Pardubice estate 43,000 fl.[1] Altogether, this sum may have represented the lower limit of the capital that the estate as an entity had invested and which it was forced to write off as a total loss.

Did this heavy commitment of the estate demonstrate its ownership? Since the archival evidence fails to make any mention of formal ownership, the best that one can do is to draw inferences. Decisions concerning the estate as well as the factory were made in Vienna by the Emperor, as possessor of the rights of usufruct over the estate, or as his agent, Baron Toussaint. On the estate the officials obviously saw these fiduciary relationships to the factory as creditor to debtor. But they had to follow the orders of their superiors in Vienna and therefore were frustrated in their efforts to collect the large debt that they claimed from the factory. Under these conditions the question of formal ownership becomes unimportant. For the estate itself this industrial enterprise proved to be a constant drain in resources as well as an uncomfortable co-inhabitant of its territorial space. The main benefit that the estate hoped to derive from the factory was the ready sale of locally grown wool, though its quality was considerably below that of the Spanish Merino variety, the main ingredient of the product as imported from Verviers and other west European centres of fine-cloth production. In 1759 there is clear evidence that this fact was recognized, although it must have been apparent many years before. In that year a new organizational arrangement was created in which the so-called Military Cloth and Baize Warehouse (*Militär Tuch- und Boy Magazin*) in Vienna began to play a new and important role. From this point on, the main raw material was Spanish Merino wool for which the Warehouse advanced funds for purchase abroad. Even more than the Pardubice estate, the Warehouse — itself an agency of the central government — was the medium through which this enterprise was kept alive with the hope of achieving eventually permanent health.

Clearly, Toussaint occupied a vital position. A writer who described the topography of Bohemia district by district in the 1780s has it that his death in 1760 was largely responsible for the decline of the factory.[2] While this assertion is not supported directly

[1] HKA, red no. 891, f. 646–64, 30 Jan. 1764.

[2] Jaroslaus Schaller, *Topographie des Königreichs Böhmen*, XI (Prag & Wien, 1789), 48.

by the documentary evidence, it does place the emphasis on the entrepreneurial function. Given the available knowledge and techniques at the time, was it wise to create a fine woollen enterprise in the Habsburg lands and if so was Kladruby the best place that could have been found for it? An affirmative answer to the first question is posited on the Mercantilistic notion that industrial self-sufficiency was desirable and that it could be best achieved by recruiting workers from those areas where the imported product was actually manufactured. These first steps were carried out with dispatch and caused no special difficulty. Although the next step of settling the foreign craftsman in an urban woollen centre seemed equally logical and simple, it proved to be abortive in the face of the strong hostility with which the Belgians were greeted. Since the officials of the central government were not prepared to abandon the project, the choice of a new location became critically important. Should they have opted for another town where the workers could operate in a setting fairly similar to that they were accustomed to in Verviers, where they generally laboured for the most part in their own workshops? Instead they were brought to a completely rural setting far from any town and moreover collected in a centralized workshop or protofactory, under the direction of one person. Knowing how often government officials and writers spoke of the recalcitrant spirit of guilds, one might suspect that the decision-makers had from the start not held high hopes for success in Jihlava and quite naturally took the first opportunity to propose a more protected sanctuary.

In the light of past experience the decision to locate on the Pardubice estate seemed reasonable. It was not the first time that this estate had been suggested as the location of a woollen factory. In 1720 an anonymous proposal to that effect had found a favourable reception from government officials, only to be demolished in a sharply worded memorandum from the then chief administrator of the Bohemian royal estates. Very likely the proponent had the Waldstein woollen mill, founded five years before, in mind as a model.[1] Did Westerhold, the Emperor or Toussaint know about this particular proposal or had they considered any other relevant experience before they settled for the location in Kladruby? The point is a moot one; the documents are silent.

[1] A. F. Pribram, *Commerzcollegium*, 129–136.

Entrepreneurial Error

Emperor Franz Stephan and Toussaint had both had previous experience with industrial undertakings. In 1736, the year in which the future emperor and then Duke of Tuscany married Maria Theresia, he also purchased two estates, Holič and Šaštin, located on the western border of present-day Slovakia. On Šaštin he placed a large-scale cotton enterprise which shared the cotton-producing monopoly for the entire Monarchy with a state-owned cotton factory in Schwechat, outside Vienna. Both firms went into private ownership in the 1750s. Even with special privileges, both the Šaštin and the Schwechat enterprise experienced numerous problems. At Holič Franz Stephan founded in the early 1740s an earthenware works, which remained in the hands of the imperial family for about one hundred years.[1] At any rate, whatever mistakes Franz Stephan and his advisor Toussaint made in the Kladruby enterprise should not be ascribed to their ignorance. By the same token they were not obligated to accept the recommendations of Westerhold and Bailoux. Nevertheless, they should have been able to rely on the technical competence of these experts. It is therefore disappointing to find that the quality of the water turned out to be detrimental to rinsing and dying whereas the two locators insisted on the opposite.[2] Possibly Westerhold and Bailoux found the water to be worse at other places.

Another factor that the locators probably assessed incorrectly relates to the labour force. The existence of a large pool of spinners in the vicinity of Kladruby had been put forward by Westerhold as one of the positive factors. But what they spun was hemp and flax for coarse weaves. It was a significant error on the part of Westerhold and Bailoux if they assumed spinning to be a homogeneous skill applicable to all fibres. The basic techniques of spinning flax and wool were the same, but the spinner used the Saxony spinning wheel for flax without trouble whereas the large hand-operated wheel was preferred for wool all over Europe at that time. If the Saxony wheel operated by a treadle was used in the area, the fineness and uniformity of the yarn required for woollen goods could not be achieved. Moreover, the peasant women on the Pardubice estate are primarily occupied with field work during the summer.

[1] Anton Špiesz, *Manufakturne obdobie na Slovensku 1725–1825* (Bratislava, 1961), 26–36; Mikoletzky 'Holics und Sassin'; Mikoletzky, 'Franz Stephen', 246–52; Mainuš, Vlnařstvi, 157.

[2] HKA, red no 891, 6 August, 1762.

Their hands being constantly in the sun subjected them to cracking of the skin and therefore caused substantial initial problems when spinning began again in the autumn. For coarse yarns this might be relatively unimportant; for the spinning of fine wool, however, great harm might result. In the Eupen–Verviers–Monschau area, with which Bailoux was familiar, pastoral agriculture predominated, allowing for the woman's hands to remain more supple all the time.[1]

The decision to locate the fine-woollens protofactory in Kladruby seems to have been primarily conditioned by factors connected with production and little attention seems to have been paid to the marketing side. Labour, raw materials and foodstuffs were expected to be readily available so that their procurement would prove to cost less than in an urban place. Domestic wool from Pardubice and nearby estates would merely require care in the selection and processing, a proposition that proved to be a serious and costly delusion.[2] The estate itself would of course gain greatly not only from the sale of the raw materials to the woollen mill but also from the sale of foodstuffs to the workers. Moreover, numerous poor inhabitants would find employment, thereby improving their standard of living.

The Problem of Sales

Even if the cloths had proved to be high enough in quality to compete with the imported product, sales would most likely still have provided some problems. Since the decision-makers concentrated mainly on the factors of production, they seemed to have ignored the locational relationship of the industry to the potential market. This is where the absence of a merchant's opinion was damaging to the decision-making process. The population in the vicinity of Kladruby could of course not provide a market for fine cloth, a luxury article reserved for the apparel of the upper classes. Consequently, transportation facilities should have been among the decisive locational factors. Although the Elbe river flowed past Kladruby, it was not navigable; overland routes were difficult and whatever 'roads' existed were far away. It may have been common in the mid-eighteenth century to ignore this factor in the Mercantilistic–Cameralistic literature and therefore in the thinking of the

[1] Ernst Barkhausen, *Die Tuchindustrie in Montjoie, ihr Aufstieg und ihr Niedergang*, (Aachen, 1925), 64–6.

[2] HKA, red no. 891, f. 106–15.

protagonists but the industrial centres in England were growing up on the basis of local and original demand, as the Manchester industrialist John Kennedy pointed out in the early nineteenth century.[1]

Basic to the strategic decision to establish the fine-woollen cloth industry was the assumption that a large market awaited the output of enterprise like that located in Kladruby. Since the import of fine cloth was known to be large, there was certainly every reason to believe that a modest enterprise of six-loom capacity could easily sell its entire output. In fact, however, this proved to be another delusion. Internal and foreign fairs and weekly markets, the traditional places for the sale of goods, proved completely disappointing. Bailoux's one documented trip to a fair in 1751 seemed to have been sufficient to kill his ardour for any similar future excursion.[2] Instead, agencies of the government and the imperial estates were forced to provide direct aid for the sale of the goods manufactured in Kladruby — all without permanent success, however. The central government took the general attitude that it was the patriotic duty of every subject of the Empress to purchase goods manufactured within the Monarchy, whether they were as good and cheap as the imported product or not. It recognized that new industry might not be competitive with the foreign manufacture but that was part of the cost that had to be paid to achieve economic development. Beyond that, the state considered it part of its function since it embarked on a strong development drive, to employ in the aid of sales coercion within the Monarchy and diplomatic effort abroad.[3]

This all-out effort had disappointing results. Given the low level of the bureaucracy and the consequent ineffectiveness in having orders carried out at all levels, it is not surprising, for example, that Army regiments were still buying fine cloth abroad in 1772 after more than twenty years of decrees and direct orders that they were to buy only domestic cloth.[4] In 1750 the government issued a decree that military needs for cloth were to be met through the Military Cloth and Baize Warehouse in Vienna which was to order the cloth from domestic sources. If the type of cloth was unobtainable through the normal commercial channels, the Warehouse was

[1] Kennedy, 'Observations . . . on the Cotton Trade', 116 f.
[2] SUA, ČDKM v Pardubice, 7 Dec. 1751.
[3] K. Pribram, *Geschichte*, 78–83.
[4] Adolf Beer, 'Die österreichische Handelspolitik unter Maria Theresia und Joseph II', *Archiv für österreichische Geschichte*, LXXXVI (1898), 9.

empowered to finance both individual masters and entire guilds.[1] When the Kladruby enterprise faced one of its do-or-die crises in 1759, the Military Cloth Warehouse in a 'last and desperate attempt' to help the enterprise from going under was ordered by Maria Theresia to finance the purchase of Merino wool and to be responsible for the sale of the finished cloth.[2] The military aspect in this contract was conspicuously absent. The Warehouse succeeded in selling its fine-woollen cloth only through force; even then, it had to allow a discount, resulting in large loss to the government.[3]

The episode in which the Military Cloth Warehouse became involved in the factory had rather interesting aspects. The contract incorporating this arrangement was between the Warehouse and Bailoux himself, but it was so full of qualifications that Bailoux had little freedom of action. An official of the estate, acting for Baron Toussaint, was to control the stock of Merino wool and the stock of finished cloth. As soon as a piece of cloth was finished it had to be kept in a special place, and whenever twelve pieces of cloth were completed they were to be transported to Vienna. This arrangement indicated the suspicion and distrust with which the officials in Vienna treated Bailoux. Payment was to be made after delivery of twenty-four pieces, the expected output of one month. Half of the proceeds were to be credited to the advance that the Warehouse made for wool and the other half would go primarily toward the cash payments that had to be made, for example, wages. These latter conditions seemed quite generous since the central government through the Military Warehouse made available at cost 103 sacks of Spanish wool, equivalent to over 15,000 pounds, for which it paid 19,749 fl. 30 kr. Even this large-scale effort on the part of the government proved to no avail. As already mentioned, the merchandise produced in this way had to be forced upon unwilling merchants.[4]

Coerced Customers

Among the largest customers during the 1750s were three Jewish communities in Bohemia, which in 1755 were 'persuaded' to purchase altogether 26,000 fl. of woollen cloth. At the minimum, such an order would have kept an efficient ten-loom plant busy for

[1] Hermann Fechner, *Die handelspolitischen Beziehungen Preussens zu Österreich* (Berlin, 1886), 223.
[2] HKA, red no. 891, ad. 14 April 1761.
[3] HKA, red no. 1, f. 275–6.
[4] HKA, red no. 891, ad. 14 April 1761.

fifty-two weeks.[1] The Jewish communities of Kolín, Nový Bydžov (Neu Bidschow) and Mlada Boleslav (Jung Bunzlau) were the designated buyers. It would be interesting to know why other communities, especially the large one in Prague, were not included. It is also intriguing that these three communities were saddled at the same time with the forced purchase of a large quantity of iron from Zbiroh, another large estate belonging to the Emperor. At any rate the two hundred Jewish taxpayers of Kolín, next to Prague one of the largest Jewish communities in Bohemia, agreed to accept 9,000 fl. of woollen cloth in addition to a large quantity of iron. The Jews of Nový Bydžov — numbering about 600 — were assigned 7,000 fl. and those of Mladá Boleslav 10,000 fl. of Kladruby cloth in addition to stipulated amounts of iron from Zbiroh.[2] The Jewish communities as a body in Kolín and Novy Bydzov and presumably Mladá Boleslav were permitted a twelve-year period in which they could pay off their debt and from the third year on were required to pay interest of 5 per cent. By 1766 the community of Kolín had only paid 9,500 fl. of its 14,000 fl. debt; whether the other two communities had paid all is unknown.[3] These were clearly forced sales reminiscent of the more famous actions of King Frederick II of Prussia who helped in a similar way to keep several factories in Berlin in operation.[4]

As in Berlin, Christian merchants were not immune to similar persuasion; they were favoured in so far as they had to take a smaller percentage of the goods in question. When the Military Warehouse was disbanded in 1762 its stock of the Kladruby factory cloth was divided among the cloth merchants of the Monarchy, despite their strong objections. A partial list shows that Vienna merchants were obliged to accept over 10,000 fl., Trieste nearly 6,000 fl., Graz about 4,500 fl., Linz nearly 4,000 fl., Brno about 3,000 fl. and Bolzano (Bozen), Krems and Ljubliana (Laibach) each about 1,500 fl.[5] The central government abhorred actual force, as one official who

[1] At an average price per ell of nearly 2 fl., about 13,000 ells or 520 pieces of 25 ells each were ordered. An efficient productivity per loom, as experienced in Verviers, was one piece of cloth per week. The Kladruby factory was unable to produce at that rate.

[2] SUA, ČDKM v Pardubice, 27 Dec. 1755; 23 July 1755, 'An Herrn Bailoux . . . ' See also Tobias Jakobovits, 'Jüdisches Gemeindeleben in Kolin (1763–1768)' *Jahrbuch der Gesellschaft für Geschichte der Juden in der čechoslov. Republik*, I (1929), 332.

[3] Jakobovitz, 'Kolin', 344.

[4] Otto Hintze, 'Ein Berliner Kaufmann aus der Zeit Friedrichs des Grossen', *Historische und politische Aufsätze* (Berlin 1893), 115 f.

[5] HKA, red no. 891, f. 213–20.

threatened to throw some unwilling merchants of a particular town into jail found out in a sharp reprimand, but it was not at all averse to means short of such drastic action. Generally, the regional commercial councils would call in the leaders of the various cloth merchants' communities and show them sample swatches along with the price lists and at times 'took' the orders.[1]

With a market for fine cloth as shown by the large amounts of foreign goods that entered the Monarchy, what prevented at least some unassisted sales? Was it a deliberate plot, as Bailoux insisted, on the part of the merchants who preferred the traditional foreign channels of trade? Or might it have been, as the merchants asserted, that poor quality and high prices were responsible? Assuming that the merchants had at least a partially sound case, why could the quality not have been raised over a period of more than a decade? In the beginning, the factory manager unquestionably faced major problems. He was to make use of native wool, which, by all evidence, was far inferior to the Spanish Merino wool from which fine cloths were made in Verviers. Unfortunately, even after the expensive foreign raw material was brought in at government expense the cloth did not reach a satisfactory quality. Was the lack of skill of the workers responsible? Without question there too lay a reason for the initial problems, for the Verviers artisans were to train the peasants on the estate. After attempting this process for several years, some success might well have resulted. The evidence is to the contrary. In the end the rather questionable talents of Bailoux as an organizer have to be examined. Even though one must tolerate and respect 'temperamental artists', as Maria Theresia admonished her officials, the manager was apparently unable to develop the required techniques for his job, greatly complicated as it was by the necessity of having to deal with an hierarchical manorial bureaucracy and with a labour force that was largely composed of Czech peasants. Bailoux may not have been an embezzler, as the manorial authorities accused, but he certainly was a poor manager and businessman.

Ruin in Kladruby

Towards the end of 1760, Bailoux, *Directeur de la Manufacture de Drap de Kladrup en Boheme*, saw his factory within two fingers (*deux doigts*) of total ruin unless the Empress intervened. In an eloquent if somewhat verbose petition, he spelled out his difficulties, none of

[1] HKA, red no. 891, 10 Nov. 1765.

which were of course of his own making.[1] It was an audacious and rather injudicious attempt on the part of the Belgian master to place the blame for his problems on the officials of the Military Cloth Warehouse. Maria Theresia and presumably her consort refused to accept the death of this enterprise and to write off this venture as a noble experiment in industrialization. Consequently investigations and deliberations were begun to discover the causes of failure as well as to suggest steps for amelioration. The Court Commercial Council in Vienna under the presidency of Count Rudolph Chotek was forced to tackle this obviously unpleasant problem. Recognizing that there were great difficulties to be encountered in the establishment and continuation of a fine cloth factory, the members of the Council felt it nevertheless inappropriate that such an 'immodest' person was complaining. The best solution would be if one or more Viennese merchants could be persuaded to take over the enterprise. This was unlikely because the merchants were more than satisfied with their traditional commission and credit arrangements. Moreover, there was none who was able to take 50,000 fl. from his own business and invest it without interest. This left the government as the only alternative. It would have to continue, the councillors feared, to take on the risks which the private sector accepted with alacrity in west European countries where industry was better developed and the mercantile community was stronger. More tolerant by far than her advisors, the Empress ordered that 'this industrious worker' should be strongly aided. In addition she requested a broad review of the condition of the fine-cloth industry and specifically wished to be informed of the methods that should be employed to increase the sales of this product.[2]

In this way Bailoux himself initiated the events that brought an end to his enterprise. The end itself, however, came with the demise of the Military Cloth Warehouse, the agency upon which the manager of the Kladruby factory had heaped such scorn. On 1 September 1762 it was dissolved, most likely for reasons totally unrelated to the Kladruby enterprise. This was after all a year prior

[1] HKA, red. no. 891, ad 4. Juni 1761.

[2] HKA, red no. 891, 14 April 1761; 31 Dec. 1761, 'Allerunterthänigster Vortrag des . . . Commercien Directori,' the head of the 'Commercial Directory.' Count Rudolf Chotek referred to Bailoux's proposal as ' . . . die Vorspiegelungen diesen unruhigen Fabrikanten . . . '. Maria Theresia called him at the same time, 'nützlicher Fabrikant' and indicated that she was willing to tolerate ' . . . die persönlichen Fehler derley Künstler . . . '.

to the formal conclusion of the Seven Years War, which marked the practical end also of any thought of military adventure to reconquer Silesia, a province now firmly in the hands of the Prussian King. The reduced needs of the military apparently made the Cloth and Baize Warehouse unnecessary.

Given the determination of the Empress to force the enterprise to succeed, what was to be done with the Kladruby factory? Its main support had been removed with the dissolution of the Military Warehouse, which had really been no more than a transitional device to bring the enterprise through some bitter trials and which seemed to have little beneficial effect other than keeping the plant in operation. The options that were considered included improved operation at Kladruby under Bailoux, leasing out the woollen mill to an experienced outsider and moving the enterprise to a new location. Despite the Empress's expression of tolerance of Bailoux's conduct, there was little likelihood that he would be allowed to continue in Kladruby. His activities had proved to be so questionable that a 'comptroller', who was directly responsible to Toussaint, was installed. Without his approval no material could be issued from the storeroom. Despite the strong repugnance that the Court Commercial Council showed for Bailoux and their conviction that he was incapable of managing the enterprise successfully, the Empress ordered that further investments be made — beyond the 50,000 fl. already provided — including 2,000 fl. for a Dutch press and for a dyehouse and equipment. The final crisis came in 1763 when the comptroller reported that there were no materials, no work, and no food. Some people were sick and some had already died from starvation.[1]

Another and rather intriguing possibility was then explored. In July 1762 François Biolley and his son came to Kladruby. The head of one of the largest woollen cloth manufacturing firms in Verviers, where all the larger enterprises were controlled by him and his relatives, Biolley had come at the request of his business friend, the Prague banker Johann Baptist del Curto.[2] Del Curto, a native of Chiaverra, Italy, had by then resided more than sixty years in the Habsburg Monarchy and had frequently served as an intermediary, especially in financial matters, for the imperial family and the government.[3] He was also a member of the Bohemian Commercial

[1] SUA, CG, Com 1755–72, A–1763, 30 Jan. 1763.
[2] Haus-, Hof-, und Staatsarchiv, Poschakten, J. S., Karton, 6. f. 492–4.
[3] SUA, Sal no. 192, pp. 551–66, 22 Mar. 1951. No. 168, pp. 111–17, 26 July 1736, 'Nobilitation.'

Council and was therefore familiar with the problems at Kladruby. Del Curto promised to bring together a company of investors if Biolley were willing to take over the plant.[1] Biolley sent a set of sample swatches of fine woollens manufactured by his plant in Verviers in order to demonstrate his ability in this field. From the outset, however, he had planned to send a competent manager rather than operate the plant personally.[2] The project never came to fruition.

Why the 60-year old Biolley and his 'sickly' son did not take over the factory is unknown. His more active son was at the time mayor of Verviers and presumably had little interest in this foreign adventure. After the attempt had had to be abandoned of having a Belgian manufacturer operate the factory, even if from afar, another tack was attempted. Why not have the major potential customers acquire the factory? Would not sales be assured if the Society of Cloth Merchants in Vienna (*Tuchlaubenverwandten*) were to be owner of the woollen mill? Inquiry there brought forth a decidedly negative response. The factory was too distant from Vienna, the merchants knew little about manufacturing and most of their members did not possess sufficient funds for such an endeavour.[3] What was then left was the last option, that of moving the factory to a new location. This was eventually carried out under the auspices of Johann Josef Kehrnhofer, a government official in Brno and managing director of the Moravian Loan Bank (*Mährische Leihbank*).

Summary

Fifteen years had elapsed between 1749 when the forty craftsmen from Verviers were deposited in Jihlava and January 1764 when those that had remained, augmented by several native Bohemians, packed themselves and the pitiful remains of the woollen-cloth factory in Kladruby into a number of creaky wagons for a cold trip to Brno. Had anything of value been accomplished in this interval? How much had the programme of economic development been advanced by the adventures of Bailoux and his Verviers band? Was the move to the town of Brno the final admission that a considerable entrepreneurial error had been committed in giving the factory a bucolic setting far from the corrupting influences of a city?

[1] HKA, red no. 891, f. 168–73, Prag 31 May 1762.
[2] HKA, red no 891, f. 168–73, Prag 31 May 1762. '... welcher niemals gesinnt seyn würde, sich aus Niederland in Persona zu heben, sondern lediglich einen dem Werk vollkommen gewachsener Factor hierher zu senden ...'
[3] HKA, red no. 881, f. 69–78.

That the venture was not considered a total loss is indicated by the mere fact of the transfer of equipment, stock and personnel to Brno. To be sure, this may have represented more an act of faith by the Empress than a rational decision. The transfer in fact provided the new enterprise with numerous liabilities that continued to delay success. On the other hand, the fifteen-year experience unquestionably contributed to the learning process in the industrialization of the Habsburg Monarchy.

What were the causes of failure? Were they predictable and could they have been easily avoided? The rural setting and the managerial inability of Bailoux were unquestionably major causes. Although both factors were liabilities, neither need to have proved overwhelming. Since the sales of fine cloth depended on a national market, the lack of demand on the local level had no effect. The scarcity of skilled labour was serious but could be remedied through training, a task that was in fact partially accomplished. Transportation problems, however, must have provided some difficulties, although none of the persons who examined the enterprise mentioned this question at all. More often the investigators pointed to the manager as the culprit. They did not ignore the special conditions resulting from the likely friction between the manorial officials and the factory personnel. There were, of course, mitigating circumstances. The manager's task was made immeasurably more difficult by the requirement to make fine-woollen cloth from native wool, that is, to make silk purses from sow's ears as the proverb reminds us. This became a patent impossibility. For a while coarser grades of cloth were produced as the large orders for the three Bohemian Jewish Communities in the mid-1750s indicate. But even when excellent imported wool was procured and turned over to Bailoux at no risk, sales being absolutely assured, he was unable to produce goods of a desired quality. By that time, in 1759, he may have been thoroughly demoralized, however, having been subject for years to frustrating conditions which were exacerbated by direct enemy action.[1]

Bailoux himself saw a conspiracy as the cause of his downfall. When it was not manorial officials, it was hateful merchants, who used every excuse to continue their harmful trade with foreign suppliers. Bailoux was no ignorant, uneducated craftsman. His appeals to Maria Theresia were well-written in flowing French and

[1] In 1757 he had been forced to flee when the Prussians, during the Seven Years War, overran Kladruby and destroyed part of the factory.

very imaginative. He may have been paranoid, but according to the testimony of Jean Thys several years later he was an able dyer and knew the cloth-making craft well. One should have expected him to be able to function well at least as a production boss once the responsibilities of purchasing and sales were lifted from him. In fact, he failed on all accounts. Had the quality of cloth manufactured under his direction not been of such uniformly poor quality one might have been more willing to accept this conspiracy theory.

A large part of the responsibility for the dismal showing of the Kladruby enterprise should devolve on the decision-makers in Vienna, above all on Toussaint who had had years of experience in the handling of industrial undertakings on an absentee basis. Why did he not relieve Bailoux of his managerial responsibilities when the Belgian proved himself unfit? Was he overtaxed with numerous other tasks during this time? The answers are moot at this point for lack of evidence.

Since a number of native workers had been trained in the factory to become skilled workmen, at least some positive result was achieved, albeit at a very high cost. Moreover, many errors were exposed and it would presumably become easier for a reformed organization in a new setting and under new control to avoid them.

Chapter III

THE URBAN FACTORY

A new entrepreneurial decision had to be made. Irrespective of the causes for failure in the Bohemian village, the long-range conditions under which the enterprise operated had to be changed decisively. While the rural location seems, in retrospect, to have been harmful, the memorandums that dealt with the subject were far more critical of the personal and the organizational elements. Consequently, the major points of focus for the present chapter concern the willingness and ability of particular persons to direct the enterprise, the institutional structure through which the direction was to be accomplished and the role that the government agencies played in the process.

One of the last persons to make an on-the-spot inspection of the Kladruby plant, Johann Anton Kehrnhofer, became also the vital figure through whom a fundamental change was effected in the enterprise. It was moved to the city of Brno. Kehrnhofer was ordered in August 1762 by the Empress to conduct an investigation of the plant in Kladruby. These actions came as a consequence of a detailed report that a member of the Bohemian Commercial Council had prepared on the pitiful condition of the factory.[1] A Prague merchant by the name of Melchior Kern had been dispatched by the governor of Bohemia to examine the enterprise in June 1762.[2] It is not completely clear why Kehrnhofer, who provided essentially the same analysis, had to be dispatched to Kladruby two months later. One likely reason was that he was expected to provide solutions to the problem. The officials in Vienna who suggested his assignment were aware of his interest in industrial development and knew that he had been engaged in other efforts to establish the manufacture of the types of woollen textiles that were imported into the Monarchy. They may from the start have harboured the hope that Kehrnhofer would in fact volunteer to take over the sick enterprise. Whether they believed that it was necessary to transfer the equipment, personnel and materials of the plant to Brno is subject to speculation. When Kehrnhofer did indeed propose such a re-location to

[1] HKA, red no. 891, f. 223–6, 6 Aug. 1762.
[2] Haus-, Hof- und Staatsarchiv, Poschakten (J.S.), Karton 6, f. 497–511.

Brno, there was no recorded opposition in Vienna among the government officials. On the contrary, all signs point to the likelihood that they welcomed this move.

Kehrnhofer as First Entrepreneur in Brno

Since part of our method of examining the process of industrialization in Brno follows Schumpeter's emphasis on the innovating entrepreneur, we can begin with a brief discussion of Kehrnhofer. How far he fitted the Schumpeterian model may be questioned since he probably made relatively few long-range decisions on his own. If the model is expanded somewhat to include the decision-making process whether exercised by an individual person alone or in combination with an entire group, then Kehrnhofer's case is relevant both in his function as head of the Moravian Loan Bank from its foundation in 1751 and his efforts to establish the fine-cloth factory in Brno in the years 1763 and 1764. At the very minimum, he set the tone of operations in both organizations. Both institutions were innovations for Brno as well as for the Habsburg Monarchy as a whole. In order to try to understand his motivation and his actions in his entrepreneurial function, information concerning his background would be extremely important. Unfortunately, there is very little available.

When Kehrnhofer undertook to bring the fine-cloth factory to Brno in 1763, he was a sickly, old man in his sixties who had already devoted forty years of his life to government service.[1] At the time of the founding of the Bank, he was the cashier for the local office of the government revenue administration (*Mährischer Banco-Gefällen Cassa-Verwalter*).[2] How long he had served in this position is unknown nor is there any information whether he occupied previously other side-occupations. After 1751 he did in fact continue to function as a government official while at the same time heading the Moravian Loan Bank and even being inscribed in the municipal mercantile court of Vienna as the head of the firm Johann Anton Kehrnhofer and Company.[3] The registration in Vienna may have

[1] HKA, red no. 816, f. 454 ff., 22 Feb. 1763.
[2] Ibid., f. 1–30, Jan. 1751.
[3] Archiv der Stadt Wien, Merkantil-& Wechselgericht 1760–1850, #4, f. 3K, 30 Juni 1757, Diese Anzeige samt inligender Firma bey der Canzley aufzubehalten . . . dero priv. Mährischen uns unter der Firma Johann Anton Kehrnhofer & Companie zu administrirten anvertrauten Leihbank . . . Niederlage in Wien Buchhalter David Mayer aus Lindau [hat] Vollmacht.

been only a technicality for the branch office of the Moravian Loan Bank there. It need not mean that Kehrnhofer was operating a firm for his own account but this implication cannot be simply dismissed.[1]

According to dissident shareholders who made use of the proposed acquisition of the fine-cloth factory to air their views, Kehrnhofer was dictatorial, arbitrary and irresponsible. These charges were particularly made by the permanent committee of the Moravian Estates, representing 8,000 fl. of investment, which the Estates had formally committed to the Loan Bank.[2] Their main complaint was that Kehrnhofer, merely an administrator and book-keeper of the Bank, had in fact, committed it to a course of operations that, according to them, had severely reduced the potential profits of the firm. He had concentrated on the economic development obligation of the charter to the almost total exclusion of the mortgage provision, which they felt promised a much greater return on their investment. The available evidence indicates that the Permanent Committee was correct in stating that Kehrnhofer took his economic development responsibilities more seriously than his mortgage banking ones, but in this way he was indeed operating within the framework that Maria Theresia and her officials had intended for the Loan Bank. As the Empress herself wrote on one of the memorandums dealing with these discussions, the Loan Bank was above all to aid industry and for that purpose she wanted the government's share in the Bank increased.[3]

It was small wonder then that Kehrnhofer carried the day in 1763 when challenged by shareholders who contested his leadership of the Bank. But in fact his days were numbered. Degelmann, the official of the Court Commercial Council most involved in these affairs, while supporting the manager of the Bank remarked on his age and on his poor state of health.[4] Kehrnhofer died in 1765, after having been dismissed from the Bank, an impoverished man whose widow was devoid of funds for her husband's burial and who therefore had to petition to the Empress to meet these expenses.[5]

[1] On a subsequent occasion he insisted that he was merely acting on behalf of the Loan Bank when he was requested to pay certain fees in Vienna in connexion with his activities. Higher echelons in the central government supported his stand and he therefore won his point. HKA, red no. 816, f. 251–7, 7 Jan. 1762.

[2] Ibid., f. 369 ff, 27 Juni 1763.

[3] Ibid., f. 364 ff, 22 Oct. 1763. She referred especially to *Fabrikanten*, which should within the context not be translated as industrialists but to mean skilled workers as well as their employers.

[4] Ibid., f. 494–508, 28 Juli 1763.

[5] HKA, red no. 73, 20 Juni 1766.

The Moravian Loan Bank

If Kehrnhofer died poor, he was not the first nor the last innovator to meet such a fate. The question arises how much of an innovating entrepreneur he actually was. It is difficult to discover what role he played in the founding of the Bank. The actual authors of the plan seem to have been two noblemen, both government officials and both of whom became industrialists of note themselves.[1] One of these was Heinrich Cajetan Freiherr von Blümegen, who was at the time one of the highest governmental officials in Moravia and a strong supporter of the so-called Haugwitz reforms.

Whether the organization of the Bank was in conformance with the proposals made by Wilhelm Freiherr von Schröder in his well-known book of 1686 on methods of increasing the welfare of the Austrian Monarchy, as has been asserted by one author, may be doubted.[2] Schröder favoured a note-issuing bank whereas the Moravian Loan Bank was essentially an investment and mortgage bank. Moreover it acted to a large extent as a provider of finance for small producers and carried on no traffic in commercial notes, the latter being another characteristic of Schröder's proposed bank. Schröder seemed also to prefer the private sector of the economy for industrial development.[3] The Moravian Bank, on the other hand, clearly was an instrument of the state from the beginning even though many of its shareholders were private persons. Its activities in the first two decades of existence were a testimony to the fact that there was little private entrepreneurial motivation in the Habsburg Monarchy without a strong prod from governmental authorities.

How closely the organization of the Bank followed any known model, whether contained in writings or in reality, is difficult to ascertain. It may have been unique or merely a pragmatic adaption of past experience. The well-known large banks in the mid-eighteenth century, such as the Bank of England, the Bank of Amsterdam or the Bank of Hamburg were not directly involved in industrialization efforts and could not therefore serve as models for

[1] Fritz Hönig, 'Schröders Bankprojekt', *Zeitschrift für Volkswirtschaft und Sozialpolitik*, II (1893), 520; Mainus, *Vlnařstvi*, 163 ff. One of Blümegen's factories was on his Letovice (Lettowitz) estate near Brno and the other on his Kettenhof estate near Vienna. The other nobleman was Johann Jacob Baron Neffzer who organized a flannel factory on his Heralec (Heraletz) estate in Bohemia.

[2] Wilhelm Schröder, *Fürstliche Schatz- und Rent-Cammer* (Leipzig, 1686).

[3] L. Sommer, *Kameralisten*, II, 99–107.

the Moravian Bank.[1] On the other hand, the Loan Bank may have borrowed from the experience of the Municipal Bank of Vienna, founded in 1703 for the specific purpose of managing the public debt of the central government. Being completely under the control of the central government, the Viennese bank was forced to supply funds from time to time to several large enterprises, including the so-called Oriental Company, for purposes of state policy.[2]

That the Moravian Loan Bank was in fact an instrument of government policy becomes more apparent by virtue of the ownership of shares as well as by the provision of its charter. A listing of shareholdings from the year 1763 reveals that the central government through its agency, the Court Commercial Council, owned ten per cent of the concern. Half of the shares were purchased after 1756 when Maria Theresia directed the government to add to its holdings so that the Bank could be more effective in aiding industrial development. This decision was partly caused by the fact that private investors especially those from the business community did not readily step forward to take advantage of this opportunity to come to the aid of their country. It is interesting, for example, that two businessmen who were reputed to be the richest in the city of Brno did not participate in this venture. On the contrary, the bulk of the capital came from governmental bodies such as various municipalities, the Jihlava clothmakers' guild and from noblemen and governmental officials. Brno's own share in the Bank was the largest of the municipalities and was apparently pushed through the city council by the mayor, Beranek, against considerable opposition.[3] This act was typical of what we have earlier suggested as being an important element of the more or less tolerant social atmosphere in Brno, creating for it the conditions that raised it above its fellow towns. Progress, although strongly opposed by some vested interests, did in fact have a chance in Brno.

While it might be unwise to use today's terminology, the Moravian Loan Bank with a paid-up capital of 124,000 fl. — a formidable sum for its day — functioned very much like a bank for economic

[1] Cf. J. G. Van Dillen, ed., *History of the Principal Public Banks*, (Reprints of Economic Classics, New York, 1964), 79–123, 125–60.

[2] H. J. Bidermann, 'Die Wiener Stadtbank', *Archiv für österreichische Geschichte*, XX (1859), 425, 428, 432; Viktor Hofmann, 'Beiträge zur neueren österreichischen Wirtschaftsgeschichte. Erster Teil. Die Wollenzeugfabrik zu Linz an der Donau', *Archiv für österreichische Geschichte*, CVIII (1920), 418 ff.

[3] Jindřich Chylík, 'Prvni obchodní banka u nás', *Časopis Matice Moravské*, LXIX (1950), 265.

development in our own time. Given the institutional tools available in the middle of the eighteenth century, the Loan Bank performed its functions efficiently. Many of the investors were rich persons, with high propensities to save. On the other hand, the Bank in its operations provided incomes for people with a high propensity to consume, thus creating the conditions for a multiplied stream of national income. Through its commercial and industrial financing activities, the Bank provided craftsmen with a sense of security which they had not hitherto enjoyed. As a result of its superior organization and its more innovative attitude, it began to expand the market for Moravian goods. For this purpose it sent representatives to reconnoitre both within the Monarchy and outside it in order to discover new markets. It also operated a lottery so that it could gain more investment funds and at the same time to help in finding outlets for its merchandise. Lastly, and very important, it began to publish a newspaper and it set up an information office (*Frag Amt*). One of the primary conditions for creating a wide market within the Monarchy for domestically produced goods was that merchants should know what articles were being produced and at what prices, for even if the mercantile community were not hostile to home manufacturers, the absence of information would militate against their placing purchases in the right places. These functions the Moravian Loan Bank carried out well, as the president of the Court Commercial Council in Vienna testified.[1]

The semi-public character of the Moravian Bank has already been demonstrated by the distribution of shares. From the beginning, moreover, it was intended that the Bank should work closely with the Manufacturing Office (*Manufakturamt*) whose chief civil servant was one Procop.[2] At first separate, but soon incorporated into the Moravian Commercial Council, the Manufacturing Office was meant to be the specific instrument for improving the industrial potential. One of the ways in which the Bank and the Manufacturing Office collaborated was by financing a trip to Italy in 1754 undertaken by Procop and Count Alois Podstatsky, a major shareholder in the Bank and president of the Moravian Commercial Council. Judged by the expressions of satisfaction in Vienna, the venture was highly successful, leading to a second such trip, this time Procop

[1] HKA, Böhm. Comerz, fasc., 49, red no. 789, f. 127, 9 Feb. 1775 '... die Lehenbank ... einzig und allein vor jetzo in ... Mähren im Stand ist, ein Waaren Negocium sowohl in den Kays. Erb- als Frembde Länder ... einzuleiten ...'

[2] HKA, red no. 816, f. 81–104, Brünn, 20 Aug. 1761.

accompanying Count Carl Haugwitz, son of the all-powerful chief minister in Vienna.[1]

The Bank was not only concerned with encouraging Moravian commerce and industry; it also participated in the efforts to build up Trieste and Livorno as major entrepots for Habsburg goods to replace Venice and Hamburg. It established a permanent warehouse in Trieste, where it stocked a sizeable inventory of various textiles. Moreover, the Trieste Company, a large trading company organized by the central government, was also to have been a shareholder in the Bank, thus testifying to a close connexion between the developing port on the Adriatic and the Moravian urban centre.[2]

At the same time that it was trying to create a larger market for Moravian goods, the Bank was also busily engaged in fostering domestic enterprise. It acted to improve the quality and increase the quantity of the raw material by inducing estates to plant flax, for example, and superintended the work of the widely dispersed peasant-spinners.[3] Several guilds worked on its orders and it also financed the recruitment of some Netherlands workers. Even before the Kladruby fine-woollen mill came into the picture, Procop and Kehrnhofer had suggested the installation of a twenty-loom woollen fabrics factory in Brno.[4] By the time the vital decision to transport workers and equipment from Kladruby to Brno to set up a fine-woollen cloth factory was made, then, the Moravian Loan Bank could look back on considerable achievement. It had sold directly thousands of pieces of textiles as far away as Transylvania and, indirectly by way of Trieste and Marseilles, even to America, where some linens from the factory of Count Blümegen on his Letovice (Lettowitz) estate had been sent about 1763 after they had found no purchaser in Europe. At the same time it continued to serve as an important catalyst for greater industrial activity in Moravia by aiding craftsmen and by participating in some of the new larger-scale enterprises like Blümegen's and a flannel factory owned primarily by Baron Neffzer and located on his Heralec (Heraletz) estate.[5] At the same time, it could pride itself on having

[1] HKA, red no. 789, f. 124 ff., 9 Feb. 1755. See also, August Fournier, 'Eine amtliche Handlungsreise nach Italien in Jahre 1754. Ein neuer Beitrag zur Geschichte der österreichischen Commercialpolitik', *Archiv für österreichische Geschichte*, LXXIII (1888), 228. August Fournier, 'Handel und Verkehr in Ungarn und Polen um die Mitte des 18. Jahrhunderts', *Archiv für österreichische Geschichte*, LXIX (1887), 360 ff.

[2] HKA, red no. 789, f. 189.

[3] K. Pribram, *Geschichte*, 81–2.

[4] HKA, red no. 816, f. 81–104.

[5] Ibid., f. 300, 309.

provided a 6 per cent annual dividend to its shareholders in addition to re-investing 6,000 fl. of its own surplus each year.[1] All this however was not sufficient to avert a major managerial crisis which resulted in the expulsion of Kehrnhofer and in the acquisition of the Bank by a company of Jewish financiers. Thus the Moravian Loan Bank, already unique for many of its accomplishments, became further so when its ownership was assumed by persons whose religious beliefs prevented their inhabiting houses within the walls of the city of Brno.

The sacrifice of Kehrnhofer as manager apparently resulted in no immediate change of direction in the policies of the Bank. The Moravian contingent of shareholders had been especially indignant about his lack of interest in the highly profitable lending business and his greater devotion to the economic development obligation of the charter.[2] Altogether, in the 25-year period from 1751 to 1776, only 472,000 fl. was lent out on mortgages but the Bank sold over 11,000,000 fl. in goods.[3]

Nevertheless, several basic changes had occurred. Instead of government officials, the Bank was now managed by private enterprisers, though they were still closely attached in their interests to the central government. Löbel Hönig, a member of this company, also was the head of a consortium that on 1 January 1765 received a ten-year lease for the tobacco tax (*Tabaksappalto*) covering Bohemia, Moravia, and some of the Austrian provinces.[4] In a Christian country where non-Roman Catholics were at best reluctantly tolerated, Jews were severely controlled. Thus to the state agency established to supervise the Bank, there was now added a 'sub-delegation' through which the new leaseholders had to operate. The 'sub-delegation' voted the shares of the Jewish company at stockholders' meetings. In every other way, however, the Jewish enterprisers were allowed to act out their normal role as businessmen and managers of the Bank. The device of a 'sub-delegation' was installed primarily to mollify the Brno merchants, who had been complaining about this Jewish pollution of their city and who had wanted to operate the Bank themselves. Being too poor, however, to raise an investment capital of over 100,000 fl. and being certainly

[1] Ibid., f. 494–508, Wien, 28 July 1768.
[2] Ibid., f. 369 ff.
[3] Hönig, 'Schröders Bankprojekt', 523.
[4] A. F. Pribram, *Urkunden und Akten zur Geschichte der Juden in Wien*, (2 vols., Wien and Leipzig, 1918). See also Michael Hainisch, 'Das österreichische Tabakmonopol in 18. Jahrhundert', *Vierteljahrschrift for Sozial- und Wirtschaftsgeschichte*, VIII (1911), 408 ff.

unwilling to guarantee a 9 per cent return on the investment as was the Jewish company, the Christian merchants were forced to acquiesce in the new situation.[1]

The Jewish Company and the Factory

The 'enemies of Christ', as the Brno merchants called the Jewish company, were less interested in ruining the local patricians than they were in advancing their own tobacco business. Having to take on the woollen mill was an unpleasant requirement, which they at first hoped to be able to turn over to the Jihlava clothmakers' guild. According to this plan, the Jihlava guild was to operate half of the factory, that is, 1½ looms and the Loan Bank the other 1½ looms.[2] How that feat was to be accomplished is not at all clear even though the Loan Bank was to be responsible for all the sales. The apparent architect of this scheme was a government official in Jihlava by the name of Schöps, who promised also to see to it that at least ten looms for fine cloth would be installed in Jihlava or elsewhere in Moravia. This peculiar scheme, although agreed to by the representatives of the Loan Bank and by those of the clothmakers' guild who formalized their act with splendid seals and signatures, proved to be abortive. Soon afterwards, Schöps was involved in a bitter dispute with the Jihlava guild and left government service.

Obviously, the government officials still harboured thoughts of having the Moravian cloth centre directly involved in the innovation of manufacturing fine-woollen cloth within the Monarchy. They hoped, apparently, that during the fifteen years that had intervened since the Verviers artisans had first arrived in Jihlava, the guildsmen had recognized the error of their ways. That the Jihlava masters were obviously experts at manufacturing cloth is clear, but why they should have been expected to know how to operate a factory is unexplained. Their experience prepared them only for manufacturing on a small scale and in individual workshops. To be sure, the government officials may still have entertained hopes that the factory would prove to be no more than a temporary expedient, a training institution whose pupils would take their implements back to their homes and set up shop there. The European world at the time of Adam Smith was, after all, not yet willing to concede defeat to the factory and its implications of enslavement to control and discipline.

[1] HKA, red no. 816, f. 543–9; 550–3; 558–63; 568–91.
[2] HKA, red no. 891, f. 570–73, Wien Juni, 1764.

Although the woollen-cloth factory eventually came into the hands of private persons, the entrepreneurial influence of the central government remained strong for many years. There is therefore no doubt that this particular industry owed its existence to the efforts of the central government. The brief but vital intervention of the Moravian Loan Bank raises the question often posed by economic historians relating to the innovating and initiating role of banks in the industrialization process.[1] Since it was basically a bank in name only, its activities provide little evidence on this point. At best it supports the thesis that government intervention is of primary importance in the industrialization of backward countries. The Habsburg Monarchy in the mid-eighteenth century could clearly call upon resources far greater than those available to any individuals. Not only could it take superior risks but it was able also to reduce these risks by virtue of the coercive power possessed by governmental institutions, which in this case it used for the purpose of sales, creation of a labour force and making equity capital available.

Entrepreneurial Function of the Government

Some writers have called the enterprise state-owned. If one considers the ownership of buildings and equipment as the basic criterion, this statement is correct for the first sixteen years in Brno. The case in favour of this proposition is made still stronger since strategic decisions relating to internal management and financing often were made at government request or at any rate only after consultation with state agencies. But in terms of legally binding contracts, the firm was now in private hands. The government acted only as an outside supervisory force not unlike a large investor who wished to see that his capital was safeguarded, but who preferred to leave operational decisions in the hands of management. One might also consider the state's role to be analogous to that of a sleeping partner who required detailed reporting from the operating partners because he had a large fiduciary interest in the firm. Lastly, one might view the company simply as leaseholders whose lease could be cancelled when they did not adhere to the conditions laid down in a contract by the owners. For analytical purposes there may be some use in settling on one of these categories. Compared

[1] Cf. Rondo Cameron, *Banking in the Early Stages of the Industrial Revolution* (New York, 1967); see also Rondo Cameron, ed., *Banking and Economic Development*, (New York, 1972).

to the predicament encountered in settling such a question for the factory while it was in Bohemian countryside, the picture in Brno was much clearer. There was now a definite contract, whereas formerly Bailoux, the Belgian master, was considered the entrepreneur in only a vague sense. The conditions at Kladruby were so indistinct that it would be difficult to assign ownership of the enterprise to either the state, the Emperor personally or the Pardubice manor. By the same token, Bailoux could be considered simply as an employee supervising the cloth works even though the pertinent government officials, the Emperor and Maria Theresia, pretended that the Belgian master could fulfill entrepreneurial and ownership functions. At any rate, the questions of ownership and of the strategic decision-making function were cleared up considerably in Brno. Nevertheless, some ambiguity remained until 1780 when a definitive contract was concluded with the central government turning complete control over to the private operators.

Maria Theresia was without question stubbornly committed to making this enterprise work; one leading historian of Habsburg economic history called it the government's pet child (*Schooskind*).[1] Since she blamed much of the failure in the Bohemian village on the indifference of the Court Commercial Council, she ordered that the government agencies undertake more decisive action. Her purpose in requiring stronger government intervention was not only oriented toward the establishment of the fine-woollen industry. She intended also to extricate the government from a province that was more properly the function of the private sector of the economy. It was for this reason, among others, that the relationship between the firm and the government was formalized in a contract on 1 July 1764 to run for the following twelve years.[2]

The formal parties to the contract were the Moravian Commercial College represented by its president Count Leopold Schlick signing for Empress Maria Theresia, and the sub-administration (*Unterverwaltung*) that is, the leaseholders of the Moravian Loan Bank on the other hand. This contract imposed certain entrepreneurial conditions upon the sub-administrators as operators of the factory. They were required to begin work immediately with the personnel and equipment that had been transported from Kladruby to expand

[1] Adolf Beer, 'Studien zur Geschichte der österreichischen Volkswirtschaft unter Maria Theresia, I. Die österreichische Industriepolitik' *Archiv für österreichische Geschichte*, LXXXI (1894), 119.

[2] HKA, red no. 891, Document #110.

their capacity as fast as possible. Any persons who wished to be instructed in the special art of manufacturing fine-woollen cloth had to be taken into the factory. Since it was well known that new enterprises in general and this one in particular had difficulties in selling their goods, the government committed itself to support the factory's efforts by having the military purchase the products. At the same time the firm was also confronted with a major entrepreneurial handicap. It was forced to accept the stock of finished goods as well as the equipment that had been used in Kladruby. The value assigned to the equipment was related to the state of repair in which it was found. Raw materials and goods in various forms of being finished were however assigned values at cost, which proved to be harmful since much of the stock was in bad condition and the finished goods could not be sold at the nominal value. Even given the attitudes of the time it was shortsighted for the government, prepared as it was to invest so many resources in this industry without seeing immediate returns, to impose such a heavy burden on the new enterprisers who in addition to being reluctant to accept the task were completely inexperienced in administering this type of concern.

Although the new company was assured that it would be able to exercise complete managerial discretion, an *ad hoc* state supervisory organ was also created especially for the factory. Combined with Maria Theresia's injunction that the commercial agencies were to exercise greater interest in the factory than they had shown when it was established in Kladruby, this resulted in considerable interference, especially in forcing the enterprise to expand swiftly.

The Eager Entrepreneur

For nearly three years the enterprise limped along until an energetic, if rather foolish young man, applied for the privilege of operating the factory. At first he had planned to take the factory over himself, but in the end he was joined by five cloth merchants of Brno, a group that seems to have been far more reluctant than young Köffiller. With almost visible relief, the Jewish company turned the troubled enterprise over to the new group by declaring themselves willing to take a considerable financial loss for the good of the commonwealth. Nevertheless they tried to be reimbursed, but they quickly gave up this attempt. They were, in fact, much more interested in the operation of a tobacco factory, which they had started in Brno in connexion with their tobacco monopoly.

The change from the reluctant company to the eager entrepreneur occurred in the years 1767 and 1768. Complications resulted immediately. Köffiller, the key man in the new group, was the elder son of one of Brno's wealthiest burghers, Johann Michael Köffiller, who had died in 1756. The father seems to have fitted into the category of the self-made man. Born in Carinthia, he was first reported in Brno in 1730 and in the following year was accorded the rights of a burgher. This rapid acquisition of citizenship suggests that he was not destitute when he arrived in the Moravian capital. While there he amassed a considerable fortune as a lender of funds and presumably supplier of material to the Russian 'auxiliary' troops that were in Moravia in the 1730s. He functioned also as a banker for the local Jesuits. A money changer and dealer in promissory notes, a wholesale merchant in the colonial trade with connexions all over Europe and resident agents in Hamburg, he also had interests in Styrian iron mines.[1] He was in addition president of the local Mercantile Brotherhood and in 1749 organized largely at his own expense a troop of fellow merchants on horseback to meet Empress Maria Theresia and her consort when they came to Brno on an official visit. Obviously socially ambitious, the elder Köffiller was a merchant for whom the appellation of somnolent, provincial businessman would hardly hold.[2]

Johann Leopold Köffiller, the son, was 24 years old in 1767, the year in which he married the daughter of a well-known lawyer in Prague who tried to move heaven and earth to prevent his son-in-law from committing a major blunder. The pleas of the father-in-law, directed to the central government authorities in Vienna, fell on deaf ears. Köffiller's youth and the fact, as his father-in-law pointed out, that experienced Jewish businessmen who would hardly pass up a profitable opportunity had forsaken the woollen mill, weighed little with government officials. And why should they heed the Prague lawyer when they were in fact making every effort to induce private capitalists and entrepreneurs to risk their funds and expend their energies in this enterprise.[3] After all, was it not the

[1] Jaroslav Dřímal, ed., *Dějiny města Brna*, (Brno, 1968), 168; Verwaltungsarchiv, Nobilitations Diploma für die Gebrüder Johann Leopold und Carl Köffiller, 18 Mai 1767.

[2] Joseph von Weinbrenner, *Patriotische Gedanken und Vorschläge über den gehemmten Ausfuhr-Handel* (second edition, Wien, 1792); Weinbrenner, a Viennese merchant, similar in many aspects to the elder Köffiller, blamed a slumbering business community in the Habsburg Monarchy for many of its economic ills.

[3] HKA, red no. 892, f. 680, 31 Oct. 1767; f. 683, 8 Nov. 1767; f. 684, 8 Nov. 1767.

Emperor Franz Stephan himself who urged the consortium of six Brno merchants, of whom Köffiller was the youngest and the richest, to acquire the fine-woollen mill?[1]

Possibly it was indeed due to the Emperor's encouragement that the six Brno merchants entered upon an undertaking that prudence would have forbidden. So anxious were government officials to induce merchants to found new industries that they were willing to stoop to blackmail. In one case, for example, a number of Vienna merchants were caught with a large quantity of smuggled goods in their warehouse. They were offered a 'Hobson's choice' alternative: jail and heavy penalties or investment in an ailing woollen-fabrics enterprise in Uničov (Mährisch Neustadt), Moravia.[2] They opted for the latter with not especially good results for themselves or the enterprise.

No hint of similar pressure is indicated in the archival sources for the Brno woollen firm. What then induced the Brno merchants, who were devoid of industrial experience, to undertake such a venture, especially one in a state of extremely poor health and so full of risk and uncertainty? Several years before, the woollen merchants of Vienna through their association the *Tuchlaubenverwandten*, had successfully given their inexperience in industrial matters as one of the major reasons why they would not undertake the operation of the factory in Kladruby.[3] Subsequent similar inquiries from government officials were also turned away.

Young Köffiller, patriotic and eager for action, seems to have made the difference in Brno. He had had a good education in business matters and had just returned from an extensive tour of Europe, the purpose of which was partly education and partly business. On his travels he tried to meet those persons who had had business relations with his father.[4] We know unfortunately little about the paternal business, but it was continued by the executors of the estate following the elder Köffiller's death in 1756.

The conspicuous absence of the father's name among the shareholders of the Moravian Loan Bank suggests the elder Köffiller's indifference to industrial development. Why then did the younger man step outside the commercial tradition that he had inherited? Was his fervour for industry actually aroused, as the diploma of nobility suggests, by his travels to Holland, England and other

[1] HKA, red no. 894, f. 637–76.
[2] Viktor Hofmann, 'Beiträge', 714–15.
[3] HKA, red no. 881, f. 69–70, 15 May 1764.
[4] Verwaltungsarchiv, Adelsarchiv, Nobilitations-Diploma . . . .

economically advanced countries? (He and his brother were ennobled in 1767 not because they were willing to innovate but because of the meritorious life of their departed father.) Or did Köffiller become an imitating entrepreneur, to use Schumpetarian terminology, chiefly because of the pressure exerted by the Emperor? The desire to please the monarch and to demonstrate patriotism cannot be dismissed as a motive. Lastly, might the youthful Köffiller have been impelled in this action by a desire to match or even outdo his father's accomplishments? How often after all are the actions of men determined by a psychological drive that relates strongly either negatively or positively to the parental environment?[1]

On the basis of his participation in the Brno woollen enterprise from 1767 to 1789, Köffiller fulfilled his entrepreneurial function with only moderate success. He contributed little in the way of innovation even in an imitative sense. This reading of his character is of course biased by the fact that the sources are all government documents, full of pleas for help. The state more frequently made the strategic decisions. Nevertheless, it was unquestionably Köffiller's enthusiasm, misguided as it may have been, that pressed the industrialization of Brno significantly forward.

Köffiller was of course not the only private businessman involved in the fate of the Brno Fine Woollen-Cloth Factory. The Jewish financiers with their primary interest in earning interest and the tobacco business have already been briefly discussed. They were replaced in 1767 first by Köffiller himself and then by Köffiller in company with five cloth merchants from Brno. There was considerable pathos and irony in this particular episode. Only Köffiller actually displayed eagerness; the five cloth merchants of Brno seemed almost as reluctant to become industrialists as the Jewish financiers. Nevertheless, the merchants actually founded their own factory at one point, after a disagreement with Köffiller.

One of their number, Franz Jakob Pachner, a member of the Brno municipal council and undoubtedly a man with considerable local prestige, became the manager of the new plant. When they organized their own woollen mill, Pachner and his partners submitted a highly optimistic plan to government officials, looking toward the early production of one thousand pieces of cloth per year. They expected considerable, material support from government agencies. Since they themselves were inexperienced in the manufacture of textiles, they

[1] Herman Freudenberger, 'An Exploration in Entrepreneurial Motivation and Action', *Explorations in Economic History*, VII (1970), 443–8.

proposed to hire as their superintendent a Netherlands master, who had been brought to Brno a number of years previously by Kehrnhofer and who was the recipient of an annual government pension. They of course hoped that the financial support for their prospective superintendent would continue and that in addition the government would supply them with an outright grant of 400 fl. for each loom that they placed in operation. This sum was large enough to permit them to purchase a loom, which with all its attachments at this time cost at most 60 fl., and to pay for the raw materials and wages for manufacturing probably four pieces of fine cloth in addition.

Additional funds would undoubtedly be required before the enterprise became self-supporting. If they were permitted to import 150 pieces of expensive woollen cloth a year at greatly reduced tariff duties, they would be able to generate the necessary flow of revenue.[1] Windfall profits of this sort could of course be more easily devoted to high-risk undertakings, a condition that may have been characteristic of the industrial revolution in England and elsewhere.[2] Although the last request was not without precedent — a Belgian manufacturer, Jean Thys, had received a similar privilege a few years earlier for the establishment of a woollen-cloth factory in Klagenfurt, Carinthia — the suspicion easily suggested itself that the proposers were more interested in preferential tariff treatment than they were in operating the plant. After all, they were primarily merchants. Consequently, the central government refused to allow the discriminatory importation of cloths, but it did agree to supply 400 fl. for each of twenty new looms.

The Amalgamated Woollen Mill

The negotiations between the government and the merchants' factory soon became negotiations for a merger of both factories. The two fine-cloth factories remained separate entities for less than a year. For one thing, Köffiller had proved a poor manager of the original factory and had moreover complicated his task greatly by taking on another sick enterprise that had been founded under government auspices. This was a velvet factory of a master from Amiens, France, who died before he was able to bring the plant into production. For another thing, there was a shortage of skilled labour

[1] HKA, red no. 892, f. 775 ff.

[2] Cf. Earl J. Hamilton, 'Prices as a Factor in Business Growth', *Journal of Economic History*, XII (1952), 325–49.

in Brno and the textile plants were competing against each other for the limited supply.

The existence in Brno of two firms manufacturing fine woollens became inexpedient, and so they as well as the plush and velvet enterprise were merged in 1768. Pachner, the chief of the Brno woollen merchants' group became manager of the combined enterprises, but Köffiller and the central government retained their fiduciary interests and their entrepreneurial prerogatives. A so-called Factory Directorate headed by a high local government official represented the central government and in a more or less loose way supervised the operation of the new firm. It interfered very little in the management of the enterprise.

A twelve-year contract between the government and the new company, dated 1 August 1768, was similar to the agreement signed four years earlier with the Jewish company.[1] It differed mainly in its emphasis on expansion and the more precise way in which mutual obligations were stated. Sixteen looms were to be in operation by the end of 1768 in the merchants' company, apart from the fourteen looms that were already set up in the 'imperial' factory, that is, the plant managed by Köffiller. The combined company was obligated by the end of the year to have altogether thirty looms constantly at work.

This type of forced expansion proved to be ill-advised. Besides the managerial problems that resulted from a larger scale of operation, especially one in which the productive facilities were physically separated from each other by a considerable distance, there were financial problems. The capital-output ratio that was generally accepted at this time called for an investment of 5,000 fl. per loom.[2] By the end of the year 150,000 fl. would thus have to be invested in this firm, a very formidable sum that the government officials recognized was well beyond its capabilities. This meant that the government officials took upon themselves a major entrepreneurial decision, which they must have known carried with it high risks of failure. They must have known that the risk factor was high if for no other reason than that they could look back upon twenty years of frustrating experience with the enterprise and its predecessor. Yet the only person who demurred seriously was the father-in-law of the young Köffiller, and he was swiftly overruled. If the Brno Six accepted this agreement without the most serious

[1] HKA, red no. 894, f. 1089–94, 1 Aug. 1768.
[2] HKA, red no. 892, f. 770 ff., 4 May 1768.

misgivings, it could only have been because they expected the government to bail them out of trouble whenever it should occur.

That the enterprisers of the fine-cloth factory should have taken this attitude is understandable in the face of other promises that the government made in the contract. Yarn supply for example, was a large problem for the textile industry in this part of Europe no less than in contemporary England. To help the factory in procuring spun yarn the government offered to establish an orphanage in Brno and to have the inmates spin at regular wages. It is interesting that the proposed solution for the spinning problem too had its counterpart in England where public authorities aided the nascent factory industry in the recruitment of child labour. The government also committed itself to recruiting more highly skilled labour, by offering to pay for the travel expenses of a dyer and a finisher from abroad and furthermore to pay a supplement to their wages by way of an annual 'pension'. As with other new industries the workers in this factory were to be free of the payment of the special fees that were normally required of craftsmen and they were also to be safe from the army recruiters. Other benefits included the erection at government expense of new fullery and the use free of charge of equipment for a dyehouse which the government had purchased only recently.The building in which the original factory was housed as well as some of the equipment belonged to the government, which permitted their use free of rental for a period of six years in return for rejecting the company's request to import a large number of cloths at greatly reduced tariff duties.

The government also committed itself in support of sales. For twenty years the fine-cloth factory both in Kladruby as well as in Brno had had serious merchandising problems. In this it was not unique; other new industries encountered the same difficulties. Merchants preferred their traditional sources of supply for many reasons, not least of which being the fact that most enterprises that were producing goods not previously manufactured in the Habsburg Monarchy were not able to equal the quality nor the price of the foreign product. Although the new industrialists and the government officials most closely associated with them disputed this contention and preferred the argument that the merchants were unpatriotically opposing them, they had to concede frequently that there was some truth in the claims of the mercantile community. At those times they insisted that society at large should willingly pay the starting costs incurred for industrial progress and that the cost would be low relative to the eventual benefits that would derive

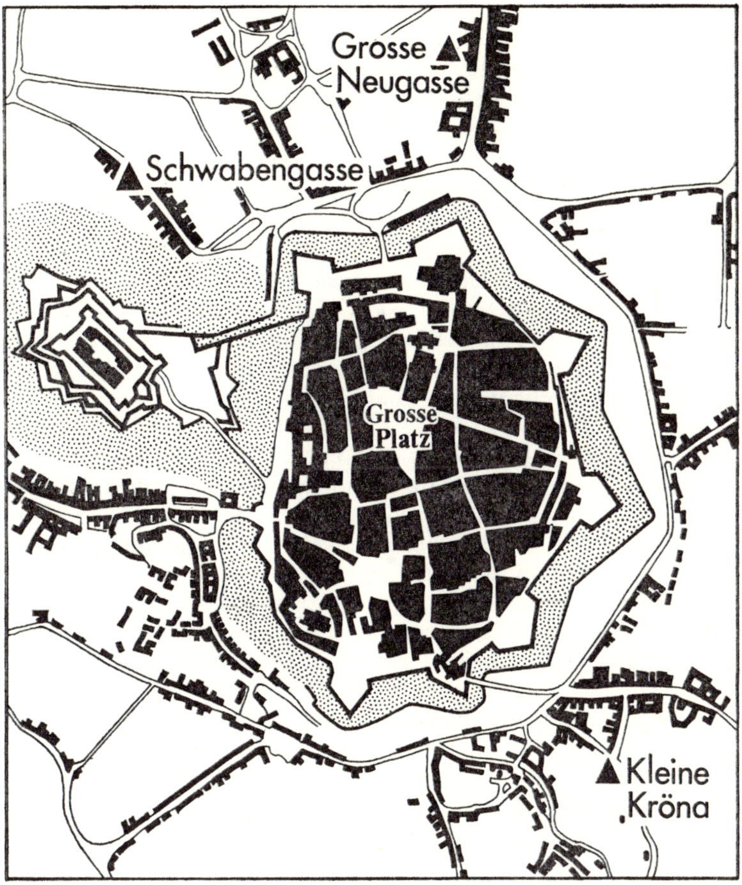

Brno in the late eighteenth century showing the factory buildings
(▲ Factory buildings)

from industrialization. In view of the bad experience with sales, the firm was assured that the government would use all its powers to aid the marketing of the finished product to the point of increasing the tariff duties on fine cloths or even of prohibiting their import altogether.

All these benefits reduced the entrepreneurial risk considerably, and so the government could press for rapid expansion. Unfortunately at the same time it added a considerable financial burden by forcing the new company to take over the debt that its predecessor owed to the government, amounting to almost 15,000 fl. This sum seems small in comparison to the 150,000 fl. investment that the firm was expected to make by the end of 1768, but it proved to be one of the major stumbling blocks.

New Time of Trouble

Trouble was not long in coming. In 1770, a year in which famine began to dominate Bohemia and Moravia,[1] three of the Brno Six were forced to declare bankruptcy and leave the firm. They were cloth merchants who had made cash investments in the firm of between 2,700 fl. and 3,400 fl. each.[2] Subsequently, there were only three, and of them Köffiller had by far the larger sum in the firm, much of it in the form of loans rather than equity. The bankruptcy of the three merchants was not directly related to the fine-cloth factory but it served to bring to light the increasingly desperate condition of the firm. An investigation that Maria Theresia ordered as a result again demonstrated the overwhelming entrepreneurial role that the government played and at the same time showed how completely divorced it had been from the day-to-day management, which theoretically was closely supervised by the so-called Factory Directorate.

Jean Thys, the Belgian woollen-cloth manufacturer who had established a well-organized factory in Klagenfurt, was the chief investigator. Finding that the liabilities exceed the assets by a considerable amount ('Passiva': 189,026; 'Activa': 161,777; difference: 27,249 fl.), he blamed the problem primarily on two entrepreneurial errors besides specifying a large number of managerial deficiencies. He felt that the pressure to expand manufacturing capacity was much too great and that the original investment

[1] Erika Weinzierl-Fischer, 'Die Bekämpfung der Hungersnot in Böhmen 1770–1772 durch Maria Theresia und Joseph II', *Mitteilungen des Österreichischen Staatsarchivs*, VII (1954), 478–514.

[2] SAB, KKT 1763, 13/208: Consignation deren aus dem vorgezeugten Cassa Buch erhobenen und von denen einem jeden Mitglied der ... Gesellschaft geleisteten Einlage.

Köffiller	3,808 fl.
Pachner	3,608
Steurer	2,782
Stimmer	1,900
Weber	2,858
Progino	3,433
	18,389 fl.

Progino, Weber, Stimmer were the merchants affected.

capital was much too small. For lack of adequate liquid funds the firm had had to purchase wool at a very high price. Moreover, on account of the pressure to produce goods, the quality of the merchandise was poor with the result that 2/5 of all the goods manufactured in the six years since the factory was established in Brno were still unsold. Thys suggested that the government write off some of the debt owed to it by the firm and that it take over the sale of the poor quality cloth by offering it at a price commensurate with its quality, with the government compensating the firm for the difference between receipt and cost of production. Most importantly, he recommended that an expert manager be found abroad to run the woollen mill.[1]

Although there was understandably much resentment of Thys's analysis both from the Brno owners and the government officials, the Belgian expert's recommendations were to a large extent adopted. Again it was clearly the central government officials, including above all the Empress herself, who made the entrepreneurial decisions. They also accepted many of the liabilities that had been incurred by the firm as a result of previous decisions. It should be emphasized at this point that the central government was in no way willing to pour funds into this inefficient enterprise without caring whether it would reach a position of greater perfectability and profitability. The Brno Fine-Cloth Factory was certainly a Mercantilistic factory but this did not mean, as some scholars have suggested, that the government which fostered it was unconcerned with its efficiency.[2] Rather than supporting the thesis that efficiency was primarily encouraged by the forces of competition, the experience of this firm suggests that the superior resources of a government provided the means of getting the best managerial services available at the time. It may even provide modest support for Schumpeter's thesis that larger enterprises can devote more resources to innovation since their greater funds reduce the risks connected with any particular entrepreneurial action.

New Era

Presumably then, the central government was again responsible for making a strategic decision of major consequence. With the

[1] HKA, red no. 893, f. 290–335.

[2] Cf. Sidney Pollard, *The Genesis of Modern Management* (Cambridge, Mass., 1965), 48. See also, Herman Freudenberger, 'On the Genesis of Modern Management', *Technology and Culture*, x (1969), 593–602.

help of a member of the Association of Cloth Merchants (*Tuchlaubenverwandten*) in Vienna who had been one of the most vociferous critics of the Brno enterprise, the firm hired a new manager. He had excellent connexions with the west German cloth centre of Monschau (Montjoie), where he had been trained and where he had married the daughter of a highly respected cloth manufacturer. The cloth merchant in Vienna, one Franz Xavery Garttner, became a partner in the firm, although there is no record that he made any investment in it other than his good offices.[1] His services may, however, have been of fundamental importance not only in procuring an able manager; equally important may have been his efforts in making Vienna the major sales outlet for cloth from the Brno factory. There is little direct evidence that he acted as agent for the firm in this way, but it is a fact that the bitter hostility of the Vienna merchants henceforth disappeared.

During the 1770s there were several other occurrences that had potentially important effects. The first of these was another of the firms' perennial crises. In this case, a new tariff law was the direct cause. In 1775, after many decades of discussion and negotiation within the agencies of the government, a general tariff law was enacted that for the first time included most of the Hereditary Lands. Moreover, it represented a sharp reversal of tactics from the highly restrictive legislation that preceded it. It greatly liberalized the conditions for the importation of foreign goods, and thus went contrary to one of the express provisions in the contractual agreement of 1768 between the government and the Brno firm. This at least was the contention of the firm which demanded to be allowed to send a circular letter to all its 'friends' declaring that if they did not continue to purchase cloths from the enterprise that stood so high in the esteem of the monarch and that was moreover so important for the continued prosperity of the country, then the liberalized provision of the new law would very likely be removed. More will be said about this problem in Chapter VII. Suffice it to say here, that the government insisted that its public policy could not be determined by private agreements. It is even questionable whether the agreement was violated since according to the record no

[1] SAB, C–12–45, f. 98 ff., 'Inventarium', 31 Aug. 1777; HKA, red no. 894, f. 1078–1116. There is some evidence that Garttner may have become a partner before the new manager was hired. In a letter written to the Emperor in 1818, Mathias Bernard Schlösser maintained that he advised Garttner in 1771 while on a business trip to hire his brother-in-law, Seitter, and for the Brno firm to begin to sell its product in the Ottoman Empire. HKA, red no. 1224, f. 479, Nov., 1818.

apparent sales problem existed at the time of the complaint. The Brno firm seemed merely to wish to prevent any problem from arising. Eventually, it claimed a loss of over 20,000 fl., resulting from the reduction in price that it had to offer in order to sell its goods.[1] Another change of importance was the departure from the rank of shareholders of two more Brno merchants. By 1777 there was only one of the original six merchants still involved in the firm. The rest had paid a very heavy price for their experience. They all found themselves in financial straits in their own mercantile business.[2]

Köffiller the Sole Proprietor

Köffiller, the sole survivor, a self-proclaimed patriot, still had his own share in the firm and in addition had advanced over 40,000 fl. in loans. Never one to lose courage despite the heavy pressure that the cloth firm's financial requirements had exerted on his own mercantile business, Köffiller reported himself pleased to have provided earnings for many inhabitants and tax revenues for the government.[3] Thus in 1780 when the agreement with the government came up for renewal, Köffiller as sole proprietor requested extensive concessions from the government to continue the firm for another twelve-year period. Although profitless during its entire existence, the enterprise had by 1780 a large manufacturing capacity of forty-five looms with an apparent need to expand further to sixty looms. The government authorities considered their role as initiator of industrialization almost complete in this instance and thus entered into a new agreement that was intended to place the Brno factory entirely in Köffiller's private hands. The new agreement called for the annulment of a 25,000 fl. loan after its expiration in 1792, provided that sixty looms were being operated. In addition, the central government authorized a new loan of 20,000 fl. at low interest from the Moravian Orphans' Fund. Other than that, it desired to relinquish its entrepreneurial function almost completely. Because of the large loans still outstanding, the Factory Directorate — the *ad hoc* representatives of the Moravian Commercial Council established in the 1760s to supervise the enterprise — continued a loose supervision over the firm.

[1] SAB, C–12–45, f. 712–33, 29 April 1780.
[2] Ibid., f. 168 ff., 3 Aug. 1778.
[3] Ibid., f. 712–33, 29 April 1780.

Whether through the Directorate or through other means, the central government seems to have continued to have had a strong influence on this enterprise until its demise in 1789. From the very beginning, the central government had desired to accomplish two goals with this factory — it wanted to eliminate the country's dependence on foreign suppliers and at the same time be in a position to export its own products. By manufacturing at home what previously had been imported, the movement of bullion abroad would be prevented and by exporting its own goods it would bring gold and silver into the Monarchy. During the 1780s the factory was finally able to penetrate this market in a large scale, to the obvious pleasure of the government whose diplomatic staff in Constantinople aided the firm in this effort. As will be seen later, much of Brno's production during the 1780s was in the form of so-called *Londrins-Seconds* cloths, many of which were sold to Constantinople.[1] When, however, war ensued in 1787 between the Habsburg Monarchy and the Ottoman Empire, the sales of the Köffiller firm dried up almost overnight.

With all the eggs that it had placed in the Turkish basket then broken, the only recourse that the head of the enterprise saw once again was the central government. No longer, however, was the sympathetic Maria Theresia the ruler. Her more doctrinaire son, Joseph II, ordered that the laws should be observed with total impartiality. Köffiller and his firm owed money which should be paid as required. That his own action as a monarch in bringing about the war was the cause of Köffiller's difficulties carried no importance. On the contrary, he required the governmental authorities to initiate judicial proceedings against the firm when it was discovered that the Brno enterprise no longer had assets sufficient to cover all its debts, including those the state had promised to forego if the firm operated 60 looms until 1792.

Besides desiring that the government take a disinterested position *vis-à-vis* the Brno factory, Joseph II recognized that this enterprise had outlived its unique usefulness. Out of it had grown a number of other woollen-cloth factories in Brno and vicinity, factories that catered more to the domestic market that Köffiller had forsaken in favour of Turkish sales. Had Köffiller in fact made this entrepreneurial decision himself or had he followed again the suggestion

[1] *Londrins Seconds* were light-weight cloths manufactured in the eighteenth century predominately in Languedoc (France) in imitation of similar cloth made in England.

of his government? In either case his was the responsibility in the end. And so we can say with few qualifications that during the period of the second contract with the central government in the 1780s, Köffiller had become his own boss, so to speak, whether he wished to or not. His twenty-odd years in the woollen manufacturing business proved to be one huge entrepreneurial error and his father-in-law was indeed correct in warning against his involvement. For the state and for society in general he was, however, a benefactor. New enterprises were already in existence in Brno when his own expired and more were destined to follow.

Summary

By 1789 when bankruptcy proceedings threatened the woollen firm, it was known as the Köffiller factory, although Köffiller was not its sole owner. It had gone through a career of twenty-five years from the time that a few wagons in the depth of winter deposited equipment, stock and personnel for the operation of three-loom woollen plant in the courtyard of a building in one of Brno's suburbs. The leader of this forlorn group of largely Belgian workers was the manager from the time when the factory was located in the Bohemian village of Kladruby. Brought to Brno under the auspices of the Moravian Loan Bank, the woollen enterprise began its existence in the Moravian capital under a cloud. It had caused a serious rift in the management of the Bank, which resulted in the dismissal of the Bank's manager. Nevertheless, it remained under the Bank's control at the insistence of the central government, even after it was taken over by a company of Jewish businessmen, whose main interest was in the tobacco trade and in money lending. Soon, however, the enterprise was rescued by Köffiller, then a young man eager for great deeds after having completed a grand tour of Europe. He was joined in the venture by a group of cloth merchants from Brno, whose ardour was considerably less and whose financial capabilities within a few years proved to be even smaller. Although certainly lacking in entrepreneurial ability, Köffiller persevered, thanks to his wealth and to the fortunate entrance upon the scene of a new manager.

All through the period in which the woollen-cloth factory existed in Brno, the central government under the direct orders of Maria Theresia and her successor Joseph II intervened strongly in the fate of this enterprise. It can properly be called state-owned in its first years, although the Empress and her chief officials were clearly anxious to divest themselves of responsibility for it. Even after the final contract was concluded between the central government and Köffiller in 1780, the entrepreneurial role of the government did not cease completely. It was the purpose of this contract to provide a twelve-year period at the end of which the enterprise would be completely in the hands of its private proprietor. Events, some of them the acts of the government itself, overtook the firm before it was able to complete the transition to a privately owned and operated enterprise and it fell victim to the bankruptcy laws of the state.

Chapter IV

THE ENTERPRISE: INTERNAL STRUCTURE

The entrepreneurial function with its emphasis on the making of strategic decisions was to a large extent in the hands of an exogenous body, the state, whose policy as it affected the enterprise was primarily concerned with the elimination of a large trade deficit in fine woollen cloth. By itself the enterprise could not accomplish the task. Its potential optimal manufacturing capacity of forty to sixty looms, that is between 2,000 to 3,000 pieces of cloth per year, necessarily represented only a small portion of the fine woollens consumed in the Habsburg Monarchy.

Although from the start it had been a major goal of the economic policy of the Habsburg government to free the Monarchy from the necessity of importing goods from abroad, being in a position to export as much as possible was only less important. The Turkish Empire figured strongly as a potential market for such goods. In the case of the woollen industry, this meant above all the so-called *Londrins-Seconds* cloths which the French province of Languedoc was exporting to the Near East in considerable quantities.[1] About 1780 the Brno firm finally succeeded in contesting French dominance and during the 1780s its productive facilities were devoted primarily to the manufacture of this cloth. Between 1780 and 1788 the factory produced *Londrins-Seconds* equivalent to 50–67 per cent of total output. During this period its total output of all types of cloth increased considerably.

When the Habsburg government proposed to replace the foreign source of supply by recruiting workers from Verviers in 1748, the hope was that fine woollens would be manufactured within the Monarchy to replace those imported from the Belgian cloth centre. Apparently, the most frequently exported cloth from Verviers had a width of 9/4 ell, that is, more than two yards.[2] This was wider than the standard cloth the Kladruby and the Brno mills produced. Their widest cloth measured 8/4 'Braband' ell (69 cm.) and prob-

[1] Leon Dutil, *L'état économique du Languedoc* (Paris, 1911), 342.
[2] Lebrun, *Verviers*, 296 ff.

ably contained about 2,800 threads of warp yarn. They also manufactured a 7/4 width cloth with about 2,300 to 2,500 warp threads. These two types of cloth remained in the inventory of the firm from the beginning until the end. Three other types seemed to have been added in the 1770s. One of these was *Londrins-Seconds*, the lightweight cloth so popular in Constantinople and the Levant. Its width varied from 4/4 to 8/4 ell, but usually was 4/4 ell wide and about 30 ells long. Lastly, there were the 'Summer' cloths, which never became an important item, and the Bergopzoom cloth, which generally had a width of 4/4 ell. According to an inventory of 1778, the Bergopzoom cloth was valued at about 1 fl. per ell, a sum that probably represents the cost of production.[1] The regular woollens of 8/4 width averaged somewhat more than 4 fl. per ell and the 7/4 width, about 3½ fl. Size 4/4 *Londrins* averaged somewhat over 1 fl. per ell.[2] Since no price lists have been found in the archival records for the 1770s and 1780s, the sales price cannot be ascertained with absolute assurance. Moreover, it would be hazardous indeed to suggest that prices that were normal in the 1760s, when some evidence exists, would still have been valid in the following decades. Prices of Verviers cloth, still the standard by which other cloths could be measured, were rising during this period from an index of 100 in 1772 to a high point of about 199 in 1786.[3] In the present chapter the focus is on the means by which the goal of manufacturing large numbers of fine cloths was accomplished. The inquiry concerns itself with questions of the over-all management of daily affairs, as distinct from the entrepreneurial function dealt with in the previous chapter. Included in this group of questions are the institutional means by which sales and purchases were carried out and the internal organization of the manufacturing process itself. To some of these matters previous allusion has been made when they were pertinent to the discussion of the entrepreneurial function. Strategic considerations are by the nature of the extant primary sources much easier to reconstruct than questions of internal structure. None of the firm's own records have survived except insofar as they were contained in reports to the governmental authorities. In consequence of having to reconstruct the story of this enterprise entirely from written material that

[1] For table of sales of cloths, see Appendix B.
[2] SAB, C/12/45, f. 461–73, 'Inventarium . . . 31 Aug. 1778'.
[3] Lebrun, *Verviers*, Diagramme II.

passed between the firm and government agencies and among the various government departments themselves, a certain bias must be expected that would be absent if these sources could be supplemented with some that were in the permanent possession of the firm itself.

The perspective on the firm will also be somewhat affected by the formulation of our questions. Entrepreneurship and management as separate functional relationships are more the formulations of scholars in our own day, especially in relation to the huge enterprises common today. The actors and observers in the eighteenth century while not oblivious to such distinctions were nevertheless vague in their usage of such terms. Consequently, the distinctions applied in this study may have a slightly artificial flavour. They have a predominantly heuristic purpose and are therefore applicable.

The Manager

A good point of departure is the role of the manager. A profound change took place in the fate of the Brno Fine-Cloth Factory in 1772 when an experienced man from Germany accepted the position. Jean Thys, the Klagenfurt manufacturer, had recommended that a person well versed in woollen manufacturing from Verviers with a capital ready for investment in the firm of between 20,000 and 30,000 fl. be offered both a partnership and the over-all direction of the factory.[1] The new man, coming from another textile centre near Verviers and having been long engaged in the woollen industry, fulfilled at least two of the conditions that Thys had set. There is no evidence, however, that he brought any investment funds with him. His technical and managerial know-how made up to a large extent for his lack of funds.[2]

This man was Johann Bartholomeus Seitter, born in Augsburg in 1728. At some time and for an unknown reason he had migrated

[1] HKA, red no. 893, f. 270–334.

[2] There was general consensus on Seitter's capabilities as a manager, with the exception of a sharply adverse opinion on the part of the Brno clothmakers guild in 1796 and 1797. In attempting to prevent Seitter's son Matthew Abraham from becoming a master in their guild, his future fellows spoke of the young man's poor technical ability as having been inherited from his late father. They maintained that the older Seitter had gone bankrupt in the 'Netherlands' before coming to Brno where he managed to bring a flourishing enterprise to a fall. (SAB, M 2053, 3 August 1796; 31 März, 1797). It is doubtful that there was any substance to this accusation.

to Monschau.[1] In 1768, at the age of 40 years, he had married the boss's daughter. Mathias Schlösser, his wife's father, with his step-brothers and cousins controlled the entire woollen-cloth industry of the town.[2] It was an industry organized much like that of Verviers with a keen eye open to market opportunities and a willingness to take risks in the manufacture of fashionable fabrics and colours. Production was organized largely on the putting-out system, with spinning and weaving placed in the hands of peasants in the surrounding countryside and as far away as Verviers itself. Finishing and storing was done in the buildings of the 'manufacturers'. Schlösser in this way turned out about 500 pieces of fine woollens per year during the 1770s. During this time and largely because of the demands of the market for fashionable goods and precise delivery times, Monschau's industry like that of Verviers became more factory-orientated. One can therefore expect Seitter to have had the type of experience required for the Brno plant.[3] To provide as good a foundation as possible the new manager's father-in-law came with him and stayed for several months in Brno.

For the first time then the fine-woollen factory was to be directed by an experienced man who knew the internal organization of a concentrated workshop or protofactory and who was aware of the dicta of an international market. In Augsburg and even more in Monschau he had lived in an environment where business activities were relatively uncontrolled by government agencies. Monschau's history was especially noteworthy in this respect and could well have provided Seitter with lessons that stood him in good stead in Brno,

[1] HKA, red no. 893, f. 87 (6 ex Aug. 772 Böh). In this document there is a reference to the 'new managing director's' citizenship in Liège. This seems to be in error. According to other archival sources, Seitter came from Monschau and consequently a recent historian's statement that he came from Augsburg where Köffiller met him on his travels also finds no support in the archival documentation. The same author reports that Seitter's two older children were born in Monschau but that his youngest child was born in Augsburg in 1771. The latter fact hardly supports the contention that Köffiller met Seitter in Augsburg while he was on his grand tour since it took place in the middle 1760s. See W. Scheibler, 'Die Auswanderungen aus Monschau nach dem Osten im 19. Jahrhundert', in Alfons Perlik ed., *Nordrhein-Westfalen und der deutsche Osten* (Dortmund, 1962), 64 f. I am grateful to Oberstudienrat Dr H. Steinröx for having made this article available to me.

[2] E. Barkhausen, *Montjoie*, 46; Gustav G. Trautenberger, *Aus der evangelischen Kirchengemeinde in Brünn* (Brünn, 1866), 2.

[3] Cf. Herbert Kisch, 'Das Erbe des Mittelalters, Ein Hemmnis wirtschaftlicher Entwicklung: Aachens Tuchgewerbe vor 1790', *Rheinische Vierteljahrsblätter*, xxx (1965), 276–7; Max Barkhausen, 'Staatliche Wirtschaftslenkung und freies Unternehmertum im westdeutschen und im nord-und südniederländischen Raum bei Entstehung der neuzeitlichen Industrie im 18. Jahrhundert, *Vierteljahrschrift für Sozial- und Wirtschaftsgeschichte*, XLV (1958), 190–91.

for the Rhenish town had been settled by Protestant weavers who had left Aachen and by dint of their own efforts had built up a thriving industry. Seitter was a Protestant, and a number of other Protestants came with him to Brno. They would have to face a certain amount of hostility from the Catholic community as well as from a government whose official policy until the Patent of Toleration in 1781 was against the settlement of non-Catholics.

By reason of his background alone, the new manager was well-equipped to be successful where others had failed. In addition he received a handsome salary of 1,800 fl. per year besides one-fifth of the profits without having to invest any funds of his own.[1] He could devote himself single-mindedly to his task without having outside interests to impinge upon his time and effort. His predecessors in Brno all had businesses of their own to take care of, and their experience of running a textile mill or, for that matter, any other industrial undertaking was woefully wanting.

Supervisory and Service Staff

About the same time as Seitter arrived in Brno, several other highly skilled persons came to serve under his direction as foremen and other officials in the factory. He had apparently recruited them himself. Eventually they were to be responsible for the horizontal expansion and proliferation of the woollen-cloth industry in Brno when a number of them established their own factories. This in itself made the sorrow and sacrifice and wasted effort that had gone into the Kladruby and the Brno factories seem worth while. The Mercantilistic efforts of the government were thus crowned with success. For the firm itself, however, the drain of managerial talent that resulted from the proliferation was one of the major causes of its downfall. Even Seitter in the 1780s, still manager, had by then outside interests. With the willing approval of the government agencies he had founded a factory producing Turkish fezes.

That the role of the manager was of critical importance is attested by the criticisms preceding Seitter's accession to the leadership of the Brno enterprise as well as by the beneficial results in the years following it. Unfortunately, however, the exact nature of his obligations and the manner in which he carried them out is not discernible. Did he take the attitude that the masters in charge

[1] HKA, red no. 894, f. 1215–18.

of various aspects of the manufacturing process were independent? Were his subordinates acting as subcontractors or as foremen? Did the office staff operate autonomously or under specific orders from him? The major officials under the manager seem to have been the superintendent (*Werkmeister* or *Fabrique Meister*) and the factor (*Fakteur*). Both of them received the same salary which in 1771 before Seitter came was 400 fl. per year. The factor may have been in charge of the book-keeping for the firm as well as the warehousing of its stock of materials and work in progress. He may also have served as a purchasing and sales agent at times. His was without doubt a position of great responsibility but it could not have been so critically important as the role of the superintendent. The high salary seems to be more accountable in terms of the reliability and integrity that was required rather than any special expertise. In none of the analyses of the crises through which the factory went can there be found any critical comment on the factor. Book-keeping methods were probably standardized and part of a widely dispersed fund of knowledge and experience on which any enterprise could draw. The fact that this type of experience was readily available provided one of the most important ingredients in assimilating business techniques from abroad without exceeding difficulty. The names of Islinger, Dangel,[1] Flieher, Schüch and even a Czech name like Auliczek indicate that general business techniques as they existed within the Monarchy could be used.

No matter how small the factory was, a minimum office staff seems to have been necessary. Although a factor was not specified among the sixty-eight employees projected in 1749 for the original factory at Kladruby, such a position was occupied by a so-called comptroller in 1764 before the equipment and personnel was transferred to Brno.[2] With increasing size the office personnel naturally increased but far less proportionally than the total number of employees. In 1780 there were 756 employees only two factors and two clerks, or one office worker for nearly 200 employees. There were four other persons besides the office workers who made up the 'overhead' group, that is those besides the manager who were not directly engaged in the manufacturing process. They included a

[1] Dangel came from Bohemia and had the especially favourable attribute, according to Kehrnhofer, that his wife was the daughter of a fine-cloth factory inspector (*Feintuch Fabrique Inspectoris Tochter*) in Saxony. SAB, K K T 1763.

[2] SUA, CG 1731–54, A-7-1749, Westerhold. Haus-, Hof-, und Staatsarchiv, Poschakten (J.S.), carton No. 6, f. 497–511, Melchior Kern.

domestic (*Hausknecht*), a wagon driver (*Kutscher*) and two general servants (*Handlanger*).[1] These people received annual salaries.[2]

Direct Supervision of the Work Force

Turning now to the officials who supervised the manufacturing process itself, we will be examining another of the basic functional divisions of protofactories or early factories, keeping in mind, however, that further sub-divisions took place as a factory became more sophisticated.[3] By investigating these functions in protofactories like the Brno Fine-Cloth Factory in detail, the foundations for a better understanding of the evolution of the supervisory functions might be laid. The development of the modern factory must be traced carefully in the organizational realm as much as in the technological, financial and entrepreneurial. The entrepreneurial function if looked at as innovational in Schumpeter's terms is analogous to a basic invention. It has the characteristic of providing the basic parameter for an enterprise. One of its contributions to the firm may be in the form of the supervisory organization. On the other hand, the supervisory organization may have to adapt itself to the strategic goals of the firm, irrespective whether these goals are innovative or merely imitative. For the Brno enterprise it would be fair to say that it was innovational mainly in employing a manufacturing process that had not previously been used in establishing means of exploiting new markets for the finished product. Given the experience and the institutional environment of the Habsburg Monarchy, the implementation of the entrepreneurial decision to produce fine cloths necessitated a factory organization.

Technology, on the other hand, did not. In the areas in which fine cloths were manufactured with great success, factory institutions were slowly evolving; but the extensive method of production through putting-out arrangements or the guild system and open markets was still predominant. The extensive method seemed to be the primary means by which the Habsburg government hoped to realize its plans, and the factory was envisioned basically as a

[1] SAB, C/12/45, f. 727, Brünn, 29 April 1780.

[2] HKA, red no. 893, f. 333. For example, the domestic servant in 1771 had a salary of 72 fl. per year and the driver of the coach received 112 fl. in addition to a uniform. Of the office staff in that year the factor had a 400 fl. salary, his second in command 200 fl. and their assistant 80 fl.

[3] Cf. Jürgen Kocka, *Unternehmensverwaltung und Angestelltenschaft am Beispiel Siemens 1847–1914* (Stuttgart, 1969), 27.

training place. Supervisors would be the chief instructors. It was for this reason that the Brno woollen mill had to agree to train any Moravian or Bohemian craftsman who wished to learn the new methods.

These new methods were hardly revolutionary. They included more careful selection of the wool from various parts of the fleece, better cleansing and washing of the wool and greater standardization of the size and twist of the yarn. The loom that was traditionally used in Verviers was no revolutionary machine. It differed mainly from the German loom to which the Moravian weavers were accustomed in being heavier and more stable in construction. That such minor changes in technology should bring forth fierce opposition from the clothmakers of Jihlava, especially when they were constantly facing unemployment remains a social fact difficult to explain.[1] It must have been a perplexing puzzle to the government officials of the time, who continued to hope that the factory would prove to be primarily a training institution that could be dispensed with once a sufficient number of clothmakers had become proficient. At any rate, if the factory started out to be merely a training institution it soon lost this characteristic.

The instructional aspect was not the only element that fostered factory organization. There was the very important problem of quality control. In the west of England or in Leyden in Holland there was probably a wide consensus among spinners, weavers and others engaged in cloth-making as to the quality required at each stage of production as well as of the finished product. But in the Habsburg Monarchy where only inferior types of cloth were produced and where the guilds were hostile to the introduction of the new fabric, close control of the separate processes was required. Another reason for closer and more detailed supervision of work in the factory was the high cost of foreign wool. Waste of Merino wool as a result of poor work or larceny of the high-priced material were among other causes for concentrating the manufacturing under one roof and having responsible masters in control. Still, all this could have been done under an internal subcontract similar to that employed in the well-known Waldstein woollen mill in north-western Bohemia.[2]

[1] Mainuš, *Vlnařství*, 45; 25 per cent of the Moravian weavers were out of work and many had to beg for their livelihood in about 1749.

[2] Freudenberger, *Waldstein Woolen Mill*, 29.

There is at least a possibility that the organizational methods used in the Waldstein works were directly transmitted to Brno. In the late 1750s the head of the Manufacturing Office of Brno was ordered by his superiors in Vienna to visit Waldstein and observe the methods used there so that he could instruct Moravians upon his return.[1] Since an internal subcontracting arrangement was probably in use there, he may have suggested the same method for the new factory in Brno some years later, if in fact he was consulted on the problem. On the other hand, such direct transference of techniques may not have been necessary. An internal subcontracting system could have been introduced in the Brno woollen mill without knowledge of the Waldstein experience, if for no other reason than that it required the least amount of managerial sophistication. In that case the protofactory as an organizational form would simply have concentrated into a limited space the crews of a number of masters operating autonomously, as they had been doing in their own premises.

Under internal subcontracting the master was permitted much independence, possibly including the hiring and firing of workers and certainly disciplining them. If he became a foreman, however, he lost much of his autonomy and became essentially the transmitter of orders from above and part of a hierarchical ladder of authority. Such a system may have been employed in the Waldstein works in 1765 when it was visited by Jean Thys. He found masters engaged in no work of their own except the supervision of teams of workers. One master, for example, stood over three looms and a shearing master over each three pairs of shears.[2] This meant that a definite change had occurred if subcontracting was originally the rule as the archival evidence suggests. Since the Klagenfurt manufacturer commented that this system was 'expensive' the conclusion suggests itself that he for one did not approve of it. He may have applied intuitively the yardstick that Alfred Marshall proposed for measuring the usefulness of a foreman. According to Marshall the wage of a foreman, which is normally considerably greater than that of a worker, must be equal to or less than the product that the same amount of wages for production workers would result in.[3]

[1] HKA, red no. 881, f. 29, Marty, 1758.

[2] SUA, ČG Comerc. Elenchen, K-39 Carton No. 222, 18 Marty 1765: 'La Direction de cette fabrique est très couteuse. Pour chaque trois metiers, pour chaque trois paires de tondeurs, il y a un maître que sans presque rien travailler est largement payé de son inspection.'

[3] Alfred Marshall, *Principles of Economics*, 8th edition (London, 1920), 497.

It is a matter of speculation how the master functioned either as internal subcontractor or as foreman. As a matter of fact the question is still unsettled today whether a foreman pushes or pulls the worker to higher productivity or if his presence is a matter of indifference. Much depends on the skills required of workers, on the inter-connectedness of work and on the attitudes of workers in respect to their own autonomy.[1] In a protofactory like the Brno woollen mill the foreman had to fulfill an important role as teacher of new skills, but beyond that on him also depended the successful meshing of the production processes. Although this is a question of major importance, the information on the logical progression by which a piece of cloth began as raw material and ended as saleable merchandise is lacking. Unfortunately neither Thys nor any other reporter on the Brno mill had much to say about the role of the supervisory personnel. It must therefore remain moot whether the Brno factory worked on an internal subcontract system or whether its chief workers and masters acted simply as persons carrying out the direct orders of those above them. A rule of thumb that has been used in analysing other industrial plants is inoperative in this case since there is no documentation left from the firm itself. In the Waldstein woollen mill, for example, the wages for a completed piece seem to have been paid to the head worker who then presumably paid his subordinates. This was very likely also the case in many British cotton factories in the nineteenth century where the mule-spinner would receive wages out of which he paid his young helpers.

In 1771 the following were among the 'officials' who supervised the production process: the 'factory master', a master weaver, receiving an annual salary of 400 fl., the shearing master with a salary of 174 fl. and two spinning masters with salaries of 140 fl. per year. Then there was the pressing master, the dye master and the fuller, who were paid by the day but at a higher rate than other workers. The dyer and the fuller were also the beneficiaries of government 'pensions'. Those masters who were paid by the day probably themselves worked along with their assistants. This was the case before Seitter arrived on the scene in 1772; there is no evidence to suggest that conditions changed afterwards in respect to the institutional form that supervision took.

[1] Cf. Delbert C. Miller, 'Supervisors: Evolution of an Organizational Role', in Rober Dubin et al., *Leadership and Productivity* (San Francisco, 1965), 104–32.

The Labour Force

The potential manpower pool in Brno was more susceptible to the learning process than the Jihlava clothmakers were. Wool manufacture was little known in Brno prior to the establishment of the woollen mill and consequently the process of 'unlearning' old methods with often precedes learning newer ones did not present insurmountable difficulties as it had done in Jihlava. In 1732 a census of crafts revealed only thirteen master weavers in Brno in contrast to 461 in Jihlava.[1] Consequently the opportunity for organized opposition was considerably smaller and the municipal, regional and central governments could safely ignore complaints from this small vested interest, though a guild of weavers did exist in Brno and from time to time it tried to make trouble for the woollen factory.[2] In all of Moravia only one district, Znojmo (Znaim), had fewer woollen weavers and looms than Brno. A series of censuses revealed the following figures for the woollen industry in Brno:

	Masters	Journeymen	Looms
1728	139	—	135
1769	189	90	210
1775	119	106	165
1776	136	107	204
1777	179	131	182
1778	170	134	211
1779	225	136	265
1780	219	186	260
1781	201	212	288
1782	208	270	327
1789	63	45	163

Sources: for 1728, Mainuš, *Vlnařství*, 38–40; for the other years, the censuses are found in HKA, red no. 796.

The censuses after 1769 were probably more accurate but they were also, unfortunately, less informative. The 1769 census gives values for the production of each branch of industry. The product of the Brno district was less than one-fifth of that of the whole area

[1] Mainuš, *Vlnařství*, 38–40.

[2] Cf. J. Šmída, 'Brněnské textilní cechy v první třetině 18. století' (Brno textile guilds in the first third of the 18th century), *Časopis Matice Moravske*, LVIII (1934), 287–95. In 1721, there was a guild of weavers (tkalcí) and one of clothmakers (soukeníků).

covered, whereas the district was second in population.[1] The 1769 census also reveals one interesting fact that could have been as helpful in the introduction of industrial innovations as the absence of strong vested interests. Almost every industry counted in Moravia was represented in the Brno district. This indicates that the district had a broad spectrum of technologies and conditions, and may therefore have been more open to different ways of doing things and more used to a greater mobility between various occupations.

Since there is detailed information on the place of origin of the workers in the fine cloth factory only for the first four years in Brno, it is difficult to estimate how well the labour force in the area assimilated itself to the new enterprise. There seems to have been little migration from further away.[2] When the factory was in Kladruby in 1761, all the workers either came from Verviers or had been trained by the Belgian craftsmen.[3] This at least was what Bailoux reported to the government, but he was trying to impress the Empress at this time to continue the operation of the factory under his direction and he may have been somewhat liberal in stating that altogether seventeen weavers had been trained and that all of them were inhabitants of Kladruby and its environment. If this was the case, then Bailoux and the Verviers craftsmen would have been very successful in transferring their techniques to the Bohemian village. There may have been some truth to it, since it is known that a Jewish businessman had woollens manufactured in Kladruby after the factory's departure. But it was coarse cloth and not the fine quality that Bailoux supposedly introduced. Nevertheless, if the enterprise in Kladruby continued to manufacture woollen cloth and was not used simply as a screen behind which the owner illegally collected the best native wool for export, as the Bohemian Commercial Council suggested, then the old Bailoux enterprise left at least some benefits behind.[4]

On the other hand, Bailoux's effort at Kladruby viewed simply in terms of transmitting an advanced technology can be considered

[1] The total product given for 1769 was 4,371,066 fl. and Brno district's share was 789,530 fl. HKA, red no. 796, 'Mährische Landes Aufnahme oder Manufacturs-Haupt Tabelle Pro Anno 1769'. Its population was about 208,000, Henryk Grossmann, 'Die Anfänge und geschichtliche Entwicklung der amtlichen Statistik in Österreich', *Statistische Monatsschrift*, N.F. XXI (1916), 384.

[2] Josef Vytiska, 'Brněnska průmyslová oblast v první polovině 19. století', (The Brno industrial territory in the first half of the 19th century), *Brno v minulosti a dnes* (Brno in the Past and Today), V (1963), 340.

[3] HKA, red no. 891, ad 17. Dez. 1761, 'N.N. 1 et 2'.

[4] Klíma, *Manufakturní období*, 349 f; HKA, red no. 794, f. 163 ff.; HKA, red no. 48, f. 292 ff.

a dismal failure. After more than a decade he was only able to produce craftsmen with skills good enough to manufacture coarse cloths. Cloth of the quality to compete with the product imported from Verviers he had never been able to manufacture. At first he had the excuse that he was asked to use inferior Bohemian and Moravian wool for the manufacture of a product that the successful manufacturers of Verviers and elsewhere were making of Spanish Merino wool. He was still unable to have his workers manufacture good fine cloths when all the wool was Spanish Merino and moreover five out of the fifteen weavers employed in 1761 had come from Verviers.[1] Except for one weaver who had come from France, the remaining ten had been trained by the Verviers weavers in Kladruby. That the cloth was still too poor to sell without coercion was consequently a serious indictment of Bailoux and his staff. It might mean that they were unable to give proper instruction or possibly that they themselves were not sufficiently skilled to be regularly employed in Verviers and had therefore left for greener pastures.

The Places of Origin of the Workers

The first list of workers in the factory in Kladruby is of limited value for purposes of comparison with two other lists from the 1760s. In the latter lists, specific names with places of birth were given, whereas the first list prepared by Bailoux gave only first names for those born abroad and these names were not always the same as those reported on the subsequent lists. This point is of some importance because it gives rise to the possibility that some of the old workers who came from Verviers had left and new ones from there had been added. The five weavers from Verviers who worked in the factory in 1766 were very likely not among the group of forty-odd persons who left their native city in 1748–9 for the Habsburg Monarchy. One of the five, aged 18, could have been brought as a baby by his parents, but the others, aged 30–35, must have arrived subsequently.

It is interesting in this respect that an enumeration of workers by name in 1767 discloses that four of the five were still in the factory and that in the meantime three new weavers from Verviers had been added. Moreover the lists of workers for 1766 and 1767 also reveal that the work force had heterogeneous origins. In 1766, for example, two weavers originated from Silesia, one from Eupen, one from Kladruby and one from Seligenstadt in Germany.

[1] HKA, red no. 891, 17 Dec. 1761.

Not until the following year, that is after three years of operation in Brno, is there a record of a weaver from that city, and he was an apprentice. Even more startling is the fact that fully six weavers employed in 1767 were reported to have come from Liberec, a woollen centre in northern Bohemia rivalling that of Jihlava and nearly as strongly dominated by a clothmakers' guild. Despite the general opposition of guilds to factories, the Liberec guild had obviously permitted these journeymen to accept employment, a permission that was necessary if the weavers expected to work for guild masters in the future or became masters themselves.

One may well wonder why the guild in the distant woollen centre permitted work in a factory while that of Jihlava only some thirty miles away would not. If the *Inventorium* reported the places of origin correctly, then a very interesting change occurred between 29 April 1767 and 30 June 1767, for in April six journeymen weavers were announced to be coming from Jihlava.[1] The Jihlava weavers may indeed have come and like others from there and from other Bohemian and Moravian cloth centres may have left the employ of the woollen works because they were unwilling to work 'Netherland' looms. In January 1767 Jacob Delimont, the superintendent of the factory, ruefully wrote in a letter to the Moravian Commercial Council that for weavers who had been trained on the 'German' loom, the 'Netherland' loom proved too difficult and that such workers regularly left within two weeks.[2] This may be the reason why the large Flemish loom, which was most likely identical to the 'Netherland' loom, was not adopted in central Europe despite having been in use in Flanders as early as the thirteenth century.[3]

Unfortunately, no detailed information as to the place of origin of the workers is to be found in the records after 1772 when Seitter began to put the organization on a new basis. There is little doubt that the work-force was increasingly recruited locally. When Kehrnhofer brought the factory to Brno, he clearly expected no problem with the hiring of workers, since the town was full of able-bodied beggars. Yet in Jihlava in 1749 half of the skilled cloth workers in the town had no work but they would not join the Netherlanders. Similarly, in Kladruby a large work force became

[1] SAB, KKT 1763, 12/207, 29 April 1767, Dobruška.

[2] SAB, KKT 1763, 12/207, 29 April 1767, Delimont.

[3] Walter Endrei, *L'évolution des techniques du filage et du tissage du moyen âge à la revolution industrielle* (Paris, 1968), 82. If Endrei is correct in saying that the Flemish loom was introduced in Jihlava, it was no longer in operation in the eighteenth century.

available only when duress was used, despite the fact that the peasants were extremely poor. In Brno labour did not spring readily to the fore despite the known plight of a large number of people in the town. How many times since then and in how many places in the world has this experience been multiplied!

Technological Diffusion

To a large extent the manpower problem revolved around the introduction and diffusion of a new technology. Over a twenty-year period from about 1750 to 1770 the skilled craftsmen from Verviers had been attempting to bring about the desired result by demonstration.[1] This period may have been a necessary time of preparation for a society that strongly resisted change and for manpower that was not very much motivated by economic incentives. To assess how easily a society accepts and adapts itself to innovation one would have to examine the entire cultural inventory so that one could understand what mental connexions had to be formed to accept new ideas. How well were members of Bohemian and Moravian society conditioned by their background to imitate those who, like the Verviers craftsmen, were brought in to teach by their example?[2] Such an assessment would have to be made separately for the rural setting of Kladruby, and the urban environment of Brno.

We may presume that the absence of clear technological and economic progress of this woollen mill over its long existence did not invalidate its contribution. The many frustrating years may have been the necessary prerequisite for successful innovation. At any rate the Moravian Commercial Commission was pleased to report considerable success to its parent body in Vienna. According to a 1773 memorandum only six of the 721 persons employed by the factory were foreigners.[3] This and subsequent reports on the workers

[1] Warren C. Scoville, 'Minority Migrations and the Diffusion of Technology', *Journal of Economic History*, XI (1951), 347–60. Scoville, in a preceptive article on the diffusion of technologies, suggested that such a method was superior to one in which individuals as teachers played the dominant role. On its face the evidence here presented does not support this thesis and may even provoke an opposite conclusion; for after two decades of effort the quality of workmanship was still poor. Scoville omitted any time constraint altogether but if we introduce the time factor, his proposition may still prove valid.

[2] Cf. H. G. Barnett, *Innovation: The Basis of Cultural Change* (New York, 1953), 11, 12, 16, 39, 40, 50. See also Nathan Rosenberg, *Technology and American Economic Growth* (New York, 1972), 31, 32.

[3] HKA, red no. 894, f. 1086, 11 Sept. 1773 (43 ex Nov. 773 Böhm).

employed by the firm are unfortunately not as detailed as those for the 1760s in which names and places of origin appeared. It may have been owing to the fast growth of the factory or possibly the lack of interest among governmental officials that the firm reported in a more abbreviated fashion on its employees, thus preventing one from making more conclusive comparisons. From a 1769 report one can ascertain that twelve of the thirty-two skilled workers then employed came from outside the Habsburg Monarchy and many of the sixty-eight spinners and spoolers were members of the families of the foreign craftsmen. If in 1773 there were actually only six foreign workers in the factory, then a notable change had taken place.

The Thys Factory: A Comparison

The small number of non-natives employed was in sharp contrast to the woollen mill in Klagenfurt which served as its model. Jean Thys brought to Klagenfurt about twenty weavers from the Netherlands, presumably from Verviers.[1] His woollen cloths enjoyed an exceptional reputation whereas Brno's products were still not universally accepted, a fact that may reflect the inferior level of skill that the native workers displayed. The Brno firm was under much greater pressure than the one in Klagenfurt to demonstrate the government's wisdom in investing so heavily in it. Since it was among the primary goals of the Mercantilistic government of Maria Theresia to find employment for the native population, the Brno enterprise may have gone further than Thys in Klagenfurt to accommodate the officials and to worry less about the quality of the product.

In the end this reliance on local workers may actually have paid dividends. It may have proved to be an efficient method of fostering general industrial development in late eighteenth century and nineteenth-century Brno, while the Klagenfurt factory, where dependence on foreign craftsmen continued, did not spawn any such development.[2] Paradoxically, the successful woollen mill in Klagenfurt may deserve the comment often levelled at mercantilistic enterprises: it was a hothouse plant which withered away once external protection and support was withdrawn. Created in 1762 under the most auspicious conditions imaginable for the time, favoured by the expertise of its founder and benefiting from

[1] HKA, red no. 442, f. 688, 21 Jan. 1774.
[2] Karl Dinklage, 'Klagenfurts industrielle Entwicklung', in Gotbert Moro ed, *Die Landeshauptstadt Klagenfurt* (Klagenfurt, 1970), II, 236–9.

governmental largesse that included a 100,000 fl. interest-free loan, it experienced few of the ailments of infant industries known to the Kladruby–Brno factory.[1]

In 1773 its founder died and his son Franz Rainer von Thys operated the factory. Although the woollen mill existed under his direction for at least another twenty years and still continued to produce high quality cloth, it was reduced in size.[2] Significantly, however, it did not induce in Klagenfurt the forward or backward linkages that might serve as a basis for industrial proliferation. That the Thys firm ceased its leadership position in the Habsburg woollen industry may be attributable to the relatively mediocre abilities of the younger Thys; it may, however, also have been the result of a lack of interest on the part of the central government in Vienna. The elder Thys had apparently set up the enterprise in a sound enough position so that the momentum carried it forward in a reasonably efficient manner. In Brno, on the other hand, the 1770s proved to be troublesome despite the change in leadership. Is it possible that the fumbling and floundering of the Brno enterprise proved to be an important contribution to the learning process in the area? In the long run, might the errors of this enterprise have provided more opportunities for potential innovators than the smoother operation in Klagenfurt? If so, Kenneth Boulding would be vindicated in making his semi-humorous remark that 'nothing fails like success because you don't learn anything from it'.[3] This may have been one of the reasons why Klagenfurt as late as 1929 was not an industrial city, as one writer proudly proclaimed.[4]

The Waldstein Factory: A Further Comparison

Before looking at other specialized workers in the Brno factory, we should cast a brief glance at the weavers in the third fine-woollen cloth mill in the Hereditary Lands of the Habsburg Monarchy. Founded in 1715 in Horní Litvinov, its purpose, too, was to manufacture fine woollens. And like the two factories that followed it several decades later, it brought in weavers and other skilled

[1] Herman Freudenberger, 'Three Mercantilistic Protofactories', *Business History Review*, XL (1966), 172.
[2] Dinklage, 'Klagenfurts industrielle Entwicklung', 238 f.
[3] Kenneth E. Boulding. 'Fun and Games with the Gross National Product — the Role of Misleading Indicators in Social Policy', in Harold W. Helfrich, Jr. ed., *The Environmental Crisis* (New Haven, 1970), 160.
[4] Erwin Stein, ed. *Die Städte Deutschösterreichs*, Vol. IV, *Klagenfurt* (Berlin, 1929), p. 341.

craftsmen from the Belgian and Dutch centres. A number of weavers from the Bohemian town of Česká Lípa (Böhmisch Leipa) were still working in the factory in 1764.[1] They were undoubtedly members of the local guild of clothmakers and must have had the permission of their corporate body. They would probably not be following the Netherland method of weaving, in which case the innovation brought from abroad at considerable expense would have fallen victim to the secular resistance of workers intent on their traditional ways. It would then explain the seemingly ill-informed statement of Franz Rainer von Thys that his father was the first to operate a woollen factory which used the Netherland methods in the Hereditary Lands.[2]

Social Attitudes

It is also of interest to consider whether the workers from Verviers brought their social attitudes along with their technology. While the weavers from the Belgian town did not belong to a guild, they operated on an individual basis much like the guild masters in the Habsburg Monarchy. In this respect they very likely retained a greater feeling of independence and were less susceptible to supervision than other skilled workers like the cloth finishers. The latter were among the first to find themselves working in premises belonging to an employer whether in England, in the Netherlands or in the Habsburg Monarchy. Most probably the reason was that the results of the finishing process, although of less intrinsic value in the strength and quality of the cloth, were more visible to the naked eye and therefore more vital than weaving in the sale of goods. By bringing finishing directly under the supervision of the employer and into his premises, an important step was taken in the development of the modern factory.[3] Might this have provided finishers quite early with a feeling of being simply workers who had nothing but their services to sell? If so, a strike of shearers in Verviers in 1759 might reflect that they had a collective interest like modern labour opposed to that of their employers.[4] Despite a strike against their employers they may have been less resistant to discipline than weavers who frequently continued to work in their own living

[1] HKA, red no. 733, 26 Mar. 1764: See also, Freudenberger, *Waldstein Woolen Mill*, 46.

[2] HKA, red no. 442, f. 1239 ff. Wien, 6 Dec. 1781.

[3] Cf. Jennifer Tann, *The Development of the Factory* (London, 1970), Lebrun, *Verviers*, 269.

[4] Lebrun, *Verviers*, 260–2.

quarters. The central accounting office in Vienna objected when Köffiller proposed to evict the weavers from their apartments in the factory and to convert the rooms completely into working quarters. The officials of that department pointed out that it was customary for weavers to combine work and living space. They saw no benefit in the proposed separation and considered it merely an unwarranted increase in the investment of the firm.[1]

Weaving was an important factor in measuring the capacity of the plant. It also was one of the largest components in the wage bill, with only the wages of the spinners to challenge it from time to time. A ubiquitous occupation in all of Europe, spinning had no formal standing as a vested interest inside or outside the factory. There were no spinners' guilds. Everyone could spin from childhood to old age, irrespective of gender. Work was carried on in a sporadic fashion, serving frequently as a filler for time when other tasks had been attended to or when darkness or inclement weather prevented other work. The techniques were simple, depending mainly on the dexterity of fingers in the manipulation of the fibre. Nevertheless, spinning was one of the major problems that plagued the Brno factory and its predecessor. The Moravian factory was not unique in experiencing this problem. A few decades earlier, the British inventor, Lewis Paul, remarked that 'weavers were often forced to remain unemployed for want of such particular sized yarns as were suitable to their occasions'.[2] Paul may have been referring to cotton yarn; he would have been equally justified in making the statement about woollen yarn. The procurement of woollen yarn proved to be a major problem even in England, where the hand-loom weaver, who predominated well into the nineteenth century, was forced to waste much time searching for warp and weft yarns.[3]

Spinning

The spinning wheel employed in the Brno woollen mill was undoubtedly the large hand-driven wheel that was already fairly well known in the Middle Ages.[4] It was preferred to the so-called Saxony wheel, whose foot treadle provided motion for the wheel.

[1] HKA, red no. 892, f. 679, 14 Nov. 1767.

[2] As quoted in W. English, *The Textile Industry* (London & Harlow, 1969), 9. See also, among others, Carl Heinrichs, *Die Wollenindustrie unter Friedrich Wilhelm I* (Berlin, 1933), 361.

[3] W. B. Crump, *The Leeds Woollen Industry 1780–1820* (Leeds, 1921), 29.

[4] For an illustration of this implement see Freudenberger, *Waldstein Woolen Mill*, plate 11. See also 'The Spinning Wheel', *Ciba Review*, 28 (1939).

The wheel's function, in turn, was to move the flier and spindle. The Saxony wheel was used most effectively with yarns for linens. The particular merit of the larger hand-driven wheel was the instantaneous control that it supposedly gave to the spinner, who merely held on to one of the spokes of the wheel to halt the spindle's movement and who could control the speed of the spindle in any way she pleased. Spinning jennies, which were admirably suited for the woollen industry, were used by English manufacturers already in 1780.[1] The first documented appearance of a mechanical spinning machine in Brno is in the inventory compiled in 1793 on the death of a local woollen manufacturer. It was a new machine, not yet completed and its constructor was out of funds so that there was a legal question about when, if ever, it would be made functional.[2]

The reluctance of producers in the woollen industry to adopt new methods is well known. Nevertheless, it is curious that material incentives were not substantially increased in order to introduce a more adequate supply of woollen yarn. Since the society that is being examined was highly traditional, even monetary incentives would not necessarily provide a higher quality yarn and might not even have had much effect on the quantity. Jean Thys, that model of a rational woollen manufacturer, discovered this in his own enterprise in Klagenfurt. Despite paying wage rates 15 to 25 per cent higher than those in the Low Countries, he was still not able to get enough yarn of the required quality.[3] To alleviate his problem, he

[1] Crump, *Leeds Woollen Industry*, 7; R. P. B. Beckinsale ed., *The Trowbridge Woollen Industry* (Devizes, 1951), xviii.

[2] Archiv zemského hlavního města Brna, Pozůstalosti, no. 533, Offermann, Johann Heinrich, sen.

[3] HKA, red no. 891, ad 227/1764, Mémoire pour le degraisement des draps . . . ;

Tabelle des prix de filage

pour un echet de chaine	à Eupen	à Aix	Verviers	à Cladroup	
de 24 macques blanche	3 2/3	3 2/3*	......	......	4 kr.
de 24 macques tiente	4 1/6	......	4 3/8*	4 7/8*	4½ kr.
echets de trame					
de 24 macques blanche	3 1/4	3 1/4	......	......	3½ kr.
de 24 macques teinte	3 3/4	......	3 3/8*	3 3/4**	4 kr.

Sur cette tabelle il y a la reflection à faire que les prix sont calculis selon le lours respective des different pays. Le ducat qui vaut icy f. 4.7 1/2 vaut à Eupen, Aix La Chapelle, etc. f. 5 jusque f. 5.10; a Verviers f. 4.30 jusqua f. 4.37 1/2. Ce que fait une difference de plus de 22 pour cent pour Eupen, Aix-la-Chapelle et de plus de dix pour cent pour Verviers.

2do La mesure de 24 macques est de premier institution des fabricques, et les fabricants d'Eupen. . . .

une fileuse ou un filiur peut filer par jour deux echets de chaine et gagner pas consequent 8 Kreutzer deux et demi et trois echets de trame et gagner ainsy 8 et dix kreutzer. . . .

* de 22 macques ** 20 macques

employed masters whose duty it was to train spinners; once they successfully completed their course of instruction they received spinning wheels and other equipment free of charge.[1] It was for reasons of this sort that the enlightened government of Maria Theresia felt it necessary to step in to raise the level of proficiency all over the Monarchy.

In order to improve both the quality and the quantity of yarn a so-called Spinning Ordinance was issued in November 1765.[2] In order that '. . . loyal subjects, especially the rural population, have a chance to augment their total income . . .', the establishment of spinning schools was ordered throughout the Hereditary Lands. Local authorities and guilds were to finance the schools which were to operate from October to March during the two years following the publication of the decree. All children between the ages of seven and fifteen who did not know how to spin were obligated to attend these schools, unless the children were 'needed' at home by their parents. Within a period of four weeks the children were expected to become proficient and during this time a wage of two kreutzer per day was to be credited to each child. Following the training period, the child was obliged to spin at home and the authorities were to make weekly inspections and to make reports to the government. Premiums of 50 to 150 fl. were promised to the most diligent officials. As an additional incentive marriages between girls who had spun steadily for two years and journeymen were to be permitted and guilds which forbade journeymen to marry were expressly enjoined not to discriminate against those who took advantage of this provision. Finally, idlers and beggars were to be placed in spinning houses for periods of three to six months and to be given free bread and water in addition to their earnings from spinning. Neither parents nor local authorities proved very co-operative, even after the decree was republished in strengthened form in 1766.[3] Local authorities seemed at first willing to establish schools but soon found that even the supplying of light and heat was too great a burden.[4] The Moravian Commercial Council however did aid the establishment of spinning schools by providing funds for at least fifteen such institutions.[5]

[1] HKA, red no. 442, f. 523.
[2] *Codex Austriacus*, VI (Wien, 1777), 763 ff.
[3] Ibid., 831.
[4] HKA, red no. 892, f. 875 ff. Brünn, 28 Nov. 1768.
[5] Ibid., f. 815 ff.

That the need for yarn was desperate is indicated by the proposal of two Moravian government officials that a special mark be placed on the clothing of all beggars in the street who legitimately required this mode of earning their living, while all others were to be detailed and forced to spin.[1] They also suggested that certain localities be assigned to the Brno factory and all other yarn collectors be prevented from invading such precincts. This was actually done in 1768 when all spinning schools that had been established within three Austrian miles (about 21 km.) of Brno were obliged to spin for the Brno fine-woollen mill.[2] Whole areas in which all the yarn produced was assigned to a particular enterprise were not unknown in the Habsburg Monarchy; the Linz woollen factory and the cotton enterprises at Šaštin and Schwechat had similar privileges.[3]

All these efforts were not sufficient to ensure the factory with an adequate supply of yarn, and complaints continued to come from the management of the firm as late as 1780.[4] The invention of a spinning wheel on which two threads of yarn could be spun simultaneously proved no help.[5] Although the Brno burgher who invented it received a 250 ducat reward from the government in 1777, no mention of it can be found in the documentation on the Brno woollen factory.

Spinning machines having not yet been introduced and neither wage incentives nor laws like the Spinning Ordinance resulting in a sufficient supply of yarn, factory managers found refuge in cruder means of coercion. In England they talked about 'apprentices' and the workhouse poor that were assigned to various enterprises; in the Habsburg Monarchy orphans provided part of the labour force to spin yarn. This period was of course notorious in England as well as in other European countries for the exploitation of children and other disadvantaged persons in industrial work.[6] In contrast to the

[1] Ibid., f. 565 ff., Brünn, 1 Sept. 1767.

[2] HKA, red no. 3.

[3] Cf. also Horst Krüger, *Zur Geschichte der Manufakturen und der Manufakturabeiter in Preussen* (Berlin, 1958), 134. In Prussia so-called spinning villages were assigned to certain enterprises.

[4] HKA, red no. 894, f. 418–39, Brünn, 19 Mai, 1780.

[5] Bedřich Šindelář, 'K nejstarším pokusům se stroji v brněnských textilních manufakturách na přelomu 18. a 19. stoleti' (To the oldest efforts to introduce machinery in the Brno textile industry at the turn of the 18th and 19th centuries) *Časopis Matice Moravske*, LXXVI (1957), 73–4.

[6] See *inter alia* Frances Collier, *The Family Economy of the Working Classes in the Cotton Industry 1784–1833*, ed. R. S. Fitton, (Manchester, 1964), 38–46; George Unwin, *Samuel Oldknow and the Arkwrights*, ed. W. H. Chaloner, (Manchester, 1968), 170–5; Krüger, *Zur Geschichte*, 141–4; John Goodchild, 'Pildacre Mill: An Early West Riding Factory', *Textile History*, I, 3 (1970), 339.

English experience where local government organized child labour, the Habsburg central government was a direct party to this traffic in human beings. The Habsburg officials readily recognized the need for cheap labour in the spinning of yarn as afforded by orphanages, penal institutions and work houses. The Moravian government had an orphans' fund constituted by the excise on chocolate and cocoa beans. The company insisted that the labour of orphans was essential. Orphan-spinners would assure them a steady supply of a standard quality of yarn, while they claimed that other spinners devoted the spring, summer and autumn to working in the fields. In supporting the management's request for the control of an orphanage in Brno, the 'Factory Directorate' emphasized the need for direct industrial discipline. Experience had taught conclusively, the 'Directorate' stated, that people were sleepy and unwilling to work, especially in Moravia, and that it was extremely difficult to convince the peasant of the usefulness of this type of industrial work.[1]

Equally as critical as a steady flow of yarn to the factory was that the factory could not provide spinners with wool until there were specific orders from customers. This was so because the firm produced coloured cloths for which the wool had to be dyed prior to spinning. Such fashion goods (*Modewaren*) depended on the idiosyncrasies of market demand and understandably the company wished to keep its inventories of different coloured yarns as low as possible.[2]

By 1783 the factory no longer required the spinning of the orphans and other work had to be found for them.[3] At about the same time, the Klagenfurt woollen mill complained that it was almost forced to shut down when the military orphanage of that city was liquidated; it had to recruit a large number of female spinners in Carniola and settle them at considerable expense in the buildings of the factory itself.[4] Among the reasons for the opposite experiences of the woollen mills in Brno and Klagenfurt may be that Brno's population was growing and was willing to send its children to the

[1] SAB, C/12/40, 163, 762: Zudeme Lehret die Erfahrung überzeugend, wie schläfrig und unthätig das Volk besonders in dem Lande Mähren beschaffen seye; wenn es auf die Einführung einer Industrial-Nahrung ankommet; In massen annoch in frischen Angedencken beywohnen wird, was für Mühe es erforderet habe den Landmann von dem wahren Nutzen derley Industrial-Verdiensten vollständig zu belehren. . . .

[2] Ibid.

[3] SAB, C/12/45, f. 266–7, Brünn, 1 Sept. 1783.

[4] HKA, red no. 442, f. 1254, 23 Dec., 1781.

factory to augment family earnings, whereas in the smaller city of Klagenfurt this process had not taken place. As a general rule children's houses (*Kinderhäuser*), similar to the 'prentice houses' in England, were still kept by factories located outside cities in the early decades of the nineteenth century.[1] The Brno factory might have been able to dispense with the orphans' work because it was able to recruit a sufficient supply of child labour from the increasing number of employees in the factory itself. In the tables listing employees and their families in the 1760s, all members of the family who could work were also employed at some task in or for the factory and this practice can be expected to have persisted.[2]

Preparatory and Finishing Processes

Spinning and weaving contributed more to the quality of the end product than did other processes. These can be divided into the preparatory and the finishing processes.[3] Generally speaking, the preparatory processes, including sorting, cleansing, scouring and carding the raw wool primarily required great care, while finishing — burling, shearing or cropping, fulling and pressing — put a higher premium on skill. Much of the wool was dyed immediately after it had been scoured and prior to weaving, this being necessary especially for cloth of mixed colours. Black woollens, on the other hand, were more often dyed in the cloth, in which case dyeing could be considered part of the finishing process. There are fewer references, except for some generalized complaints on poor workmanship, concerning the finishing processes compared with those to spinning, weaving and the preparatory processes. Since personal skill was the basic prerequisite for a burler and since he was among the better paid workers, a combination of monetary incentive and appeal to the virtuosity of the craft presumably were sufficient.

[1] Ludwig von Mises, 'Zur Geschichte der österreichischen Fabrikgesetzgebung', *Zeitschrift für Volkswirtschaft, Sozialpolitik und Verwaltung*, XIV (1905), 220; see also J. L. Hammond and Barbara Hammond, *The Town Labourer* (paperback ed. London, 1966), 157 who ascribe the move from the countryside to the city to technological change. Textile mills were located in the country where water power was dominant in importance and they moved to the city when steam took its place.

[2] This was common practice in England as well where entire families worked in the mills of Samuel Gregg in Styal and those of W. G. and J. Strutt at Belper and Milford, Derbyshire. In Manchester, too, the same social framework seems to have existed until greater mechanization and further division of labour inside the factory broke up the family groupings. Collier, *Family Incomes*, 43, 74–89.

[3] Lebrun, *Verviers*, 215.

With sorting, cleansing, scouring and carding, however, discipline became a more important means for performing satisfactory work.

That good dyeing, fulling, burling and shearing were of great importance is underlined by the fact that the skilled craftsmen who were recruited for that purpose often received government pensions in addition to their wages from the firm. For example in the late 1750s when there were some moves afoot independent of the Kladruby factory to establish a woollen enterprise in Brno, a young craftsman from the Verviers area who had settled in Brno was commissioned by the government to recruit a dyer and a shearer from Verviers. Their travelling expenses to Brno would be paid and they were promised, in addition, an annual pension from the government of 150 fl. in addition to their wages.[1] Despite these attractive conditions great difficulties were experienced in recruitment. One of two men enticed to leave Verviers returned home pissatisfied soon after coming to Brno. These jobs were important because of their easy visibility in the completed product. Poor dyeing, shearing that left too many hairs standing, fulling that left the fabric greasy and/or loose and pressing that did not provide the necessary gloss all made the selling of the product very difficult, even after the best of wool had been deftly spun and well woven. In one case, Thys severely criticized the management of the Brno factory for having costs for burling and shearing that were between 25 and 30 per cent lower than those in his own factory.[2]

The problems attending the introduction and diffusion of technology have been emphasized. Much of the documentation on which this discussion depended came from the period before 1772, when Seitter, the man trained in Monschau, became manager of the Brno Fine-Cloth Factory. Since complaints concerning poor quality cloth continued during his period of leadership, one may presume that the problems were not immediately solved with his coming. On the other hand, none of the subsequent crises revolved around the question of quality so much as the earlier ones had. The conclusion seems warranted therefore that the Netherland art of making fine woollens took permanent hold in Brno and that after much travail and frustration government policies encouraging industrialization proved successful.

[1] SAB, KT T 1763, 13/207, 25 Jan. 1764, Referat . . . Kehrnhofer.
[2] HKA, red no. 891, 766–9, Klagenfurt, 15 Nov. 1765.

Wages

In turning our attention now to wages and salaries, we must keep in mind that the documentation available to us is insufficient for a completely satisfactory analysis. Again it is the period up to 1772 for which there is a greater abundance of material than for the time subsequent to Seitter's assumption of power. For the earlier period, wage rates are known and estimates of annual earnings can therefore be deduced. But this tells little about the actual annual income of an operative or his family. For that one would have to know the name of the operative and the number of hours during a given week that he actually worked at a given rate, or if he worked on piece rate, which was common, the actual amount of work that he turned out. This type of evidence does exist for a number of English cotton firms for which wage books have been preserved.[1]

As things stand, one can at best approximate the number of days that an operative could work during the year, given that he was never taken ill, never had a hangover that kept him away from work, never had to wait for a previous process to be finished, and that the entire factory never had to stop altogether because of lack of orders or because a freeze or a drought made it impossible to work water-wheels or to wash wool in a flowing stream. The intermittent nature of production at this time for whatever reason had a serious effect on the annual income of a family. From time to time the records reveal hints of problems such as the demand of some of the workers to be paid half-time when they were subject to involuntary unemployment.[2]

On the whole, then, the evidence is circumstantial and various assumptions have to be made to arrive at figures for either monetary or real incomes. Such calculations become especially difficult because many occupations permitted — even in more sophisticated Britain — only sporadic work.[3] It is simply inadmissible for us to picture a weaver, for example, steadily working at his loom from dawn to dusk, day after day. The available data are at best useful for drawing upper limits of earning power. The wage rates were compiled originally to estimate production costs and they are still more useful for that purpose.

[1] See Collier, *Family Economy*.
[2] HKA, red no. 891, f. 887–918, 24 Mar. 1767.
[3] Smelser, *Social Change*, 102.

Wage Rates

	1762	1764	1771	
Weaver	7½ *kr.*	7½ *kr.*	7½–9 *kr.*	per ell
Fuller	1 *fl.*	1 *fl.*	45 *kr.*	per day
Fuller's Assistant	18 *kr.*	—	12 *kr.*	per day
Spinner	4 *kr.*	4 *kr.*	5½ *kr.*	per *Stern* or *Stahn*
Burler	30–37 *kr.*/piece	—	24 *kr.*	per day
Shearer	30 *kr.*/day	30 *kr.*/day	3 *fl.* 45 *kr.*	per piece
Spooler		18–22 *kr.*/day		
Carder			2½ *kr.*	per pound
Press master	37½ *kr.*/day	—	30 *kr.*	per day

1 fl. (gulden) = 60 *kr.* (Kreutzer)

Sources: for 1762: Haus-Hof-und Staatsarchiv, Poschakten, J. S. Karton #6, f. 497–511.
for 1763: SAB, KT T 1763, 13/207, Referat . . . Kehrnhofer
for 1771: HKA, red no. 893, f. 332–3.

Clearly piece rates make it extremely difficult to estimate earnings; even day wages do not assure a total earnings figure. A detailed listing of production costs (attested by Jean Thys to be reasonable in most respects) may allow the estimates to be more than merely wild guesses.

The cost estimate must be used cautiously. Costs for three pieces eight-quarter width (i.e. two ells) and twenty-five ells in length are broken down into individual components, the cost of wool and of dyeing being the major variables.[1] It seems that the superintendent gave standardized wage-costs rather than those for the particular pieces on which he based the calculation. Two-thirds of the costs were accounted for by raw materials, a proportion approximately that of the reports of Roland de la Platière in his authoritative encyclopedia published in 1785.[2] If it took two weeks to weave one piece of woollen cloth then the six gulden assigned to that task would have to be divided in some way between the two weavers who worked the loom. The sources for this period indicate that both the weavers were journeymen and that the factory did not follow the

[1] HKA, red no. 891, f. 763 ,ad 35/1765.
[2] Roland de la Platière, *Encyclopedia Méthodique. Manufactures, Arts et Métiers*, 1 (Paris and Liège, 1785), 334.

practice of having a young boy serve as the second man on the loom. This may mean then that the two men divided the wage equally, which would have meant 1–1/2 fl. (90 kr.) for each weaver per week or about 15 kr. per day on a six-day week. This estimate of daily earning power conforms to the wage rates reported in the table above. If the weaver was indeed able to produce one piece of cloth, 25 ells long, in a two-week period, then he would have had to weave approximately 2 ells per day. According to the piece rates reported for the 1760s and early 1770s, this would allow him to earn at least 15 kr. per day. If, on the other hand, he was able to produce one piece per week, then his earnings would double. Assertions to that effect can be found in the documentation, although they must be looked at sceptically since this rate of production seems to have required both a high level of proficiency and an efficient organization of work.[1] Verviers, one of the more efficient cloth centres in Europe, was able to boast such a record.[2] It is highly doubtful in the light of the numerous criticisms of the low level of proficiency and of organization in Brno that such productivity could have been attained.

Since the main focus in attempting to assess the well-being of a worker should be his earnings and not wage-rates or productivity, the question arises how well he was able to sustain himself with the 15 kr. per day that he was probably paid. For this purpose the most convenient rule of thumb is the sum of money that was reportedly necessary to keep an orphan alive and working about the year 1774. This information comes from the management of the Brno woollen mill, which at that time was temporarily running an orphanage, when they were demanding a subsidy from the state for each child's upkeep because contrary to expectations the orphans proved unable to earn their own keep by spinning. They claimed it took 8 kr. per day to keep a child alive and working.[3] A weaver who earned 15 kr. per working-day actually had 13 kr. per day available for consumption purposes over a seven-day week. In that case he enjoyed a standard of living that was 60 per cent higher than an orphan. This would be the case for a journeyman-weaver who was a bachelor. It he had dependants who themselves did not work, then his standard of living would, of course, be seriously diluted.

Although the estimate of the upkeep of an orphan is a reasonable standard by which to assess the welfare of others, some qualifications

[1] SAB, KK T 1763, 12/297, 29 April 1767.
[2] Lebrun, *Verviers*, 328.
[3] Allgemeines Verwaltungsarchiv, Hofkanzlei, no. 60.

must necessarily be made. The figure for the orphans may have been somewhat inflated since the managers of the firm were attempting to extract the maximum subsidy from the government authorities. Moreover, included in any realistic figure for orphans would have to be overhead charges for the salaries of officials and other expenses that would not concern a private person. The size of the worker's family is of course extremely important in assessing his standard of living. The best evidence on this question is the 1766 list of employees from which the wage-rate data have been extracted in the above table.

Four of the ten weavers then employed were married and the wife of each was also employed within the factory. Three of the four families had children ranging in age from 2 to 8, but none was reported as working. As is well-known, a child over 4 or 5 years of age was variously employed in England and elsewhere, and although this practice was certainly not frowned upon in the Habsburg Monarchy, it is somewhat surprising to find that the lowest age recorded for a worker was 10 years. The proportion of non-working dependants may indeed have been large. In a listing of employees by categories of work in 1777, the work force is given as nearly 700 and the number of wives and children, as about 400.[1] Since the spinners were listed and totalled nearly 400, the conclusion presents itself that the 'wives and children' category comprised only dependants. (It is of course possible that the firm deliberately double-counted, although this would have been a transparent trick indeed.) At least another 70 persons, besides the 400 spinners, were unmarried or without dependants; this number included apprentices, spoolers and other children. The number of workers who might therefore have had non-working dependants was at most 230, in which case the average number of dependants per married worker would have been nearly two. A family of three persons then would have to share the weaver's earnings of 13 kr. per day, when averaged over the seven-day week. This sum does not compare very favourably with the estimated 8 kr. per day that the upkeep of an orphan required.

If the wife was able to spin, she would be able to augment the daily earning power of the family by 5 to 7 kr. at most.[2] This was the earning power of the best spinners and required work on a full-time basis, so the more normal earnings of such a family would be

[1] HKA, red no. 894, f. 619.
[2] Allgemeines Verwaltungsarchiv, Hofkanzlei, no. 60, 13 Oct. 1772.

possibly about 18 kr. per working day. Children over ten years of age might then add 2–3 kr. to a working family's income. These hypothetical daily earnings estimates are based on the unrealistic assumption that all members of the family worked a full 313-workday year, that is, the calendar year of 365 less 52 Sundays. That this was the case is highly unlikely and consequently the average earnings per working day were unquestionably lower than those posited here.

Summary

The Brno Fine-Cloth Factory had a number of the characteristics of a protofactory. Almost all the manufacturing processes were under the control of a supervisory force and with the exception of a number of spinners in the countryside surrounding Brno, all work was carried on in the buildings provided by the firm. The organizational form of a protofactory had been imposed on this enterprise to a large extent to enable it to serve as a training institution for the diffusion of a new technology in Moravia. The guildsmen in this particular mystery mounted strong opposition to it wherever possible depite the fact that many of of them were unemployed and in very poor circumstances. Brno's potential labour force did not have a long tradition in the craft of clothmaking, a fact that seems to have assisted the process of adoption of the methods imported from Verviers. Nevertheless, close supervision was still required.

At first Belgian craftsmen acted as superintendents but their enterprise did not succeed. From 1772, a man trained in the west-German cloth centre of Monschau, a part of the Verviers–Aachen area of woollen-cloth specialization, brought stability to the factory. With him came a number of other men from the same area. They served as supervisors in the factory and many of them eventually became industrialists in their own right.

Besides focusing on the organization of work, one must also try to discovery the earnings of the workers and to estimate how well off they were. This effort can be successful only in a limited sense since so little is known of the cost of living or the standard of living of the time. One can make some comparisons and in the present case it is at least possible to speculate concerning the well-being of a family on the basis of the cost of living that was ascribed to orphans in Brno.

Chapter V

THE ENTERPRISE: EXTERNAL RELATIONS

The advent of Seitter in 1772 as manager brought about a favourable change in the internal arrangements of the Brno Fine-Cloth Factory. Twenty years of fumbling and stumbling, a period that might either be considered a necessary learning period or written off as a mere waste came thus to an end. In its external relationships the enterprise experienced a similar change.

The Purchasing of Raw Materials

In 1759 a new *modus operandi* had been worked out whereby the so-called Military Cloth Warehouse in Vienna became for all practical purposes the controller of the Kladruby enterprise, which was to begin to concentrate on the manufacture of cloths made from Spanish wool. The Warehouse undertook to purchase the necessary wool at its own expense and to supply it to the factory, which would then pay by delivering cloths made from the wool. Since the connexion with a textile mill was not part of its normal function, it is not surprising that importers in Vienna and Prague were the intermediaries for the purchase of bales of wool imported into the Habsburg Monarchy through Amsterdam and Hamburg where major wool brokers were located. Besides high freight charges for transport overland for a good part of the way, there were payments to so many middlemen that the cost of the basic raw material was substantially increased. This tended to defeat one important goal of the policy makers in that it required the outflow of money and made autarky a more elusive objective. Ungratefully, Bailoux quickly pointed to this problem, and proposed that the government establish a barter arrangement with Spain by which Habsburg goods and Merino wool would be exchanged through the ports of Trieste and Cadiz. This was angrily and derisively turned down by the head of the Court Commercial Council, Count Chotek, as having been tried without success.[1] The government as well as the enterprise had to accept that the price of Spanish wool was considerably greater than that paid by the clothmakers of Verviers, Monschau and Leyden,

[1] HKA, red no. 891, 17 Dez. 1761, ad 4 vi. 1761.

areas where the trade in Spanish wool had been long established by way of Amsterdam.

Brno should have been a better location than Kladruby because of the presence there of houses with international connexions, such as that of Köffiller. Raw material procurement however continued to be a problem. Seitter's father-in-law, Mathias Schlösser provided assistance in obtaining a large quantity of Merino wool.[1] Freight costs for imported wool were unquestionably an important factor as was emphasized by the entrepreneurial decision that Thys had made in choosing Klagenfurt for the location of his woollen mill; he emphasized that the nearness of Trieste would provide him with substantial savings.[2]

Since the Brno woollen mill was the only major user of Merino wool in Moravia and one of very few in the entire Habsburg Monarchy, it seems only reasonable to expect that sooner or later it would start to purchase the Spanish wool itself without intermediaries and store it in its own warehouses. Thys, in his 1771 report on the condition of the enterprise, intimated that insufficient liquidity had prevented the firm from taking this desirable step. Between 1732 and 1780 over 800 cwt. of Spanish wool had been directly purchased (*verschrieben*), with the bulk of the purchases made in 1773 and 1774,[3] while a total of 2,417 cwt. was supplied to the firm in the same period from various agricultural estates within the Monarchy. After 1774 the price of Spanish wool rose sharply, reportedly by as much as 30 per cent. Large quantities at this high price were apparently purchased. The capital tied up in this asset contributed to another of the many serious crises in the company's history.[4] Fortunately, however, domestic wool of good quality was being produced so that the pressure of illiquidity on the firm was somewhat reduced. Over one-third of the domestic wool came from the estates of Prince Liechtenstein, whose interest in improving the breed of sheep in the Habsburg Monarchy predates the efforts of the government itself.[5] Although writers on the subject do not judge these attempts to have been really successful until after 1800, the presumption seems clearly warranted that the herds of sheep in the

[1] HKA, red no. 893, f. 1086 (43 ex Nov. 1773 Böhm).

[2] HKA, red no. 442, f. 55.

[3] SAB, C/12/45, 'N', 29 April 1780, 'Extract von verschrieben und verarbeiteter Ausländischer vornehmlich Spanischer Wolle.'

[4] SAB, C/12/45, f. 39–60; HKA, red no. 893, f. 637–76.

[5] Ignaz Hübel, 'Die Einführung der Merinozucht in den Sudetenländern', *Zeitschrift des deutschen Vereines für Geschichte Mährens und Schlesiens*, XL (1938), 105–19.

Hereditary Lands and in Hungary supplied the Brno factory with enough wool of satisfactory quality for it to reduce its dependence on foreign supplies.[1] The exact procedure by which the purchase of domestic wool was made is not known. It is possible that the enterprise contracted for the entire clips of particular herds before the shearing took place.

Besides wool — which made up between 50 and 60 per cent or more of the cost of a piece of cloth — dyes and olive oil had to be obtained and were regularly imported.[2] As with other new enterprises in a decree of 1749, the Brno woollen mill was permitted to import raw materials free of the statutory duties and at the minimal payment of one-fourth per cent, presumably of the value, in a so-called consumption tax.[3] The tariff authorities looked with suspicion at the businessmen who held such a privilege. While the government strongly desired that merchants invest their funds in industry, it also feared that the import privileges that might accompany such a step would be abused. It seems that each enterprise had to negotiate its own schedule of products that were to be excluded from the standard import duties. The Brno firm, for example, had to pay the normal duties on its Merino wool, but dyes and olive oil as well as tools and equipment for manufacturing were exempt. Suspicions persisted that some smuggling was going on and in 1773, the Bank Administration, which collected the import duties, wanted to know why Köffiller had a large stock of dyestuffs and olive oil in his warehouse. The house of Michael Köffiller, the name by which the grocery and spice import firm was still known and which was headed by Johann Leopold Köffiller, the largest private investor in the cloth factory, was storing these goods and it was difficult to convince the tariff authority that they were all going to be consumed in the factory.[4] Whether this brief flurry indicates that the importation was done by the mercantile house of Köffiller or whether it merely meant that its warehouse served as a convenient storeroom remains a moot question. In the absence of letter books or other internal documentation the important question of managerial procedure concerning

[1] Cf. Stephan von Keess, *Darstellung des Fabriks-und Gewerbewesens im österreichischen Kaiserstaate*, 3 vols. (Wien, 1819), I, 354–59.

[2] See Appendix C.

[3] Hermann Fechner, *Die handelspolitischen Beziehungen Preussens zu Österreich* (Berlin, 1886), 222.

[4] HKA, red no. 894, f. 964–80 (27 ex Martio 774 Böhm), 14 März 1774; f. 1073–7 (13 ex Dec. 773 Böhm), 6 Dec. 1773; f. 964–80 (27 ex Martio 1774 Böhm), 14 März 1774. The normal ratio of oil to finished cloth was five pounds of oil to 100 pounds of finished cloth.

the purchasing of raw materials can only be guessed at. It would, however, seem reasonable that the factor carried on the routine purchases in addition to his other functions as book-keeper and head of the warehousing section of the factory.[1]

Selling

The factor or book-keeper may also have been in charge of the technical side of sales. In the larger sense of procuring orders for finished cloths, the manager was unquestionably the major figure. Unfortunately, there is no specific information in the records to enlighten us on this question. Since sales were of vital importance for the success of an enterprise, it would be very useful indeed if more detailed evidence for the manner in which sales efforts were carried out in the eighteenth century were available.

For the small master in Europe the typical method for selling his goods was to appear at the periodic markets and fairs. In Yorkshire the cloth weavers had organized cloth halls to offer their wares. There they were purchased by merchants who then carried them to other places for further sale. Even where larger undertakings were involved, such as in Verviers, the large-scale putter-out was primarily concerned with the mercantile function. He presented his goods or samples at the larger international fairs such as in Leipzig or Frankfurt am Main. That he worked on the basis of samples is attested to by the fortunate survival of a set of over 300 swatches of different types of cloths in various colours that the Verviers manufacturer François Biolley sent to officials in Vienna about 1760 when he evinced some interest in the Kladruby factory. They were swatches that had been designated for use at the fair in Frankfurt am Main and Biolley had them forwarded to Vienna to demonstrate his ability as a manufacturer of fine quality goods.[2] The Brno enterprise also used the method of presenting swatches to prospective buyers. Although there is some evidence that it offered its wares at fairs, the documents are silent on whether entire pieces or merely sample swatches were sent. In the early 1750s Bailoux did make a brief foray into the competitive world with several pieces of cloth. He met such total failure that he never made a similar attempt. His

[1] Cf. Kocka, *Unternehmensverwaltung*, 97. Kocka reports that even in the 1860s it was common for book-keepers to be in charge of purchasing and sales. He gives the case of Siemens and Halske.

[2] Haus-Hof-und Staatsarchiv, Poschakten, J. S. Karton 6, f. 489–91: 'Assortment in Frankfurt Ostermesse 1762.'

successors did not find public markets a particularly good method of selling their goods either.

Salesmen travelling to prospective customers were another means to convince merchants to purchase goods from the firm. An interesting case was a trip made by the Reverend Victor Riecke, pastor to Brno's Protestants, most of whom had come to the city to be employed in the woollen mill. Riecke's main purpose in travelling through Hungary in 1787 was to raise money among Hungarian Protestants for his congregation. Since his church in Brno was also an investor in the Brno woollen-cloth firm, he felt it apparently only natural to take orders and to send back intelligence concerning the reputation of the firm among its potential customers. At the same time he had young Seitter along with him so that the son of the manager would become acquainted with the cloth merchants.[1] There is no further evidence of commercial travellers for the Köffiller firm. On the other hand, its main competitor during the 1780s, the Mundy cloth works, had a person by the name of Biegmann travelling for it. A very successful salesman, Biegmann opened his own woollen factory in the 1790s. In addition, Netherland merchant houses are supposed to have sent such persons regularly for orders into the Monarchy.[2] Since these statements are not based on internal evidence they must be accepted with a certain amount of scepticism. That commercial travellers existed in England and France as early as the 1760s is suggested by some authors.[3]

Because of the problems that the Brno firm experienced in sales, it often threatened to engage in retailing. Merchant communities everywhere in the Monarchy strenuously objected to such efforts, not unique to the Brno woollen mill. Here again, the evidence is too sparse to allow even a well-informed guess as to the quantity of cloth sold retail. It is, however, possible that the warehouses which the firm kept in Vienna, Prague and Budapest did sell some goods in this way.

Government Support in Selling

The ideal solution to the problem of sales would of course have been for the merchants in the Habsburg Monarchy engaged in the purchase of fine woollens from foreign suppliers to place their

[1] Trautenberger, *Kirchengemeinde*, 137–8.
[2] d'Elvert, *Cultur-Geschichte*, 77.
[3] William E. A. Axon, ed., *The Annals of Manchester* (London, 1886), 96. Cf. also George V. Taylor, 'Notes on Commercial Travelers in 18th Century France', *Business History Review*, XXXVIII, (1964), 346–53.

orders voluntarily with the Brno firm. This was not the case whether for the reason that the merchants gave — that the Brno cloth was both vastly inferior to and substantially higher in price than the foreign product — or, as the managers in Kladruby and Brno as well as many government officials suggested, because the Habsburg merchants deliberately plotted the ruin of the woollen cloth mill as well as the other import-substituting industries that were being established. Since it was firm government policy during the 1750s and 1760s that the expansion of native industry was necessary for the continued existence and the increased welfare of the Monarchy, the merchants' arguments, however justified, were pushed aside. Government officials knew that a sizeable social cost would have to be incurred in order to realize their plan for greater industrialization and they were therefore willing to use the coercive powers of the state for the purpose. The first quarter-century of the mill's existence, from about 1750 to 1775, was replete with instances of direct sales support in the form of forcing merchants to accept a designated number of pieces of cloth. Even after 1775 the government was indirectly and at times directly involved in the sales effort. The measures undertaken by government agencies in this respect lend support to a thesis of Alexander Gerschenkron that the greater the opposition within society to particular efforts for economic development, the stronger will be the pressure that governments employ to accomplish their goal.[1]

Once embarked on a strong economic development drive, the Mercantilistic state of Maria Theresia willingly accepted its task of aiding the sales of native industry by whatever means possible, starting with the supply of information to merchants who were generally ignorant of the products produced in the Monarchy. From the supply of information it was not a far step to official inquiry into lack of purchases and then to coercion if not outright force. The commercial commissions of the various sections of the Monarchy were employed for that purpose, while abroad, diplomats became part of the sales effort.[2] Moreover, the government, as a large purchaser of goods, was the obvious first target as a market for goods made within the Monarchy.

A royal decree was issued in 1762 according to which all manufacturers, large or small, making cloth suitable for uniforms would

[1] Cf. Alexander Gerschenkron, *Economic Backwardness in Historical Perspective* (New York, 1962), 155.

[2] K. Pribram, *Geschichte*, 78–83.

have assured sales.[1] A number of regiments did buy cloths from the Brno Fine-Cloth Factory only to find them defective in numerous respects, such as being full of holes and not having the colours that had been ordered.[2] There is little doubt that the quality of the cloth for officers' uniforms made at the Brno factory was inferior to the foreign product. Nevertheless, if the industrialization programme was to succeed, officers, members of the imperial court and churchmen would have to be willing to accept this merchandise as part of their patriotic duty; unless they did so, one could hardly expect the common people to do so.[3] Actually the government had little power to force military officers to follow its dictates in these matters. Procurement of much military material was still in the hands of individual regiments.

The creation of a national market or at least a market that permitted an easy flow of goods across the borders of the various provinces in the Hereditary Lands was another very important task for the central government. There were tariffs within the Monarchy and as has been pointed out earlier a consolidated tariff for the group of lands called the Hereditary Lands was not enacted until 1775. The tariffs will be discussed further below. Merchants in different parts of the Monarchy were so used to dealing with foreign suppliers that they were ignorant of the goods being produced within their own country. To be sure, the foreign connexions were comfortable for them and changing their routines would cause new problems. Consequently, there was little reason for them to make unusual efforts to purchase domestic goods. During the period of what we might call high Mercantilism, from 1749 to about 1770, the commercial authorities of the government were charged with the task of publicizing domestic production.[4] They went about their task partly by assembling price lists giving the places where particular goods were produced and possibly also the names of the manufacturers. Such a list for 1767 states for cloth goods (*Tuchmacher Waaren*), for example, that extra fine billiard table cloth might be procured from the imperial and royal privileged cloth factories under contract to the company of the Brno merchant community (*Kais. Königl. privilegirte feine Tuch Fabriken unter Vertrag der Compagnie des Brünner Handelsstand*) at 5 fl. to 6 fl. 30 kr. per ell and that knee-carded

[1] HKA, red no. 1, f. 275–6.
[2] Ibid., f. 494–6, 23 May 1764; also, 30 July 1766, 8 Sept. 1766 and 30 Oct. 1766 for other examples of orders from regiments.
[3] HKA, red no. 890, f. 28 ff., 18 Nov. 1761.
[4] Beer, 'Österreichische Handelspolitik', p. 8.

(*kniestreichen*) cloth could be obtained in a number of towns, giving specific merchants' names.[1]

To make such mercantile information available was a most reasonable activity for a government that wished to stimulate industrialization and to become independent of foreign sources of supply. When the mere presentation of information did not in fact have the desired result, government agencies took other steps to persuade merchants of the wisdom of buying at home. In 1765, for example, sample swatches of cloth from the Brno woollen mill were sent to a number of provincial commercial commissions with the instructions from the Court Commercial Council that they were to urge merchants under their jurisdiction to purchase the cloth and that if they did not comply that there would be a good chance of the imposition of import prohibitions.[2] This was not the first time that commercial councils had been assigned such a task.

From the gentle art of persuasion it was only a short step to crude force. No one seems actually to have been thrown into jail for refusing to buy cloth from the Brno firm, though it came very close to this in one particular case. The overzealous official who was responsible for threatening a cloth merchant with incarceration was censured.[3] Overt threats or the suggestion that import prohibitions might result if the merchants would not purchase domestic goods were the main methods by which government officials tried to persuade merchants to buy at home. Even without specific threats merchants could be intimidated. One can well imagine the position in which the Viennese merchants must have felt themselves to be when they were called before a committee of the Lower Austrian Government Councillors (*Regierungsräte*) in 1760 and questioned about their reasons for not purchasing goods from the Kladruby mill.[4] Two years later they were simply ordered to buy some of the stock of the Military Cloth Warehouse. The merchants of the Hereditary Lands were then forced to acquire altogether 326 pieces of cloth valued at nearly 32,000 fl., merchandise that was admitted to be poor in quality.[5] Ten years later a similar forced sale had to be made, amounting to nearly 80,000 fl. There were precedents for such sales, such as the coercion in 1758 of money changers and merchants in

[1] HKA, red no. 796, 'General-Verzeichniss deren in dem Erbmarkgrafthume Mähren verfertigt werdenden Waaren, Pro Anno 1767'.

[2] HKA, red no. 891, f. 749–51.

[3] Ibid., f. 594.

[4] Ibid., f. 11–28.

[5] Ibid., f. 213–20, 265–70, 332–50, 356–7.

Prague who were obliged to accept inferior money, the forced sale of 2,000 pieces of woollens from the Linz Woollen Fabrics Factory in 1697 to the merchants of Vienna and the sale of cloths to a number of Jewish communities in the 1750s.[1]

There is no other similar case of an entire community being forced to purchase cloths from the woollen mill but coercion remained for many years part of the arsenal of tools with which the government helped the enterprise. The company itself would have liked nothing better than to have been appointed the sole importer of foreign cloths and for Habsburg merchants to be required to buy a stipulated quantity of goods manufactured in the woollen mill itself. In 1775, during a period of modified *laisser-faire* that had brought forth a relatively liberal tariff, the firm went so far as to propose that all cloth merchants in the Hereditary Lands be required by law to purchase between 8 and 12 pieces of cloth from the Brno mill.[2] The Moravian provincial government (*Gubernium*) supported the company in this panic reaction. In the atmosphere of greater economic liberalism then prevailing, this request was turned down, as was a proposed circular that the firm had wanted to send to all of its 'friends'. In this verbal missile it wanted to congratulate its 82 customers that the import of foreign cloth was now fully permitted but cautioned them not to go overboard in ordering cloths from abroad. If the woollen mill in Brno received no orders its personnel could no longer be kept at work. The consequent general cry for help from the one thousand persons who were kept alive through work at the factory including 300 children without parents would reach the highest authorities in the land, and their response might be to cut off the further import of cloth. The firm would therefore wish to suggest that the old friendly relations between the merchants and the enterprise continue.[3] This heartrending letter never went beyond the conceptual stage and found its appropriate resting place in the Viennese state archives.

Tariffs

The fearful activity on the part of the enterprise was induced by the promulgation of the new 1775 tariff that replaced the protectionist system of the previous decade. To call the new system

[1] HKA, red no. 893, f. 493 ff; Alfred Hoffmann, *Wirtschaftsgeschichte des Landes Oberösterreich* (Salzburg, 1952), 110.
[2] HKA, red no. 894, f. 774–86.
[3] Ibid., f. 809–10.

modified liberalism merely underlines the rigid state determinism that preceded it, for the new tariff in fact imposed high duties on the importation of most goods, including fine cloth. The projected letter to the customers of the woollen mill reflected on the one hand a continuing fear that the mercantile community was determined to kill the nascent industry out of sheer spite and on the other hand the fear of competition of any sort that the protective system had spawned.[1]

The system of protection reached its highest point in the 1760s along with the general high-water mark of Mercantilistic government activity. In 1764 coarse woollens could no longer be imported and in 1769 fine-woollen cloth could be brought in from abroad only under licence.[2] An import licence was issued to a merchant when he was able to prove that he had purchased a stipulated portion of his needs from one of the Habsburg factories. The factories often colluded with merchants by signing attestations that more cloths had been purchased from them than was the case. They hoped in this way to get into the good books of the merchants. At the same time, these purchases were offered as evidence that the product of the factory enjoyed greater confidence.[3] The policy of total prohibition had been unworkable because the supply of even poorly made 'fine cloth' was far below the market demand which was in excess of the 1,300,000 fl. of this merchandise that was annually imported.[4]

A system of import prohibitions, replaced in 1775 by a more liberal tariff, was reimposed in a more logical way under Joseph II in 1784. Joseph decreed that within a period of six months foreign goods were to be removed from the shelves of Habsburg merchants and none imported thereafter with few exceptions. Goods not produced in sufficient quantities within the Monarchy could be imported but the government was to see that even these would be soon eliminated. Only for this type of goods would the government henceforth offer financial support.[5] Joseph rounded ironically and ferociously on the errors of the system of strong government intervention that had prevailed in his mother's reign. According to him it served as an open invitation for all sorts of dishonest rascals,

[1] K. Pribram, *Geschichte*, 186.

[2] HKA, red no. 893, f. 843, 22 May, 1769; See also, Beer, 'Zollpolitik', 242, 244.

[3] Cf. HKA, red no. 893, f. 493 ff. (47 ex Majo 771 Böhm); merchants ordered half-width cloths and reported them as if they were full width; also they would order 40 ells of cloth from abroad whereas the normal length was 25–30 ells.

[4] Ibid., f. 845 ff.

[5] Paul von Mitrofanov, *Joseph II*, trans. from Russian into German by V. von Demelic (Wien and Leipzig, 1910), 446 ff.

skilled only in the art of drawing funds out of the coffers of the state, to mislead well-meaning officials like the Counts Joseph Kinsky, Rudolph Chotek and others who had supreme responsibility over these matters.[1] While Joseph may have been correct in referring to the waste that attended these efforts, they did in fact succeed in laying the foundation stones on which Joseph's more discriminating policies of internal *laisser-faire* and external exclusion could be based. The period that he derided proved to be the learning opportunity for Habsburg society. In the case of fine cloths, for example, a considerable capacity had been built up to supply a substantial portion of the internal market and potential entrepreneurs had been drawn into the Monarchy who could exploit the protective policies by establishing their own woollen mills. This will be seen more clearly in the section of this work that deals with the successor firms of the Köffiller woollen mill.

Exports

At the same time as foreign goods were to be excluded from the Habsburg Monarchy, every effort was to be made to sell Habsburg goods abroad. A main target was the Ottoman Empire. J. J. Becher, the great Cameralist at the court of Leopold I, had pushed for strong economic connexions with the Turks. As a result of his activities an Oriental trading company was founded in 1667, which met with only indifferent success by the time it was dissolved in 1683, the year in which Turkish armies besieged the city of Vienna.[2] The greatest chance for opening the Turkish market presented itself in 1719 when the Ottoman Porte was forced to sign a commercial treaty highly favourable to the Austrians along with the Treaty of Passarowitz.[3] These treaties established among other things, a permanent interest in the Balkans that was not erased until the demise of the Austrian Monarchy in 1918. For various reasons, it took many years before Habsburg merchants were able to show any positive results.

For one thing, Greek–Turkish merchants were superior to the Austrians in trading between the two empires and they also dominated the commerce of Hungary, of which the Habsburgs were

[1] K. Pribram, *Geschichte*, 396–400.

[2] Herbert Hassinger, 'Die erste Wiener orientalishe Handelskompagnie 1667–83', *Vierteljahrschrift für Sozial-und Wirtschaftsgeschichte*, XXXV (1942), 1–53.

[3] *Handlungseinverständniss*, 17–23.

rulers.[1] For another thing, Habsburg industry was ill-equipped to dislodge the French from the pre-eminent position they had long enjoyed in the textile trade with Turkey. Woollen cloth imports to Turkey from France, above all those manufactured in the province of Languedoc, increased from 1½ million gulden per year in the first half of the eighteenth century to 5½ million gulden by 1771.[2] It was therefore sheer lunacy, as an Austrian merchant expressed it in 1781, that the general idea was still entertained in Vienna that all inferior merchandise could be sold at great profit in Turkey.[3] By the 1780s the efforts to make the Ottoman Empire a major market for Habsburg products nevertheless began to bear fruit, especially as far as the Brno fine-woollen cloth factory was concerned. As early as the 1750s Austrian diplomats had taken samples of woollen cloth manufactured in the Monarchy and tried to interest businessmen in Constantinople in using the Monarchy as a major source for industrial products.

Even though the ambassador to the Porte and businessmen like the one quoted above pointed to the inferior quality of Habsburg goods, at least one mercantile house in Constantinople was apparently prepared in 1781 to contract for the entire output of the Brno firm.[4] While the woollen mill wisely refrained from entering into such a binding contract, in the 1780s it concentrated on this most profitable trade and allowed its rivals in Brno to service the domestic demand, greatly expanded after the imposition of the new protective tariff in 1784.[5] At one stage the firm asked for diplomatic protection for their main commercial agent, one Giamgioglou, to whose honesty and integrity the Austrian ambassador von Hebert had already attested before the Ottoman authorities in the face of assertions to the contrary by Dutch and French interests.[6] But this was no trouble at all compared to what befell the company as a result of the war between the Habsburg Monarchy and the Ottoman Empire in 1787. Inconclusive as a military operation, the war

[1] Cf. Anton Špiesz, 'Die orthodoxen Handelsleute aus dem Balkan in der Slowakei', *Balkan Studies*, IX (1968), 381; Trojan Stoianovich, 'The Conquering Balkan Orthodox Merchants', *Journal of Economic History*, XX (1960), 214–313.

[2] Marianne von Herzfeld, 'Zur Orientpolitik Österreichs unter Maria Theresia in der Zeit von 1740–1771', *Archiv für österreichische Geschichte*, CVIII (1920), 224–8.

[3] Hans Halm, *Habsburgischer Osthandel im 18. Jahrhundert*, (München, 1954), 15.

[4] HKA, red no. 881, f. 4–7, 29 Marty 1758. In this memorandum complaints of Turkish and Italian merchants appear concerning the poor quality of *Londrins Seconds* cloths manufactured in the Habsburg Monarchy.

[5] HKA, red no. 894, f. 345–52 (20 ex Novembri 1781 Böhm) Wien, 4 Okt. 1781.

[6] Ibid., f. 277–93 (18 ex Januario 1785 Böhm), Wien, 13 Jan. 1785.

proved to be an utter disaster for the Brno enterprise; suddenly its orders dwindled to nothing and it was forced to close its doors. It would be overstating the case to say that the drying-up of the Turkish market was the sole cause of the debacle that overtook the Brno firm. In the past its problems with sales had been frequently a question of a poor quality product. This time the product seemed to be in demand but now the fate of the woollen factory had become entangled in the foreign affairs of the state.

The Sales Record

By 1780, when the first really big shipments were made to Constantinople, the Köffiller woollen enterprise had established a very respectable sales record.[1] The tables below give some figures. The discrepancies between them for 1777–8, 1778–9 and 1779–80 cannot be explained.

Total Sales 1772–1780 in Pieces of Cloth

1772–3	1773–4	1774–5	1775–6	1776–7	1777–8	1778–9	1779–80	Total
555	614	530	768	813	653	1014	1016	5963

Source: SAB, C/12/45, f. 715 'Von eingelaufenen Commissionen und abgesetzten Tüchern nach abgenommen alten Tuchlager.'

Total Sales 1777–1788 in Pieces of Cloth

	Types of Cloth					
	8/4	7/4	Summer	Londrins	Bergopzoom	Total
1777–8	160	326	28	192	277	983
1778–9	157	255	13	262	270	957
1779–80	224	296	12	298	358	1,188
1780–1	131	188	40	686	379	1,424
1783	169	246	44	1,144	646	2,249
1784	201	162	50	1,783	710	2,906
1786	219	236	73	1,669	510	2,707
1787	345	505	95	1,433	435	2,883
1788	309	217	145	1,077	475	2,223

Sources: SAB, C/12/45 and M-2110 (numerous folio pages). These data are derived from monthly reports that the firm was required to submit to the central government because of the large loans that it had received. The records are incomplete. None were found for 1781–2 and those for 1785 are fragmentary. 1786, 1787 and 1788 are calendar years; other years usually ran from 1 June to 31 May.

[1] For further details see Appendix B.

Sales figures can be provided only from 1772 when Seitter became manager and from which time one can safely assert that the firm was on a fairly sound footing. During his first year in Brno, Seitter was able to report the sale of 555 pieces of cloth, nearly half of them going to Vienna and over 100 pieces finding outlets in Brno itself. By 1780 over 1,000 pieces of cloth were being sold per year, the proportion going to Vienna exceeding one half but the percentage remaining in Brno having sunk considerably. Except for two years there was a steady growth of sales during the 1770s. The year 1774–5 provided some problems when the liberalized tariff was enacted, and there was a reduction in sales from 614 pieces in 1773–4 to 530 in the following year. The year 1777–8 also proved to be a bad year for the firm, when two of the partners were forced to leave the firm.

Capital Requirements

At this point the vital question of financing will be taken up. It is an involved question, especially if the Kladruby mill is taken into account as it must since so many of the Brno firm's troubles stemmed from that unhappy inheritance. First, an estimate must be made of the capital required for the operation of a woollen mill. Second, all the available data on the sources of the financial support will be assembled. The financial data are somewhat suspect since the firm was repeatedly requesting funds from the government and therefore probably attempted to draw a picture that would be most beneficial to its case.

For a woollen mill of the size that the Brno Fine-Cloth Factory achieved in the 1770s and the 1780s, a considerable fixed investment as well as a large amount of circulating capital was necessary. The projections that preceded the location of the woollen works in Kladruby in 1749 and its transfer to Brno in 1764 agreed that an initial investment per loom of 5,000 fl. was required. This estimate may have included high starting costs both in the way of the wasted materials and wages attending the learning process of a new factory labour force and the high fixed investment in buildings, dye vats, fulleries, etc., whose contribution to the cost of a piece of cloth would be reduced as the production of goods increased. If an investment per loom-capacity of 5,000 fl. was reasonable in the 1740s and the 1760s, then a change seems to have occurred in the 1770s to go by an estimate composed by the government officials comprising the 'Factory Directorate' concerning the capital that would be needed for a 60-loom factory.[1] In 1770 they suggested a total sum of 214,000 fl. or over 3,500 fl. per loom. This estimate is difficult to use for present purposes because the stated fixed capital requirements had a double-base: they include the equipment already available in the Brno factory apparently at their acquisition cost and then superimposed the cost of new facilities and equipment on top of them. Moreover, the estimate also assumed that raw materials for one year's production would have to be purchased and wage and other costs for this purpose would have to be advanced. It is possible that the larger sum that was suggested in 1749 and 1764 for each loom-capacity also included a longer period of time over which the enterprise would have no cash flowing into it from the sale of goods.

As further evidence for the investment required per loom the inventories for the 1770s can be effectively used.[2] For example, in the 1777 inventory assets were given as 139,632 fl. which would mean that for each of the thirty-five looms then in operation assets of about 4,000 fl. had to be provided. The inventory of the following year reveals aggregate assets of only 135,444 fl. Forty looms may have been operated during that year. If this number is correct, assets per loom were about 3,300 fl. but if only thirty-five looms were being worked, then the average would have been closer to 3,600 fl. Since fixed assets did not vary markedly, the difference in these figures would have to be explained by changes in the stocks of raw materials, work in progress and finished goods located in a number of different warehouses. If it is correct that the investment per loom was lower in 1778, it may have been the result of an improvement in the condition of the firm, probably due to a reduction in the assets tied up in stock. The ratio of assets to workers changed similarly, since the number of workers did not seem to increase very much if at all during this time. For the 700 persons employed by the Köffiller woollen mill during the 1770s, the average assets per worker were about 200 fl. If the assets per worker dropped with increased production, then one of the conclusions to be drawn is that there previously was a considerable amount of slack in the plant. This must certainly have been the case since the woollen mill could easily afford to have workers wait for work; payments were almost always on a piece-work basis. Without question, moreover, the plant

[1] HKA, red no. 893, f. 513–14, Brünn, 18 Dec. 1770.

[2] The following inventories have been used for this purpose: 1 Aug. 1776, HKA, red no. 894, f. 658–61. 28 Hornung, 1777; f. 568–89. 31 Aug. 1777, SAB, C/12/45, f. 98–107, 31 Aug. 1778; f. 461–73. 31 Aug. 1779; f. 360–72.

became more efficient during the 1770s with the result that fewer fixed and semi-fixed assets had to be tied up for production per worker.

Fixed Capital Investment

It is difficult if not audacious, as Lebrun suggested for Verviers, for the retrospective observer to presume that his estimates of fixed, variable or total capital requirements are close to the mark.[1] Nevertheless, the attempt should be made. Some figures for the value of the firm's buildings are given below.

Estimated Value of Buildings in the 1770s

Factory Building (Cröna)	12,732
Factory Building (Schwabengasse)	2,736
Factory Building (Grosse Neugasse)	4,000*
Fullery	720
Winter Frame Building	1,256
Building for Red Dye Mill (Röthemühle)	900
	22,344

Sources: HKA, red no. 894, f. 658–61, Inventarium 1 Aug. 1776; f. 568–89, Inventarium, 28 Feb. 1777; red no. 891, f. 670. Depreciation is not specifically included.
*Cost of the building when purchased in 1763.

The equipment account came to about 14,000 fl. in 1777 when more than thirty-two looms were being operated.[2] Consequently, the capital that had to be sunk into machinery and equipment came to nearly 440 fl. for each of the thirty-two looms which were completely usable, a figure that is comparable with the 480 fl. that was estimated for the Waldstein woollen mill in the 1760s and the lower figure of 370 fl. for the Offermann factory, one of the successor firms to the original woollen mill, in 1793.[3] It is revealing that an independent inventory of the Offermann factory, ordered by the city magistrate, valued the equipment and machinery at the equivalent of only about 286 fl. The magistrate's estimators deducted for depreciation while the management seems to have placed 'when-new' values on the equipment. Very likely this method was also used in the inventories of the Köffiller and Waldstein factories.

[1] Cf. Lebrun, *Verviers*, 381.
[2] HKA, red no. 894, f. 568–89. There were 32 usable and 20 partly usable looms.
[3] Archiv zemskehó hlavniho města Brna, Pozůstalosti, no. 533. The management of the factory placed the total investment in equipment and machinery at about 9,600 fl. An independent evaluation ordered by the city magistrate was only 7,700 fl.

In these three factories there prevailed with little doubt different levels of efficiency. It is probably a good rule of thumb that the lower the ratio of capital per loom the more efficient the management was likely to have been. Since the estimate for the Waldstein works was for a ten-loom plant and that for the Köffiller factory for a thirty-two-loom operation, considerable economies of scale must have been realized. The Offermann firm was a quite profitable enterprise in 1793 when its owner died. Neither the Waldstein nor the Köffiller woollen mill could boast a similar accomplishment, thus providing at least a *prima facie* case that they were not so well run as the Offermann enterprise.

Circulating Capital

It is also quite difficult to assign values to the amount of variable or circulating capital that was required. For Verviers, Lebrun estimated that a twenty-loom factory producing 1,000 pieces of woollen cloth of 24 ells length each, would necessitate in the mid-1770s about 82,000 florins (Liège currency) or about 41,000 fl. in Habsburg currency per year for wages and salaries and the maintenance of buildings.[1] Presumably, this sum would not include any charge for imputed interest on funds tied up in fixed and circulating capital. Comparing this estimate with the costs assigned in 1765 to the making of a piece of cloth in the Brno woollen mill, one finds that the costs assigned in Brno were considerably lower.[2] Wages and salaries as well as overhead expenses came to about 28 fl. If, however, the expenditure for dyes, oil, glue and soap were added, then the resultant figure would be close to 40 fl., which conforms well with the average of 41 fl. that would have been the case with the factory of Verviers producing 1,000 pieces of woollens per year. It would also accord with the 'Factory Directorate's' projection in 1770, assigning 36 fl. per piece to costs other than wool.[3] Very likely however, both the cost sheet of 1765 as well as the projection of 1770 understate the costs by a considerable amount.

In a report to the central government, the firm stated in 1773 that it paid out 700 fl. per week to its 721 employees.[4] According to a tabulation made in 1780 of all the cloths that were sold during the fiscal year 1773–4, 555 pieces left the factory. If one accepts the

[1] Lebrun, *Verviers*, 381.
[2] HKA, red no. 891, ad 35/1765.
[3] HKA, red no. 893, f. 513–14.
[4] HKA, red no. 894, f. 1086–96.

figure of 700 fl., then a sum of 36,400 fl. was paid out to the employees in the plant during that year. Dividing that sum by the 555 pieces reported to have been sold gives average salary and wage costs for each piece of 66 fl., nearly twice the sum that has been derived from the other internal evidence cited above. Even if the 66 fl. figure was completely accurate, it was probably on the high side compared with the years that followed, since 1773 was the first full year for the new manager and old inefficiencies could have been expected to persist, while the report was made in order to impress government officials with the size of the firm.

The evidence suggests that the cost of labour in the Brno plant was about 1 fl. per worker per week or the equivalent of 20 sous (*Stüver*) in Liège currency.[1] When compared with the average wage of 15 sous for contemporary Verviers, it is apparent that wage costs in Brno were possibly 33 per cent higher. This fact could be easily explained by the substantially higher level of efficiency in the Belgian woollen centre, a fact that can be clearly seen from the estimated fifty pieces that were produced by each loom per year as opposed to about thirty-four pieces which the 'Factory Directorate' projected for Brno in 1770. Moreover, in the theoretical projection that Lebrun made for a Verviers factory producing 1,000 pieces of cloth, only 300 workers had to be employed whereas the Brno plant reported more than double that number. In assessing the capital requirements for a plant in Brno one must be aware of the inefficiencies attendant to new industries in general and certainly of the Brno factory in particular.

Sources of Capital Fuuds

A woollen mill employing about thirty-five looms had to be able to call upon assets of between 130,000 and 160,000 fl. This was partly necessary in order to finance the sale of cloths, the average period of time for which credit had to be given being about one year.

The Verviers cloth sellers at times had to offer as much as eighteen months credit to their foreign buyers and therefore Habsburg merchants were used to generous credit terms. Manufacturers in the Belgian city also received good credit terms from their Dutch suppliers of wool, so that they did not need to tie up very large sums in purchase of Merino wool. The Brno firm, too, was able to buy much of its wool on credit, although the length of time that was allowed for payment is not known. In the inventories of the early 1770s the

[1] Lebrun, *Verviers*, 381.

Amsterdam firm of Bongard & Kullmann was owed as much as 11,000 fl. for Spanish wool. Similarly a number of estates owned by noblemen such as Prince Liechtenstein carried the Brno woollen mill for large quantities of wool. In one inventory the Tišnov monastery appears both as a lender of funds and as a creditor for wool purchases. The data are not sufficient to assess accurately whether the Brno firm like the woollen manufacturers in Verviers was able to effect a trade-off between the sums that it owed for wool and the debts that its customers in turn owed it.[1] Bits of evidence suggest that the Köffiller company was frequently faced with imbalances forcing it to pay its creditors while being unable to extract payment from its debtors.

Besides being in a poor position between its suppliers and its customers, the Köffiller firm also had other difficulties in obtaining funds. The contribution of banking to the fate of the woollen mill has already been discussed. The Moravian Loan Bank served well as a channel for innovation in bringing the fine-cloth factory to Brno, but after the dismissal of Kehrnhofer and the eventual acquisition of the plant by Köffiller and his associates the Bank had no further connexion with it. Even while Kehrnhofer was still in control, his appeal for funds went to the central government. Moreover, as pointed out earlier, the Moravian Loan Bank did not accept deposits and therefore cannot be considered a bank in the normal commercial sense.

Since there were no other banks in Moravia and since there is no evidence whatever that the Brno firm received funds from any other banking source, it is clear that banking had little effect on this case of industrialization. On the other hand, it was not financed by a profit inflation, that is, a substantial gain over many years from high sales prices while wages remained relatively low. Lebrun contends that this was the case in Verviers and is therefore able to support E. J. Hamilton's thesis on this subject.[2] Undistributed profits rather than loans from capitalists provided the source for Verviers's industrialization. In Brno — as in the Habsburg Monarchy generally — persons who possessed excess funds were loath to invest them in industry and instead preferred government bonds and real estate. Thus private individuals who were interested in industry had to carry the burden of industrialization. Frequently such persons were aristocrats and others like Köffiller who considered it their patriotic duty or who wanted to be in the forefront of progress.

[1] Cf. Ibid., 380 f.
[2] Ibid., 376 f.

At other times, they were merchants and government officials who were coerced into subscribing to new industrial enterprises. This seems to have been the case with Köffiller's five partners, all cloth merchants in Brno. The most important source of capital in the Habsburg Monarchy and certainly in the case of the Brno Fine-Cloth Factory was the central government.

Equity Financing by Private Persons

Following the discussion of the insignificant financial contribution made by the Moravian Loan Bank, the next concern is the participation of private persons who made funds available to the Brno enterprise. Above all, the paid-in cash equity investment in the firm should be considered. For all practical purposes, the factory was wholly owned by the government prior to 1768 when Leopold von Köffiller and his five compatriots merged their two separate companies. In the 1771 balance sheet, the company's six members were reported to have paid in a total of 20,000 fl. in cash.[1] In a summary compiled in 1780 the firm reported that the six shareholders together had an equity of 20,941 fl., of which 2,475 fl. represented the salary of one of them as manager for 2½ years. He as well as two of his fellow shareholders included in their portion of the equity unspecified interest payments that they had allowed to accumulate. As a result, one must be sceptical about the size of the cash payments that the partners made into the equity fund.

The capital investment of the partners represented only a small portion of the total investment in the firm. Outstanding among those who lent money to the concern was Leopold von Köffiller, who was also one of the principal shareholders and the only one of the company to remain an owner until the end. In 1768, when the company was formed, he had lent 20,500 fl. in addition to his contribution to the equity fund. Three years later he provided another loan of 22,000 fl. Including the interest that he had left in the firm, he was a creditor in 1780 to the extent of 48,752 fl.

Little evidence can be located concerning the contributions that other partners made to the capital fund or whether they made loans to the firm. The Viennese merchant Garttner's association as a partner with the Brno enterprise seems to have been short. He apparently severed this relationship in 1773, although he remained a purchaser of the firm's products. His partnership seems not to have included the payment of any money into the capital fund or

[1] HKA, red no. 893, f. 547–9.

the making of any loans. Seitter was a partner in name only, as far as any direct monetary contribution was concerned. The sole owner of the factory in 1780 when he negotiated a new contract with the central government, Köffiller was fortunate enough to have another man join him in that year. Unfortunately we know almost nothing concerning Alois Edler von Schweikhard's participation in the firm, except that he was one of the unhappy survivors who had to experience the painful bankruptcy proceedings in 1789.[1] By that time there was a third shareholder in the firm, since Madame Emanuele Haunold von Marvancy had become a partner in 1784.[2] She was apparently no longer alive in 1789; the heirs of the lady were included in the category of creditors of the second degree for the amount of 11,711 fl.[3] Whether this represented the original share of Mme Marvany, or included interest payments, or was a loan cannot be ascertained.

Loans by Private Persons

Altogether the firm borrowed 189,560 fl., including 65,000 fl. from the government, between the years 1768 and 1780. During this twelve-year period it paid 36,215 fl. in interest charges.

Debts Incurred 1768–1780

Date Incurred			*Date Repaid*
1768	Baron v. Jungwirth (Vienna)	fl. 20,000 @ 5%	1771
1768	Herr v. Weinbrenner (Vienna)	14,000 @ 6%	1771
1769	'K.K. Schulden Cassa'	25,000 @ 5%	—
1769	Graf Wilh. v. Waffenberg (Olomouc)	5,000 @ 4%	1775/77
1769	Graf Ignaz Chorinsky (Wessely)	4,000 @ 5%	1771
1769	Carl Edler v. Köffiller (Brno)	16,000 @ 5 & 6%	1773 (3,000)*
1769	Carl Sauter	4,800 @ 5%	1773/4
1769	Olympius Rosenkranz (Brno)	5,000 @ 5%	1771/7
1769	Franc. Maria Rosenkrantz (Widow) (Znojmo)	3,000 @ 5%	1776
1774	Paul Kobeck (Vienna)	10,000 @ 5%	1776/7
1775	Adam Isaac Arensteiner (Vienna)	42,760 @ 8%	1777/8
1775	Orphanage Fund (Brno)	40,000 @ 4%	—
		fl. 189,560	

Source: SAB, C/12/45, f. 712–814 'C'. *13,000 fl. left to be paid in 1780.

[1] Schweikard was made a knight (*Ritter*) in 1781 and in 1790 became a *Reichs-Freiherr*, indicating that he was not harmed very much by the Brno debacle. Adalbert Ritter Karl von Dobra Voda, *Der Adel von Böhmen, Mähren und Schlesien* (Prag, 1904), 327.

[2] Meister, 'Köffiller', 68.

[3] SAB, M2110, f. 577.

This table does not reflect the borrowing activity of the firm completely accurately. For example, a 1771 balance-sheet reveals that one of the lenders, Carl Sauter, had actually made 5,500 fl. available, of which 600 fl. had been repaid by 1770.[1] A somewhat similar error may have slipped in the account of Adam Isaac Arensteiner who in an inventory statement dated 21 August 1779 was still recorded as a creditor for 1,000 fl.[2] Despite such errors the table is still useful as an indication of the date when loans were made, the interest rates charged and the types of lenders. Among the lenders omitted from the table for reasons unknown was the Tišnov (Tischnowitz) monastery which had lent 9,000 fl. at 5 per cent, a debt that fell due in March 1771 but for which there is no date of origin recorded.[3] As will be noted from the table, among the lenders there were several noblemen such as Waffenberg and Chorinsky, neither of whom was known as having been especially interested in supporting industrial undertakings. Most of the bourgeois lenders, with the possible exception of Arensteiner, did not have any particular reputation for favouring industrial development. Arensteiner was a rich Jewish businessman, one of very few Jews allowed to live in Vienna, and a wholesaler and financier at the Imperial Court. In the 1780s one Nathan Adam Arensteiner, very likely a son or a nephew, was cited in a government document as a person who had strongly supported domestic industry.[4]

As a rule, Jews did not wholly support the industrialization efforts of the government at this time. In this respect they followed the precept of their Christian compatriots. One of the lenders, von Weinbrenner, was a conspicuous exception to this rule. A prominent skin merchant (*Rauhwarenhändler*) in Vienna, he is best known for the sharp critique to which he subjected the merchants of the Monarchy in a book first published in 1781.[5] A wealthy man, he claimed to have made a profit of 31,000 fl. from his business in 1764 and in 1786 held a 70,000 fl. investment in a woollen factory in Uničov.[6] He condemned the Habsburg merchants for being ignorant and unenterprising. As can be seen from the table, his interest in the Brno woollen mill did not last long and his pressure on the firm to repay the loan was one of the major reasons for the

[1] HKA, red no. 893, f. 548–9, 31 Aug. 1770.
[2] SAB, C/12/45, f. 360–72, 31 Aug. 1779.
[3] HKA, red no. 893, f. 548–9.
[4] A. F. Pribram, *Urkunden*, 1, 338, 364, 404, 597, 608.
[5] Joseph von Weinbrenner, *Patriotische Gedanken.*
[6] Archiv der Stadt Wien, Merkantil Gericht, B7–1 Fasc. 3, no. 7 and no. 41.

crisis into which the Brno enterprise was plunged in 1771. He also invested in the successor firms.

We have some information on persons who lent money to the firm in the 1780s; since they were the unfortunate ones who had claims at the time of the bankruptcy. When Köffiller negotiated a new contract with the government in 1780, he boasted of having no creditor other than the government since 1778.[1] He must have considered the 13,000 fl. debt owed to his brother as not being worthy of mention since it was within the family and it was placed in the annual inventory statement of 1779 under the category of 'Capital Account'. In the same category there also appeared, however, the 1,000 fl. that the Köffiller firm still owed Arensteiner and the Jewish businessman was not a partner in the company. Köffiller hoped at the time that the government would reward him for his patriotic efforts in keeping people at work and would finally destroy the opposition of Habsburg merchants to domestically produced goods not only by lending him a further 20,000 fl., which it did, but also by presenting him with gifts. He wanted a 10,000 fl. building and a further 10,000 fl. for twenty-five new looms. Since the government was not quite that accommodating, he obviously had to find the funds elsewhere. The two new partners Edler von Schweikard and Frau Harnold von Marvancy apparently were not able to bring sufficient funds into the firm and it was therefore forced to borrow money from others.

Most of the information comes from the bankruptcy proceedings after 1789 and they do not always show when a debt was incurred. Toward the end of the firm's existence an industrialist of great note, Freiherr von Badenthal, managing director of the large Schwechat cotton mill, lent 156,000 fl., probably from the funds of the cotton firm. He was fortunate or as a good businessman a very fine risk averter. Countess Maria Brigitta Canal underwrote 100,000 fl. of this sum in March 1789 and the Köffiller firm signed over to Badenthal 36,000 fl. that was owing it from two good debtors. In the end, Badenthal, acting for his cotton firm, was a creditor for only 20,000 fl. Several other aristocrats were among the lenders to the Brno firm. Among them there was a Baroness Spindler, who held a first mortgage for 15,000 fl. and several persons whose loans were not secured, including Count Auersperg, 15,000 fl., Count Karl Rudolf von Braun, 5,000 fl., Countess von Kanaren, 16,000 fl.,

[1] SAB, C/12/45, f. 00712 ff. 'Pro Memoria', 5 May 1780.

Freiherr von Ottenfels, 26,200 fl. and one von Vriorsky who had lent 5,000 fl.[1]

What this incomplete listing of creditors suggests is that direct investment in shares of the company for profit or loss was at all times minimal. Most of the capital was raised by loans from the government, Köffiller himself and several other wealthy persons. It is somewhat strange that the Moravian Loan Bank was completely uninvolved, even though it continued to prosper.[2] Even if it resigned its innovating function with the dismissal of Kehrnhofer in 1764, it did not have to cease to make loans to industrial undertakings. How the lenders and the borrower were brought together is not completely clear. It probably happened through intermediaries, often the Jews who were attached to many aristocrats and who acted as financiers and purveyors at Court.

The Government as Investor

One of the largest investors was of course the government, on whose initiative the whole venture was undertaken in the first place. It is clear that the government hoped to serve as a catalyst but had no desire at any time to become the owner of the enterprise. At the same time, it was deeply interested in having the woollen mill succeed and therefore used its own financial resources whenever necessary.

For the twelve or so years in Kladruby the estate itself provided loans but no equity investment. Between 1755 and 1756 Bailoux received 9,225 fl. in loans, partly directly from the manorial administration and mainly (7,211 fl.) from its orphanage and church funds.[3] These loans were essentially temporary advances against manufactured goods and were to be repaid as soon as possible. No interest charges appear to have been made. This type of financing seems to have continued on an increasingly acrimonious note. In 1757 Bailoux received 4,844 fl. but paid back only 4,604 fl. Baron Toussaint, the head of the imperial estates, ordered in 1758 that Pardubice was to make no further advances to Bailoux without express permission from Vienna. Presumably Toussaint and his subordinates in Vienna were becoming tired of doing Bailoux's chores such as collecting debts that merchants owed for the purchase

[1] SAB, M 2110 f. 236, Brünn, 4 Oct. 1791; f. 817–26, 31 Mar. 1789 'Protocoll'.
[2] Chylík, 'První obchodní banka', 274 ff.
[3] SUA, Pardubitzer Akten, V–II–18, f. 48–52, 13 Okt. 1756.

of cloths.[1] To be sure, these were times of war; the Prussian enemy was often near Kladruby and at times overran the village, once destroying some of the equipment at the plant. These extenuating circumstances make it more understandable that the manorial administration was advancing funds for the weekly wage bill.[2] Moreover, by this time there was fairly conclusive evidence that Bailoux was incompetent as a businessman. Consequently the governmental authorities in Vienna found themselves in a dilemma; they were unwilling to dissolve the enterprise but knew no way of bringing it to its feet.

When this question was finally settled in favour of transferring the whole operation to Brno, it turned out that Bailoux and/or the enterprise were so heavily in debt to the Pardubice estate that the chief steward (*Oberamtmann*) incarcerated Bailoux, impounded the stock of materials and goods and would not even allow Bailoux's wife to leave. Altogether at least 48,000 fl. seems to have been owed. After 5,000 fl. had been paid the chief steward was willing to release Bailoux's wife. It took all the persuasion that could be mustered by the government official who came to Kladruby in January 1764 to fetch Bailoux and his family and the belongings of the woollen mill in addition to the direct orders from government officials in Vienna, before the chief steward relented.[3] No further word is to be found on the remaining 43,000 fl. debt.

The original building in Brno was purchased by the government for 4,000 fl.[4] Repairs and extensions to it in subsequent years brought the total cost to about 16,000 fl. In 1780 Köfiller was permitted to purchase the building for 3,000 fl.[5] In the meantime the woollen mill was to have paid a rental to the government amounting at first to 100 fl. per year, which was certainly far below the alternative income that 4,000 fl. would have brought in on the financial market place. In 1793 during the bankruptcy proceedings against the firm, this building was estimated to be worth 24,330 fl., a sum that obviously included improvements and probably took into

[1] Ibid., f. 69, 5 July 1758.

[2] Ibid., f. 70–2, 15 Dec. 1758; f. 56, 4 Jan. 1758; f. 67, 14 Jan. 1758; f. 65, 14 Juni 1758.

[3] HKA, red no. 891, f. 646–64, 30 Jan. 1764.

[4] HKA, red no. 891, 12 Mar. 1762.

[5] Ibid., f. 396–405, 6 Dec 1763; f. 680, 20 Mar. 1765; red no. 893, f. 669 f. 12 Nov. 1767; f. 1142–51, 11 Oct. 1773; red no, 894, f. 414–15 (9 ex Oct. 780 Böhm.).

account a mild inflation that had occurred in the Habsburg Monarchy in the intervening years.[1]

During the 1760s the government purchased several other buildings including the so-called *Teichtmühle* for 4,500 fl. This property was to serve as a dyehouse and fullery.[2] The government also turned over to the woollen mill the so-called Fischer house in the Schwabengasse suburb, which it had bought originally for a plush and velvet factory. With various repairs and improvements, this building cost the government about 5,000 fl. Thus altogether over 25,000 fl. of public money was being devoted to the buildings of the Brno Fine-Cloth Factory in the 1760s.

The government also supplied the firm with a number of fairly large loans. The concern was forced to accept notes payable to the government amounting to over 26,000 fl. for equipment of questionable value and materials (together 7,000 fl.) and a large stock of poorly fabricated cloths that had to be offered for sale at much less than manufacturing costs (19,000 fl.).[3] This inheritance from the Kladruby mill came as a painful surprise to the new owner, who had expected instead to receive a government loan of at least 20,000 fl.[4] This sizeable encumbrance and the bad reputation of its predecessor which continued to dog the new enterprise were major reasons for its extremely troubled existence during the first decade in Brno. In 1769 the government finally took steps to reduce the pain somewhat by making available to the firm a 25,000 fl. loan at four per cent. They were reluctant to do so because they were in the process of presenting the firm with an outright gift of 8,000 fl. In accordance with the 1768 contracts the Brno woollen mill was to receive a gratuity of 400 fl. for each of twenty looms placed into operation by the company formed by the fine-cloth merchants of Brno.[5]

Equipped with more money, its sales supported by the direct efforts of various government agencies and protected from foreign competition by an outright import prohibition, the firm still floundered around uncertainly. New management eventually in 1772 brought a semblance of stability to the woollen mill, but it was thrown in a frenzy in 1775 when a more liberal tariff law was enacted. It was then able to extract a 40,000 fl. loan at four per cent,

[1] SAB, 'Protocoll welches auf Anordnung der k.k. M. S. Landrechte vom 9. Febr., 1793 . . . .'
[2] For locations of the buildings, see Appendix A.
[3] HKA, red no. 891, Wien, 14 May 1767, Hofbuchhalterey.
[4] HKA, red no. 816, f. 454 ff.
[5] HKA, red no. 893, f. 845 ff.

money that had lain idle in the Moravian Orphans' Fund. Government officials agreed that private money was extremely difficult for industrial undertakings to raise.[1] Factories were admittedly poor risks and the officials contended furthermore that money flowed in too large quantities to government treasuries and to charitable institutions as opposed to private investments.[2] By this time the factory still owed the government about 9,000 fl. of the original loan for equipment, materials and stock of cloth from Kladruby. It had also received an outright gift of 8,000 fl. and loans amounting to 65,000 fl. Now it was attempting to have 25,000 fl. of the loan converted into a gift, claiming that the government had gone contrary to agreement by opening the import of fine cloths to foreigners without impediment, albeit at a high tariff.

By 1780 the contract between the central government and the Brno firm had run its required course of twelve years and a new *modus operandi* was to be established. Primarily because of the liberalized tariff of 1775, which went contrary to the contract of 1768, the government finally agreed to cancel the 25,000 fl. debt on the loan contracted in 1769. The cancellation would take effect from 1792 on condition that the firm had kept sixty looms in operation throughout that time. A loan of 20,000 fl. at four per cent from the Moravian Orphans' Fund was made to the firm so that it could expand its productive facilities from the forty-five loom capacity in operation in 1780 to sixty looms, which all concerned considered the desirable goal. Government buildings and equipment were also sold to the enterprise at a fraction of their cost. In return, the government emphasized that it would not offer any further special treatment to the Brno firm, which was to be almost completely on its own.[3]

For a number of years the hopes raised in the negotiations for the agreement of 1780 seemed to be warranted. The absence of much material on this period in the archives testifies to the euphoria in which the firm was operating until the sky suddenly fell in 1788 with the dismal concomittants of the Turkish war. Köffiller then as before rushed with pleas of desperation to the government only to be met by the austere presence of the Enlightened Monarch, Joseph II, who ordered that things were to be allowed to run their course and bankruptcy proceedings should not be interfered with. The firm

[1] HKA, red no. 894, f. 930–40.
[2] Ibid., f. 720–2; 756–9.
[3] SAB, C/12/45, f. 712–814.

had received enough support over the years from the government and there were by then a number of other fine-cloth factories in Brno, as will be discussed below, so that the loss of one would do no irreparable harm. In part it was this rather rigid attitude that plunged the firm into the bankruptcy from which it did not emerge intact. Once private creditors made their claims, government officials discovered that debts owed to the state were no longer covered by assets and that bankruptcy proceedings should therefore be pressed.[1]

Summary

In its external relations the Köffiller woollen mill and its predecessor were heavily dependant on government support. The enterprise at Kladruby began its existence about 1750 with the hope that it would be able to use domestic wool from the imperial estates in Bohemia, but this hope proved vain. Subsequently in 1759 an agency of the central government took on the task of procuring Spanish wool at its own expense and even of supplying funds for wage payments. When the woollen mill was transferred to Brno it severed this arrangement, which had included sales of its products as well as procurement of raw materials. During its first years in Brno it continued to encounter difficulties both in the supply of raw materials and the sale of finished goods and frequently called on the government for support. The protective arm of the central government was especially obvious in sales where on at least two separate occasions Habsburg merchants were forced to purchase defective goods made by the woollen mill. It was also apparent in tariff policy, which went from outright prohibition in the 1760s to modified protection in 1775 and back to almost complete exclusion of imported fine woollens in 1784. In the financing of the enterprise the government too played a prominent role. As owner of several of its buildings and of some of its equipment, the central government also favoured the factory with loans totalling 85,000 fl. Besides the Habsburg government there were some private persons who invested in the firm. Most prominent in this respect was Köffiller who with his brother lent over 50,000 fl. at one point. At the time of bankruptcy the investment from private persons exceeded 200,000 fl.

As was the case in other protofactories, the capital requirements for fixed assets and for variable assets were quite high compared

[1] HKA, red no. 894, f. 247–57, 185–233.

to traditional, small workshops. In extended manufacturing as it prevailed under the aegis of guilds and/or putters-out, a large concentration of resources in manufacturing was not required. At the same time, primitive factories such as that at Brno needed large sums of money at a time and place when the institutional means for such a purpose were still largely lacking. Nevertheless in this particular case considerable resources were made available both from government and private sources.

Chapter VI

BANKRUPTCY AFTER FORTY YEARS OF CRISES

Before Brno's rise as an industrial centre is discussed, a brief recapitulation is in place by way of a discussion of the numerous crises that befell the Fine-Cloth Factory, including its final demise. By then the goal announced in 1749 when skilled craftsmen from Verviers were brought to the Habsburg Monarchy had been fulfilled; in 1789 a viable fine woollen industry did in fact exist so that the Monarchy was no longer dependant on foreign suppliers. This eventual success was preceded by numerous problems and there were many critical points in time when rational determination of the facts might easily have dictated abandonment of the enterprise. Were the decisions to continue at these critical junctures correct in the light of the goal that was to be achieved? Was the goal itself worthy of considerable sacrifice of Habsburg resources or should the decision-makers have diverted the resources here employed to other branches of industry? These questions of course assume that the goal of autarky, which lay at the base of Habsburg economic policy, was itself worthy of great effort. Might not free trade with all countries and *laisser-faire* within the political unit have had more beneficial results for the welfare of the Habsburg population? Such questions go into the philosophy of political systems and are therefore largely outside our purview. Nevertheless, they deserve attention as being part of the social parameter within which policy-makers operated and which impinged seriously on the decisions they took.

The large imports of fine woollens made this industry an excellent candidate in a development scheme that looked first to stemming the outflow of bullion. It also had the further virtue of being labour-intensive. The Mercantilist–Cameralist writers of central Europe had for a century agreed that a state would prosper best when money could be kept within it and when the population could be made wealthy enough to be efficiently squeezed by the tax-collector and still retain an incentive for further work. Becher in the 1660s and 1670s may have placed less importance on governmental direction and control than did Schröder, who was active in Vienna until he died in 1686, and there may also have been minor differences in approach between Justi who left Vienna in 1755 and Sonnenfels who shortly thereafter began his brilliant career combining professional duties at the University of Vienna and leading positions as consultant and member of governmental agencies (somewhat reminiscent of certain present-day professors). But they all agreed on a number of basic principles.

In most major countries including England and France Mercantilistic writers also favoured the woollen industry (which employed the largest number of workers outside agriculture) as an industry to be aided in its development. To recruit workers from Verviers, an outstanding centre for fine woollens, in 1748 was therefore a very rational decision, given the known facts. We know from the recital in the previous chapters that sophisticated foresight, based on the present excellent perspective of hindsight, should have made Count Philipp Kinsky and Emperor Franz I Stephan cautious. If they assumed that the small increments in technical knowledge necessary for Netherland-type woollens combined with the known unemployment of native clothmakers would make the transmission of the innovation simple, they were in error. Even the complaints of near starvation of the Jihlava guild masters did not provide a sufficient incentive. But the art of social transfer of technology was even less well known and certainly less well appreciated than it is today.

First Crisis: Jihlava

Assuming that the original decision was sound, were subsequent ones equally valid? The crisis points on which failure or hope for eventual success hinged can be easily identified. They have been alluded to before but at this point they should be individually evaluated. First came the point at which the whole enterprise could have been most easily aborted. This was in 1749 after the craftsmen under the direction of Bailoux had been brought from Verviers and deposited in the woollen-cloth centre of Jihlava to teach the four to five hundred master-weavers there by example how a piece of fine woollen cloth was to be manufactured. Even without the unpleasant personality of their leader, the French-speaking craftsmen faced a doubtful welcome from the proud German masters in Jihlava, who had a long history of obstinacy. Persistent high unemployment for decades served only to heighten their opposition to the introduction of new methods. Despite the promise of secure sales for Verviers-type cloth of satisfactory quality, the masters of Jihlava saw their guests from Belgium only as competitors and parasites who threatened their existence.

Faced with the determined opposition of the guildsmen in Jihlava, the policy-makers could have allowed the Verviers artisans to return home. Instead, they decided to collect them in one group and to constitute them as a factory in a small village on the imperial manor of Pardubice. This move necessitated the expenditure of about 20,000 fl., not an inconsequential sum but small in comparison to the annual outflow of over a million gulden for fine woollens. Can the policy-makers be faulted for taking the workers out of the uncongenial atmosphere of a central European town into the rural environment of a Bohemian manor? They seem to have taken the right precautions, having dispatched two supposed experts to canvass the imperial manors and to select the one best suited. Since the Emperor had direct and absolute control over these properties, the minimum of problems could be expected there. There were other manors with industrial enterprises, possibly the most famous and also the most pertinent in this case being Horní Litvinov, the property of Count Waldstein. On the whole, therefore, the decision to move the manufacturing organization to Kladruby on the Pardubice estate seems reasonable. At the time Franz Stephan and others may not have foreseen the clashes between the factory manager and the officials of the manor, nor have taken into account the latters' propensity to sabotage the undertaking. These proved to be problems that were massive enough to lead to another time of decision.

Second Crisis: To Abandon Kladruby

The second crisis point was reached in 1761. After more than a decade the fine-woollen mill in Kladruby had succeeded only in swallowing large sums of money, amassing great quantities of goods so poor in quality that they proved to be difficult to sell even under duress, creating irritations from the lowest manorial official in Pardubice to the highest ministers and councillors in Vienna whose combined bitterness washed like angry waves at the feet of the Empress. Maria Theresia herself was kind and forgiving, displaying tolerance for the 'useful artist', as she called Bailoux. Originally Bailoux had been expected to transform himself eventually from manager to enterpriser. Instead the woollen factory remained an appurtenance of Emperor Franz and his Pardubice estate.

It would be too much to try to define actual ownership but there is no doubt that neither the manor nor the Emperor personally nor the government desired proprietorship. That the government become outright owner was one of the alternatives that Bailoux suggested; the other was that the government lend him large sums to continue operations.[1] Both suggestions were brushed aside by Count Rudolph Chotek, president of the Court Commercial Council, the first as being contrary to policy for the government to own factories and the second as having been tried with a total lack of success. As a 'last and desperate effort' to save the Kladruby factory the so-called Military Cloth Warehouse in Vienna was made to act the part of a financing and sales agent (*Verleger*) in 1759.[2]

At this point there was a possibility that a foreign manufacturer would take over. Through a Prague banker, Johann Baptist Del Curto who took care of the financial affairs of the imperial estates, one of the foremost manufacturers of Verviers became interested in the possibility of manufacturing woollens in the Kladruby factory. Had this been consummated, it would have been an early example of a multinational industrial arrangement and would have been similar to the action of the brothers Schoeller in 1817 when they left their native city of Düren in Westphalia and settled in Brno. The reasons might even have been the same; the Schoellers saw themselves excluded from their normal markets in northern Italy, which lay within the Austrian protective tariff wall.[3] Settling in Brno extended to them the benefits of protection. François Biolley, the Verviers manufacturer, probably also saw the spectre of exclusion from a lucrative market as a result of the prohibitive measures that were being contemplated. Although Biolley and one of his sons came to Kladruby to survey the situation, the plan was abandoned, possibly because Biolley was old and his son was sickly.

While the crisis of the Kladruby wollen mill was in full swing, the Habsburg government was negotiating with Jean Thys whose family had a profitable establishment in Eupen to settle in the Hereditary Lands. Thys eventually decided on Klagenfurt but it remains a mystery why the Kladruby factory was not at least suggested to him. This would seem to have been the most logical solution for its problem. Most likely, the governmental authorities in

[1] HKA, red no. 891, 17 Dec. 1761.
[2] Ibid., ad/14 April 1761.
[3] Haus-Hof-und Staatsarchiv, Poschakten, J. S., Karton 6, f. 485–7; Heinrich Benedikt, *Alexander von Schoeller 1805–1886*, (Wien, 1958), 19–21.

Vienna were by then more interested in expanding the industry than in merely having one plant placed on a going basis. Certainly throughout the 1760s officials in Vienna were putting great pressure on industry to expand. At any rate, after Maria Theresia had firmly decided that the factory must go on and the workers could not be allowed to disperse or return home, several investigators were dispatched to Kladruby to report conditions and to recommend action. The last investigator was Kehrnhofer, a government official and head of the quasi-private Moravian Loan Bank. Under his tutelage and with the strong backing of Hofrat von Degelmann, who as a permanent undersecretary of the Court Commercial Council exercised much influence, the factory was finally brought to Brno.

The crisis was resolved not without some comic and tragic by-products. Although there was a consensus that Bailoux was untrustworthy and ill-suited to be an industrialist or a manager, in the end he was placed in charge of the transplanted woollen mill in Brno. But he had difficulty in leaving Kladruby, the manorial administration having jailed him for non-payment of debt. It took a direct order from the Empress to release him. Strange too may be considered the sale of many of the implements belonging to the factory to a Jewish merchant, who planned to continue manufacturing woollen cloth in Kladruby. These episodes testify to the lack of control that the lord of a manor was able to exercise over his own subordinates. More tragic was the case of Kehrnhofer, by then already an old man of sixty-one who had shown for at least a decade an entrepreneurial spirit uncommon for his time and place. Naturally he had stepped on many tender toes. Transferring the factory to Brno was indeed an undertaking of high risk and uncertainty as to future prospects. Even without having stored up grievances many of the shareholders could have demanded justification of the move. One of the large shareholders, the Court Commercial Council, represented by von Degelmann, was able to carry the day against the sharp opposition of the Moravian Estates, another owner, while only the transfer of the woollen enterprise was involved. When a large defaulted debt to the Bank also came to the fore, probably as a result of the first rigorous accounting in many years, Kehrnhofer had to vacate his place.

Crisis Number Three: Settling in Brno

Kehrnhofer's troubles can be considered part of a new crisis immediately after the previous one seemed to have been successfully surmounted. Instead of a strongly interested person in charge of the Bank, which was now the owner-administrator of the factory, this task fell into the uninterested hands of a group of Jewish businessmen who had acquired the Bank after Kehrnhofer's dismissal. Their main concern centred on the Bank itself and on the tobacco business in which several of them were involved. Without the woollen-cloth factory, however, they would not have been permitted to acquire the Bank. Their knowledge of woollen manufacturing was clearly much inferior to that of Kehrnhofer, who had for years been trying to start a fine woollen industry.

Crisis Number Four: Partners' Bankruptcies and Large Stock

If Kehrnhofer's passing from the scene represented a crisis, it was merely part of a continuing crisis that continued to plague the enterprise for years after its move to Brno. In 1767 it left the reluctant hands of the Jewish company and passed into those of the anxious Köffiller, who was burning to do a great deed for his country's economy after having seen the accomplishments of industry in western Europe. Totally inexperienced in the management of an industrial unit, Köffiller was soon pressed by government officials to join a company of woollen-cloth merchants in Brno who had opened their own woollen mill. But the provincial merchants, like Köffiller and his predecessors, had to rely for the operational management on hired superintendents from abroad who, like Bailoux, proved unequal to the task. Finally, 1770, a bad year with terrible rains and resultant poor harvest, turned into a nightmare for the fine-woollen cloth company. Of the six partners in the enterprise, three were forced to declare bankruptcy; of those remaining, only Köffiller still had a strong financial position to fall back upon. The factory had amassed a stock of unsold goods amounting to almost 80,000 fl. The goods were poor in quality and, as it turned out, could only be sold at a sizeable discount, even under duress. Once again, the enterprise had come to a do or die position and as a result the archives contain thick folders containing the reports of investigations and recommendations.

Two reports excite most attention. The first was written by the so-called Factory Directorate (*Feine-Tuch-Fabriks-Direction*) and the second came from the pen of Jean Thys whose analysis and opinion carried great weight with the Empress and the officials in Vienna. The Factory Directorate was a small body comprised of members of the Moravian Commercial Council and instituted to oversee the woollen mill and to protect the government's large fiduciary interest in it. What were the main problems, according to its report? First, there was the disinclination of Habsburg merchants to buy native goods and their preference for smuggling foreign goods. This, combined with losses from poor merchandise manufactured in the factory accounted for much of the trouble. Secondly, there were the huge sums of money that lay 'dead' in buildings and equipment. Thirdly, the unexpected bankruptcies of three of the shareholders and in addition the demand of Köffiller, the chief shareholder, that money that he had lent be repaid so that his grocery business would not suffer caused severe financial embarrassment. In addition, there were several outsiders who had lent large sums of money and who were pressing for repayment. Since the government would not itself take over the enterprise, the 'Directorate' made several observations which it hoped would place the factory on a permanent basis. It suggested that a sixty-loom capacity would be optimal and that merchants should be forced to purchase goods from the enterprise, especially since they took every opportunity to circumvent regulations. For example, they could import only by licence and the number of pieces that they were allowed to import was determined by the number they bought domestically. What they did was to buy pieces of a half-length from Brno and then order double-length pieces from abroad. Consequently the 'Directorate' did not hesitate to propose a forced sale of the accumulated stock and also suggested that each merchant in the Monarchy be assigned a quota once the mill reached its sixty-loom capacity. To achieve this capacity the company required 156,000 fl. in funds.[1]

Maria Theresia and her councillors would not be rushed into adopting these plans. They first awaited the report of Thys, the Belgian expert from Klagenfurt. While favouring the continuation and expansion of the woollen mill, Thys was also highly critical of the manner in which it had been operating. Finding the debts of the firm nearly 30,000 fl. greater than its assets, which he estimated at about 160,000 fl., he saw no difficulty in discovering the reason for this state of affairs. The original capital investment was too small; the government pushed too hard to expand capacity; the merchandise was poor in quality and only two-fifths of that produced since its founding in Brno had been sold; a lack of liquidity forced the firm to purchase Spanish wool at high prices through intermediaries

[1] HKA, red no. 893, f. 493–521 (47 ex Mar. 771 Böhm.).

instead of directly; and then there were numerous technical faults which he detailed. These mistakes could be corrected fairly easily. He suggested a realistic value for the stock of woollens, at which it was eventually sold by assigning each cloth merchant within the monarchy a quota. He also proposed a division of the losses that had been incurred as a result of poor workmanship, feeling that the government should be responsible for that portion which Köffiller inherited from his predecessors. Lastly and most importantly, he proposed that a man be found, preferably in Verviers, who would administer the enterprise and would at the same time be a shareholder in the firm.[1] It was primarily along the lines proposed by Thys that the crisis was resolved and that Seitter became the new manager in 1772.

Although Seitter's appointment marked without question a most important turning point for the Brno Fine-woollen cloth factory, it did not eliminate the sense of tension and crisis. The archives are filled with a stream of complaints and pleadings for the remainder of the 1770s. At first the primary problem was the orphanage whose inmates were to supply the spun yarn that the company was unable to procure through more normal channels. The factory company was entrusted with its temporary control, and a question causing much correspondence between the company and government offices concerned the size of the daily subsidy for the upkeep of each orphan. All rhetoric to the contrary, a small child was unable to earn enough by spinning to subsist on. A subsidy of four kreutzer per day was finally agreed. Eventually the entire orphanage was taken away from the industrial enterprise, as it wished, and turned over to more professional direction.

Crisis Number Five: Tariff Liberalization

With the orphanage 'crisis' disposed of, it seemed that a new one had to take its place. Cries from the managers of the woollen mill that it faced destruction had been heard already in connexion with the orphanage; they became still more shrill with the enactment of a new tariff system in 1775. The company claimed that this went contrary to its contractual agreement with the government. This statement produced a contemptuous response. The government in the enactment of its policies was not bound by private contracts, even when it itself was a party, was the reasoning of the officials in

[1] HKA, red no. 893, f. 290–335 (61 ex Sept. 771 Böhm.).

charge. The cause of the uproar was the fact that the prohibitive system, which had been found unworkable and which did not achieve its purpose, was set aside and a more liberal system allowing for less difficulty in the importation of goods was put in its place. Moreover, the tariff of 1775 was also the first real attempt to enclose the 'Hereditary Lands' in one tariff border, eliminating at least one of the troubles that the company had complained of in the past. It had felt itself at a disadvantage when competing with Jean Thys of Klagenfurt, whose enterprise was located along with the important market of Vienna inside the previous tariff borders. In fact, the two concerns made non-competing products: Thys manufactured only black woollens and Köffiller primarily coloured cloths. This argument was consequently spurious.

The new tariff clearly had a catalytic effect on Köffiller and his associates, who at this time, one year prior to the publication of Adam Smith's *Wealth of Nations*, showed no sign whatsoever of the joys of competition. Even without the benefit of Adam Smith's famous book, economic liberals, among them Joseph II, Count Karl von Zinzendorf and Hofrat Friedrich Anton von Raab, had been instrumental in loosening the economic fetters imposed by government action. The gentlemen in Brno, however, seemed to have enjoyed the yoke of legal economic restrictions and displayed such small confidence in their product that they felt convinced that they would perish at the first breath of foreign competition. Having for years purveyed shoddy products that could be sold only with the aid of the coercive arm of government, they rightfully feared that their reluctant customers would wreak vengeance on them now and institute a virtual boycott.

It was not the fear-inspiring tariff alone that caused the company to declare itself in a life and death crisis once more. The government, showing now the face of an exacting creditor instead of the doting parent, placed increased pressure on the company for payment of debts. In addition raw wool had become more expensive and the capital market had dried up.[1] Although not yet well-established in the commercial and industrial community, the Brno fine-woollen mill was in constant need of additional capital. Köffiller also wanted the government to make a formal commitment not to collect the debts that the Brno enterprise owed it. He wished to extract new funds, free of interest, from the government bodies. Strange as it may sound, he eventually succeeded in his efforts, thanks to excel-

[1] HKA, red no. 894, f. 720–2 (31 ex Julio 775 Böhn.).

lent lobbying in Vienna. Helped by government officials in Brno, the firm was able to declare itself in fine health despite admittedly high overhead costs and poor customer relations.[1] It was a dangerous game, for as the officials in Vienna remarked, if the factory was actually in so poor a condition as indicated, could any aid save it from destruction?[2] The firm weathered the storm, but the 'Factory Directorate' manned by government officials sympathetic to the company was ordered by its superiors in Vienna to keep closer watch.

The Final Crisis

One may entertain certain suspicions about the gravity of the 1775 'crisis'. There is no such doubt, however, regarding that of the late 1780s; it culminated in the destruction of the enterprise. As in the case of the other crises it was a combination of weakness within the firm and external pressures. The company's very success as innovator within the Habsburg Monarchy and especially in Brno sapped it of its best managerial talent. Government participation in the private sector of the economy seems generally most useful when it results in a demonstration effect that encourages private enterprisers to follow suit. It proved its worth most clearly in Brno where the emulators were actually trained in the mother-enterprise itself. Not unlike the deliberate and highly successful policy of Japan in the late nineteenth century, here was a case where a firm became an instrument of the government for the industrialization of the country.[3] While its programme can thus be declared beneficial in the community at large, the government exacted a substantial toll from many private individuals. It may stand as a testimony to the daemonic effect of government in business; with the downfall of its chosen instrument, there was created a basis for the efflorescence of the city and region of Brno. Could the government not have kept the original firm alive and healthy and at the same time permitted the growth of new firms? Having for many years devoted much effort and funds to the success of the woollen firm, the central government now under Joseph II was determined to force it to fend for itself. Unfortunately, it helped in the fall by taking the position of a demanding creditor, thereby becoming an example of a certain

[1] SAB, C/12/45, f. 39–46, 13 Oct. 1776.

[2] HKA, red no. 894, f. 632–4 (3 ex Feb. 777 Böhm.).

[3] Cf. T. C. Smith, *Political Change and Industrial Development in Japan: Government Enterprise, 1868–1880*, (Stanford, 1955), 55.

bureaucratic inflexibility on the part of the Emperor. Its internal weakness came, however, from the desire of its employees to make themselves independent. Such enterprising employees proved the success of the company in the larger sense of aiding the development of the economy, and at the same time proved its undoing by removing its most able officials. But could not the company have recruited and trained other able persons, as it had done so effectively with those that established themselves on their own? It might be said that the company was incapable of renewing itself, that it was in fact exhausted.

Seitter had by this time probably over-extended himself. Besides serving in the firm, he had established a factory of his own producing fezes for the Turkish market. He may have been urged by government officials to enter this branch of industry. It had long been the fervent hope of Habsburg officials that Bohemian–Moravian industry would penetrate the Turkish market. This market in fact fatally seduced the Brno Fine-Cloth Factory. The firm devoted a large portion of its productive facilities to goods for the Turkish market once it found sufficient demand there in the 1780s. This policy proved to be harmful when peaceful commerce was sharply interrupted by war in 1787, a war of unsuccessful aggression for Emperor Joseph II and one which strongly contributed to the final disaster for the concern.

Bankruptcy

How the final debacle came about is detailed in the voluminous records of the bankruptcy proceedings which lasted for several years. Despite their volume, they are clearly incomplete and tend to show a confused picture. The suggestion of some writers that Köffiller saw the approaching end when he petitioned to be made the farmer of a tax on Moravian Jews is probably no more than a snide afterthought.[1] The Brno industrialist was appointed to this post with a salary of 1,500 fl. and up to 600 fl. for travel allowances on 1 February 1788.[2] In June of the same year the government officials in Vienna may have begun to fear that trouble was brewing when they requested information on the operation of the factory from their Brno representative. Schröffel von Mansperg, the head

[1] d'Elvert, *Cultur-Geschichte*, 77.

[2] Hugo Meissner, 'Der Mährisch-Jüdische Landesmassafond', in Hugo Gold, ed., *Juden und Judengemeinden Mährens in Vergangenheit und Gegenwart* (Brünn, 1929), 67; SAB, M 2110, f. 274, 'Protocoll . . . ' 19 Juli 1794 gives the salary and travel expense allowance.

of the 'Factory Directorate', the official supervisory organ, reported that as of 1 July 1788 only fifty-five large and sixteen small looms were being used, a sharp drop from the 101 large and nineteen small looms that had been weaving cloth at the beginning of the year. The cause of this severe reduction was the outbreak of war and the resulting breakdown in the Levant trade, wrote Schröffel.[1]

At the same time Hofrat Joseph Alexander Julien Badenthal, head of the large cotton enterprise at Schwechat, became deeply involved in the affairs of the Köffiller firm. His cotton mill had lent 20,000 fl. on 27 June 1787 and he himself seems to have added 100,000 fl. on 10 July 1788.[2] He may have been merely the intermediary for Countess von Canal (née Chotek) who underwrote Badenthal's loan to Köffiller's factory out of charitable motives (*aus wohltätigem Betriebe*).[3] She undertook her act of charity as late as April 1780 at which time the deplorable state of the firm was so clear that her act was foolhardy and if really charitable made her determination in subsequent years to get every kreutzer back somewhat suspect.

Bankruptcy records are an excellent source for the economic historian, but they are unpleasant actions and the historian cannot help feeling an uneasiness as he pokes through the emaciated remains of a firm. In the process he finds it difficult to cull the sincere from the hypocritical claims and assertions and must be on his guard not to be duped by the participants. Was it premonition or knowledge that made Köffiller take steps to safeguard his personal well-being? It is not only the acquisition of the post as tax-farmer in 1788 that arouses the suspicion of corruption. Another bit of evidence is the proposal for a compromise allowing the firm to continue which he and his partner, Schweikard, circulated among the creditors in June 1789. Nearly at the end of their document the two partners suggested that Köffiller be repaid at the rate of 1,000 fl.

[1] HKA, red no. 894, f. 269 (19 ex Junio 788 Böhm.); f. 264–8 (44 ex Julio 788 Böhm.).

[2] SAB, M 21 10, f. 249, 23 Marti 1789.

[3] Ibid., f. 439–41, 15 April 1789; See also SAB, K Z 3771, f. 344–59, 16 Jan. 1798, Attorney Dr Franz Ott representing government financial interest, writes: 'Die Gräfin von Kanal welche ehedem an der Fabrik gar keinen Antheil hatte, glaubte selbe zu retten und verbürgte dem Hofrath von Badenthal seine Schuldforderung. . . . Es hatte aber die Vermittlung von . . . Kanal keinen guten Erfolg, ja es geriet vielmehr die Fabrik in noch grössere Verwirrung . . . Die Verwirrung zwischen der Fabrik, den Faustpfandbesitzern, den Hypothekar und chyrographar Gläubigen stieg . . . in der Folge so weit dass auf keine Art mehr als durch Eröffnung des Konkurses herauszukommen war, welches auch im Jahre 1793 geschah.'

per month and Schweikard 500 fl. each month, a suggestion that the officials of the Brno branch of the royal exchequer justifiably questioned.[1] Another proceeding that leaves his high, noble purpose in some doubt was the manoeuvre that permitted his wife, a wealthy heiress in her own right, to pay off some of his debts in return for the opulent townhouse that he owned.

It would, of course, be wrong to expect the ageing innovator to have retained the idealism of his youth. He had never been one of the breed of heroic individualists who stood against the world; on the contrary now in this final hour of trial for his creation he again directed appeal after appeal to his sovereign. The new tariff act of 1784, Köffiller wailed, was largely responsible for his trouble in that it allowed Belgian goods to come in freely. Should this be removed he foresaw prosperity for the widows and orphans who would be thrown out of work if the factory came to a halt. Joseph ridiculed this appeal, pointing out that the duty on Belgian woollens had actually doubled from 10 to 20 per cent of value and, moreover, that Wilhelm Mundy, one of Köffiller's former employees, had found the new economic climate so invigorating that he was now operating a 120-loom factory. Furthermore, the efforts of the government in improving the breed of sheep had paid off well so that the local manufacturers paid only half as much for wool as the Belgians for Spanish wool of commensurate quality.[2] In the end, Joseph consented to give the company three months of grace before court action would commence to force it into bankruptcy.

Attempts to Rescue the Firm

Did Köffiller merely go through the motions of saving his enterprise and had he in fact become tired after over two decades of coping with this difficult and hazardous venture? Possibly he was now disenchanted with his role as an industrialist and preferred the sinecure of being farmer of the tax on Moravian Jews. At any rate, he could be proud of a formidable accomplishment. He was the head of a very large enterprise that was still strong and enticing enough for one of the foremost textile manufacturers in the Monarchy to be casting longing glances toward it. Freiherr Julien Alexander von Badenthal, the leading figure at the giant Schwechat cotton mill since the 1770s, through large loans to the Brno woollen mill was apparently ready to expand his operations. At a meeting with the main

[1] SAB, M 2110, f. 630–4; f. 627–42, 5 Aug. 1789, k. Fiskalamt.
[2] HKA, red no. 894, f. 247–57 (16 ex Julio 1789 Böhm.).

creditors called by the government in March 1789 to explore the possibility of keeping the mill in operation, Badenthal claimed that the firm owed him altogether 156,000 fl.[1] If, as the records indicate, be began his lending activity to the Brno factory in 1787, it would be surprising that so well experienced and knowledgeable an industrialist — who in his capacity of *Hofrat* advising the government on economic matters had access to good sources of information — was not aware of internal difficulties. May he actually have entertained the thought of acquiring the Köffiller firm and thus becoming without question the greatest industrialist in the Habsburg Monarchy? The hint permitting this suspicion comes in the form of a memorandum of August 1789, well after other creditors had begun judicial proceedings against the firm. The highly-placed court official Degelmann suggested in this paper that if Badenthal were to take over the direction of the factory, the government claims would not be pressed. He made this proposal even though he had before him the minutes of a meeting in Brno at which the governor of Moravia, Count Ugarte, expressed doubt that Badenthal would take such a step. According to Ugarte, the cotton manufacturer feared that he would be suspected of having deliberately used his official position in order to bring the Brno enterprise into his hands.[2] With success at hand, did the ageing Badenthal lose his nerve? He may, of course, have been less grasping than the sceptical historian might suggest.

One of the more interesting suggestions that Badenthal made in order to prevent the enterprise from going down and at the same time to secure all the creditors from loss was for Wilhelm Freiherr von Mundy to be asked to sell 30,000 fl. of the products of the Köffiller factory. Mundy, who had made a very successful voyage from relative poverty in the Rhineland, before he came in the 1770s to work in the Köffiller plant, to his present eminence, was an old enemy. Köffiller rejected this proposal out of hand.[3] Badenthal's objective was to have assets liquefied as fast as possible and he clearly had confidence in Mundy's ability as a businessman.

It is of course possible that Badenthal was actually conspiring with Mundy to acquire the Köffiller firm. Mundy was certainly not above such machinations and as a matter of fact in the latter part of 1789 came forward with his own scheme for a solution to the

[1] SAB, M 2110, f. 817–26, 31 Mar. 1789.
[2] HKA, red no. 894, f. 236–43 (17 ex Aug. 789 Böhm.), Wien, 24 August 1789.
[3] SAB, M 2110, 31 Mar. 1789, 'Protocoll'.

debacle of his erstwhile employer. He proposed to manage the plant for three years, once it had gone through complete bankruptcy proceedings, and to share during this period the purchasing and sales functions with the state-owned Linz woollen-fabrics factory. He stated that he would require 100,000 fl. of new working capital, and that he was willing to do all this because he felt sorry for Köffiller, whose other business was not doing well either, and for Schweickhard, who was about to lose everything he had, which seems to have been an exaggeration. In return he would take one-third of the net profits. He also demanded that no attempt be made to secure new owners of the Köffiller works during this time. It would be foolish, he declared, to build further competition for himself in this way. His proposals were made orally; written stuff was not to his liking, he was reported to have said.[1] They look suspiciously like an effort at monopoly. Nevertheless, he was given a respectful hearing, but the proposal foundered soon on the inability to raise the 100,000 fl. The Emperor was against any further government involvement. As he wrote in the margin of the memorandum dealing with this proposal, the woollen industry was best served in the hands of private enterprise. Despite his dislike for the written word, Mundy wrote a letter after he had been asked for advice informing the Emperor that his efforts to recruit a rich man for the Köffiller factory had proved unavailing, mainly because it was so much more profitable to invest in government securities.

Some who wanted to save this 'useful' enterprise professed charity; others specified the common welfare. The workers wrote pleading letters to the monarch because their livelihoods were threatened, but they too received little in return to satisfy them. One proposal came to the government offices from an unusual quarter. One Florian Sigmund and another person, Gottfried Möller, in 1790 showed a willingness to operate the plant under certain conditions. Their proposal was turned down.[2] That these two men, both burghers and members of the clothmakers guild in the north Bohemian cloth centre of Liberec applied, is of considerable interest. Möller especially had shown unusual initiative quite early by raising himself from the rank of master weaver to being the most prominent cloth merchant in the town with trade connexions

[1] HKA, red no. 894, f. 218–33 (1 ex Dec. 789 Böhm.), f. 185–217 (30 ex Dec. 789 Böhm.).

[2] SAB, M 2110 f. 932–7, 18 Jan. 1790, f. 690, 23 Nov. 1789; Sigmund, Tuchfabrikant in Reichenberg.

with Germany, Switzerland, Italy, Turkey and other areas.[1] He represents the uncommon case of an innovative guild master who was honoured by his peers despite their adamant opposition to novelty. They may not have known of this proposal or if they did they may have ignored it as of no importance to them since it concerned a town far away. They were deeply antagonistic towards factories as a merchant from Prague, Johann Georg Berger, the founder of the first factory in Liberec discovered in the 1790s.[2] Möller himself proved to be one of the first imitators in Liberec by opening a factory soon after the Berger plant was officially sanctioned.

Besides the Sigmund and Möller attempt to continue the Köffiller factory, there were also proposals from the mortgage holders and from the unsecured creditors. The holders of mortgages included members of the nobility, which was also well represented among the unsecured creditors who had lent money to the firm. This is clear evidence that the aristocracy was interested in industrial undertakings, evidence that becomes especially significant when added to the many other examples of direct involvement on the part of the Habsburg nobility in industry.[3] In all of the Köffiller bankruptcy proceedings nothing strikes a more odd note than the rejection by von Badenthal of the proposal of three well-known and wealthy aristocrats to supply the necessary security for the Köffiller factory to continue to operate. Badenthal apparently did not take seriously the offers of Counts Belcredi, Mitrowski and Dietrichstein to support the enterprise. He said that he refused their offer because he would feel loath to take them to court as he expected to have to do sooner or later in order to collect the required money from them. At the same time, he was able to say that it was not payment of debts but security for the funds lent that concerned him primarily, thereby putting into question their own state of affairs.[4]

In the end it seems to have been the government that forced the bankruptcy proceedings when it discovered that a particular building on which a 27,000 fl. loan from the orphanage fund was secured was actually worth considerably less.[5] The government

[1] Joza, *Z minulosti*, 62–72.

[2] Hermann Hallwich, *Reichenberg und Umgebung* (Reichenberg, 1874), 478–5.

[3] Cf. Gustav Otruba, *Die Wirtschaftspolitik Maria Theresias* (Wien, 1963). See also, Herman Freudenberger, 'Progressive Bohemian and Moravian Aristocrats', in Stanley B. Winters and Joseph Held, eds., *Intellectual and Social Developments in the Habsburg Empire from Maria Theresia to World War I* (New York and London, 1975), 115–30.

[4] SAB, M 2110, 31 Mar. 1789, 'Protocoll'.

[5] HKA, red no. 894, f. 224 (1 ex Dec. 789 Böhm.).

officials maintained that they were bound by law to do so, although it was clear to all that in the Habsburg Monarchy the autocratic monarch was above the law. But Emperor Joseph was at this time very sick and nearing his death. The official insistence on the continuation of court proceedings may also be attributed to fears that other creditors were gaining a legal step on the government which in the end might be left out in the cold.

Was the Köffiller woollen-cloth factory worth saving in 1789? Had it not outlived its usefulness? Were those who were trying to save the firm profit maximizers or were they altruistic benefactors of society? What was the actual worth of the firm? This last question should be the easiest to answer but the evidence is confusing and conflicting. Mundy, the competitor across the town, estimated that the factory — that is buildings, equipment, goods and raw materials — was worth 308,000 fl. and that the company owed 414,000 fl. Without buildings taken into consideration Badenthal estimated the firm's worth at 179,000 fl. but the Moravian governor's office (*Gubernium*) came up with only 128,000 fl.[1] One estimate submitted by the firm but not generally accepted as valid by the creditors was as follows:

Raw wool in stock	52,641 fl.
Wool being processed	58,271
Goods in stock (Brno)	41,802
Goods in stock (Vienna)	34,737
Miscellaneous goods	804
Dyestuffs	6,841
Equipment	3,976
Forward Bills	28,400
"Gindenus"	10,000
Buildings	95,785
	332,977 fl.

Source: SAB, M 2110, f. 405, 30 Juni 1789.

The court actions of the various parties concerned has only peripheral importance for our purposes; they spelled the end of the woollen enterprise that began its innovating existence nearly forty years before. Even in failure, its success in the larger sense was clear, if only judged by the squabbling among the creditors and the spate of proposals to reorganize it and to continue its operations.

[1] HKA, red no. 894, f. 218–33 (1 ex Dec. 1789 Böhm.); SAB, M 2110 f. 373 ff. 4 July 1789.

Chapter VII

THE PROLIFERATION OF INDUSTRY

The proof of the pudding is in the eating. The proof of the success of the government's policy with the fine-cloth industry in Brno is in the industrial prominence of that city to this day. Its industrial progress came as a result of the proliferation of the woollen industry and of the linkages that attended it. For it was to service the woollen industry that manufacturers of textile machinery and steam engines settled in Brno. The expertise they developed in the production of textile machinery permitted them subsequently to branch out into the manufacture of other industrial machinery, such as for sugar beet.

Premature Efforts at Proliferation

Efforts at proliferation in the fine woollen industry actually accompanied the uncertain career of the enterprise during its first thirty years at Kladruby and Brno. Even before the fine-cloth mill was firmly enough established to provide a visible demonstration for potential imitators, there were attempts to create a fine-woollen industry in the Moravian capital. Kehrnhofer had proposed the founding of a 20-loom factory in the 1750s, well before the Kladruby transfer was even considered. For the purpose he recruited a Netherland weaver named Johann Hermann and his son and settled them in Brno in 1757. The son was dispatched to the Verviers area to try to enlist a number of workers to return with him.[1] He succeeded with only two, a dyer and a fuller, one of whom returned home almost immediately. His departure did not seriously affect the prospects of a fine-woollens industry in Brno since it coincided with the time when the equipment, workers and stock of goods were being transferred from Kladruby. Nevertheless, Jean Hermann, Jr (his father having died while the son was on his trip in the Netherlands) carried on independently with a three-loom workshop, the same size as that with which the Brno Fine-Cloth Factory itself began.

Optimistic about his future Hermann forecast for himself an immediate output of 100 to 150 pieces of cloth per year.[2] He proved

[1] HKA, red no. 891, f. 289–92.
[2] Ibid., f. 370–90, 30 Jan. 1763.

to be a poor forecaster and a disappointment to the officials in the government as well as those in the Moravian Loan Bank, who hoped for success from him. There was even a question of his competence as a clothmaker. In a competition for the best fine cloth produced in Moravia he was able to garner only the second prize, despite the fact that he was the only contestant. He excused his bad performance by blaming the fuller from Verviers, who was unfamiliar with the German equipment that he found in Brno.[1]

By January 1763 Hermann's high hopes of the previous year had been turned into poverty-stricken unemployment. Kehrnhofer considered him an unreliable fellow and refused to finance any more of his work. Based on this judgement Hermann was also unable to gain employment in the new factory. Nevertheless, a few years later, in 1767, Hermann was superintendent of the factory that the five Brno cloth merchants briefly established on their own. Even though the superintendent of the combined factories was another person, Hermann apparently continued to work in the plant, for when this man was dismissed as incompetent, Hermann seems to have taken his place.[2] He probably did not survive the changes made when Seitter became manager in 1772. Since he had acquired the rights of a burgher and in addition was receiving an annual pension of 150 fl. from the government, he should not have experienced any particular difficulties in again setting up his own workshop. Hermann's final effort at becoming a man of substance occurred in 1782, when he requested a 1,000 fl. loan from the government in order to expand. This was swiftly turned down, as might be expected in the unsympathetic climate of Joseph II's government.[3] Thus ended one branch of the tree of proliferation.

The second branch did not have a significantly better chance of survival. Joseph Jacob Delimont, who like Hermann served as superintendent of the plant for a period, also tried to make himself independent. Like Hermann, Delimont proved a great disappointment as head of the factory's internal operations. After four years of being in charge of the plant he was dismissed in 1769, the quality of the cloth having continued on the low level that Bailoux had brought from Kladruby. Having been made a burgher of Brno in 1769, Delimont was in a position when discharged from the factory to go his own way without particular difficulty.[4] Once independent,

[1] Ibid., f. 305, 28 May 1762.
[2] HKA, red no. 893, f. 290–335 (61 ex Sept. 771 Böhm.).
[3] SAB, C/12/45, f. 246–7, (10 Sept. 1782); f. 260–61, 4 Nov. 1782.
[4] Ibid., f. 2–7, 12 Juni 1769.

he demonstrated an ambition to become a great manufacturer. He entered into a six-year contract to rent a building in which he operated five looms and early in 1770 he requested a government loan of 4,000 fl. He planned to add this to the nearly 3,000 fl. that he had already borrowed privately. The Moravian Commercial Council, while not supporting his proposal for a loan, did suggest that he receive a gratuity of 400 fl. for each loom that he placed in operation, similar to the Köffiller firm. Alas, poor Delimont did not enjoy the same privileged position and was flatly turned down by the authorities in Vienna for being a man who knew his art only poorly and who had had ample opportunity to display his lack of accomplishments.[1]

To these two efforts at expansion of the woollen industry can be added a third. Lukas Plaschke, also a worker associated with the Brno fine-woollen cloth firm, approached the government in 1777 for a hand-out. He proclaimed himself persecuted by his employer and willing to establish a cloth works anywhere else but in Brno. His request received the same treatment as those of Hermann and Delimont. The government memorandum concerning his case pointed to his incompetence but also added that it was contrary to the principles of the government at that time to give financial support.[2]

Rugged Individualism: Wilhelm Mundy

These would have been pitiful attempts if they had been the only ones that demonstrated the existence of entrepreneurial talent. There would have been little or no industrial development in Brno at this time. Understandable as were their efforts to lean upon the government, since they merely followed the example of the Köffiller Fine-Cloth Factory, such economic actors were too weak to carry forward the development of the area and the industry. During the 1770s, however, men who were made of sterner stuff infiltrated. One of these was Wilhelm Mundy. He came from western Germany, possibly from Monschau, along with or at about the same time as Seitter in 1772.[3] He may have been a journeyman weaver when he came but he soon was a foreman (*Werkmeister*) in Köffiller's factory.

[1] HKA, red no. 882, f. 56–7, 74, 81, 65.

[2] Ibid., f. 279–86.

[3] B. Šindelař, 'O západoevropských odbornících v některých textilních manufakturách na Moravě koncem 18. století', (On western European specialists in several textile manufactories in Moravia at the end of the 18th century.) *Časopis Matice Moravske*, LXXVII (1958), 57.

In 1774, after $2\frac{1}{2}$ years with the firm he made himself independent.[1] Unlike the others, he made no application to the government for financial support for several years. It was not that he disdained the support of the government, for he certainly tried in 1780 and again in 1785 to gain funds from the state.[2] By 1780 he had brought his workshop to a capacity of twelve looms, a considerable feat which he had accomplished with the financial help of his mother and out of his profits.[3] The mention of his mother as a supplier of funds is especially interesting, for if she resided in Monschau she was probably not wealthy. All search for a family by that name in the Monschau region has been unavailing. In his use of his profits for the expansion of his productive facilities, he followed the same principle as the British industrialists of the time.

Of the twelve looms in operation in 1780, Mundy was forced for lack of space to place four away from his workshop and was therefore unable to supervise his entire plant. It was mainly in order to purchase a building in which he could concentrate all of his productive facilities that he appealed to the government for help. In addition he requested the officials to put a stop to the obstructive practices of the Brno clothmakers' guild and the municipal administration. Although central government officials wanted to supply financial help, they were prevented from doing so on account of a paragraph in the contract of 1780 between the government and Köffiller. No new woollen textile factories were to receive support similar to Köffiller's if they were located within one Austrian mile, that is about 7 km., of the city of Brno. Mundy must have known that Köffiller would be an antagonist. In his formal proposal for aid, Mundy extolled the virtues of Brno as a convenient location and observed that besides the Köffiller factory at least twenty of Mundy's size could easily exist there. That such a limiting provision was included in Köffiller's contract went, of course, contrary to the logic of the government's industrial policy. On the other hand, however, this policy favoured industrial growth on a more extensive and decentralized basis and was opposed to the massing of industry as well as of population in one place. Joseph von Sonnenfels, then a very influential person in the government although in no wise connected with this case, taught and wrote that industrial plants should be forced as far as possible to be located in the countryside

[1] HKA, red no. 882, f. 385, 21 and 22 Jan. 1780.
[2] Ibid., f. 385, 21 and 22 Jan. 1780; f. 459–62, 28 Mar. 1785.
[3] Ibid., f. 396.

where living costs were presumably cheaper than in towns and where therefore the cost of production could be lower.[1]

Undaunted by his rebuff in 1780, Mundy continued on his way and was able by 1785 to report that he had fifty-five looms in operation.[2] This represented about half as many looms as were working in the Köffiller factory and must clearly be considered a substantial feat especially since it was accomplished without the help of government and in the absence of great personal wealth. He asked for 30,000 fl. to expand his facilities so that he could serve the greatly increased internal market for fine woollens that resulted from the protective tariff of 1784. In addition, as with Köffiller, the problem with Mundy was in part the high cost of capital and the need to tie up sizeable resources in buildings and equipment for a large-scale enterprise. This constant thirst for capital, an increasing portion of which was imbedded in fixed investment, was of course a hallmark of the industrial revolution in England as well as elsewhere. Although the accomplishments in Brno could hardly be characterized as revolutionary in the sense of the industrial revolution in England, they did in fact represent proof of a successful policy to the government officials who supported Mundy's appeal for funds on the ground that even the immediate successors of pioneer enterprises deserved recognition and aid. They wrote with satisfaction, that the industry was far enough advanced that the state no longer had to devote the extraordinary resources that were necessary at its beginning. Supporting Mundy would place the last stone in a proud edifice that the state had begun.[3]

The officials could point with pride to Mundy's accomplishments. He was the first and only private person who had constructed so costly and important an enterprise using his own financial resources.[4] Despite all the most eloquent arguments to the contrary, Joseph II refused to allow financial support out of the public purse to flow

[1] Joseph von Sonnenfels, *Von der Theuerung in den grossen Städten und dem Mittel derselben abzuhelfen* (Wien, 1770).

[2] HKA, red no. 882, f. 479–80, 483–4, 10 Aug. 1785.

[3] Ibid. (15 ex Aug. 1785 Böhm.) '. . . der Staat nicht mehr nöthig [hat], jene ausserordentliche Verwendung auf die feine Tuch Manufaktur zu machen, welche er der ersten Errichtung geleistet hat . . . aber . . . Nachfolger nicht ohne Unterstützung zu lassen welche so zu sagen im Begriff stehen die letzte Hand an jenes Werk zu legen, so der Staat ausführen sich vorgenommen hat.'

[4] Ibid., 29 Dec. 1781. 'Dieser Mundy ist der erste und der einzige privat Mann der ein so kostbares und wichtiges Werk aus eigen anfänglich schwachen Geldmitteln durch Fleiss und Kenntniss so weit gebracht hat . . . .'

to the Brno manufacturer. This did not mean that the Emperor was antagonistic to the self-made man of Brno. In 1786 he permitted Mundy to purchase a confiscated Cistercian monastery at Tišnovic (Tischnowitz) for the minimal sum of 2,000 fl.[1] Three years later he overrode his officials when they counselled him to approve Mundy's elevation only to knight (*Ritter*) and instead presented him with the title of baron that the industrialist had requested.[2]

To expect consistency from anyone, let alone a rugged individualist like Mundy, would be too much to expect. It should not come as a complete surprise therefore that the man who proclaimed in 1780 that Brno could accommodate twenty more factories in 1786 opposed the application for a permit to erect a factory made by one of his former colleagues in the Köffiller factory. Johann Heinrich Offermann, son of the owner of a woollen-cloth factory in Monschau forced to close in 1770 apparently as a result of economic difficulties, requested permission to open a woollen factory in Brno in 1786 after no less a personage than the Emperor Joseph II had urged him to do so.[3] Offermann, like Mundy, had come to Brno at Seitter's behest about 1775 and had served in the Köffiller firm as book-keeper, factor and foreman. Mundy wrote that he feared that harm could ensue as a result of the competition of too many enterprises and he objected to the infusion of 'foreign' investment that would be part of the capital of the projected firm.[4] This point was probably the most unkind, for as the government authorities in Vienna observed in support of Offermann's application, Mundy himself could not possibly have built up a sixty-loom capacity without a great deal of credit. Köffiller supported his book-keeper's application whereas he opposed Mundy wherever possible. It seems clear that personal differences of possibly many years' standing were at play. Mundy, whom Brno's chronicler calls an arrogant man and government officials disliked for his lack of courtesy and his well-known rough manner of acting, very likely delighted in making his rise from rags to riches known to all.[5]

[1] K. Pribram, *Geschichte*, 401.

[2] Verwaltungsarchiv, Adelsarchiv, 20 April 1789.

[3] Scheibler, 'Auswanderungen', 64–73.

[4] HKA, red no. 882, f. 563–7 (21 ex Aug. 786 Böhm.).

[5] Trautenberger, *Chronik der Landeshauptstadt*, v, 196; iv, 159–60. The chronicler, a Protestant clergyman, showed in his work obvious approval of Köffiller, who despite being a Catholic, had helped to found the Protestant church in Brno. Offermann was one of the leaders of the Protestant community until his death in 1793. Mundy, who married a Freyin von Forgatsch may have become a Catholic. Also, SAB, M 2049, 16 Jan. 1792.

He probably resented those who, like Offermann, came from patrician backgrounds.

Whether the patrician background of his competitor concerned him greatly or not, there is no question that Mundy was socially very ambitious. Allied in marriage to a respected noble family, a privilege that he considered important enough to be willing to forego a dowry from his wife and instead to commit 20,000 fl. of his own funds to be inherited by his wife,[1] he died in 1805, the owner of three factories and of two manorial estates, with assets totalling over 1,638,000 fl.[2] Two of the factories were located in the vicinity of Brno and the third (with a capacity of thirty-two large looms), had been established in Teschen in 1798 at the request of Duke Albert von Sachsen-Teschen and with substantial financial support from him. He was Mundy's creditor for 201,027 fl.[3] The list of Mundy's major creditors at his death contained, besides Duke Albert, a number of other interesting names including Baron von Badenthal, who had been so prominent in the Köffiller bankruptcy to whom he owed 16,000 fl., Baron von Weinbrenner, the articulate merchant of Vienna who had been the cause of an earlier crisis, in 1770, in the Köffiller firm, with over 25,000 fl., and General Field Marshall von Brady, who participated in the formation of a textile machine manufacturing firm in Brno. Of Mundy's total liabilities at his death about half were to noblemen. Somewhat over 71,000 fl. was owing to a governmental agency, the *k.k. Religions Fond*, an agency in charge of property confiscated from religious organizations and the remainder to commoners, most of them probably merchants in Brno and Vienna. The listing in the inventory does not identify the various accounts very clearly but it seems that Mundy was the sole owner and did not share the responsibilities with any partners. His creditors had consequently most probably simply lent funds to him or extended some credit. Three accounts had notations appended that they were for notes payable (*Wechsel*) and it seems therefore that these sums amounting to nearly 300,000 fl. were short-term credits.

This reporting of Mundy's creditors has the purpose of emphasizing the difference in quantity and in quality between it and the

[1] SAB, fasc. 13/340. Josepha Freyin von Mundy died 18 Jan. 1792. She gave birth to two children, Wilhelm and Wenzel.

[2] SAB, Moravsko-sleszke zemske pravo, sign. 13–701, Vilem Mundy.

[3] The source for this statement is the inventory compiled after Mundy's death. It is not clear from it whether the Duke was an investor for profit or loss or whether he merely lent funds or gave credit for goods purchased, such as wool.

Köffiller firm. In the Mundy business the role of the government was not absent but it was much muted. Among the accounts-receivable there were a large number of army regiments, testifying to considerable sale of cloths. This business seems to have been more forced upon the woollen manufacturer than looked for. At any rate, Archduke Karl, an army commander, felt that Mundy should have been supplying larger quantities.[1] The account of the *Religions Fond*, which seems to incorporate a loan, was not exceptionally large in comparison to other creditors. The participation of the nobility was sizeable, testifying to its ability to make liquid funds available to profitable business undertakings.

Mundy had indeed succeeded in a big way and with his success the industrial policy of the central government adopted in the middle of the eighteenth century had demonstrated its value. Unfortunately, after his death a shrivelling process began, in part because of the absence of adult heirs to continue his enterprises and because of the demands of the creditors. For the textile factories themselves, the liabilities were greater than the assets. Apparently, the estates that he had purchased were untouched.

Further Horizontal Expansion

Brno's fate as a woollen cloth manufacturing centre was fortunately not in the hands of Baron Wilhelm Mundy alone. The factory built by Johann Heinrich Offermann was at the time of Mundy's death in 1805 very much in the picture and was destined to enjoy a prosperous existence into the early twentieth century. Offermann, the man about whose potentially harmful competition and whose dependence on foreign capital Mundy complained, was nevertheless able to establish himself successfully in 1786. The foreign capital to which Mundy referred emanated from a Nürnberg businessman, Johann Jakob Herzogenrath, who apparently used this means to recoup the potential losses that he expected from the interruption of his trade connexions with Brno resulting from the

[1] HKA, red no. 883, f. 49, 17 Feb. 1802. Archduke Karl complained in this memorandum that Mundy was not supplying enough cloths for the army despite the fact that in the Archduke's opinion, Mundy had this obligation as a result of having received the Tišnov property at a low price. Mundy averred, on the other hand, that the only obligation that he incurred as a result was to finance his brother's operations there for a period of two years, i.e. until the factory was self-sustaining.

prohibitive tariff of 1784.[1] With the unknown amount that Herzogenrath lent to him and his own life-savings of 3,000 fl. Offermann was able to open a modest factory.[2] He also benefited from the generous credit terms that Herzogenrath offered him for materials that he purchased directly from the Nürnberg merchant. Offermann was able to purchase Spanish wool from Amsterdam suppliers on long credits through Herzogenrath's intercession.[3] Seemingly rather inactive or at least unsuccessful as a businessman for the first forty-three years of his life Offermann unfolded notable creative abilities between 1786 and 1793, the year of his death. For one thing, he married — in 1782. Marriage may have been one of the factors that provided the incentive for Offermann to enlarge his factory from the four original looms to about twenty-eight looms by 1791, at which point his firm commanded a capital investment of nearly 100,000 fl., only 15,427 fl. of which had come from abroad, as the pertinent document archly adds.[4] Offermann was at this point requesting the legal designation of *Landesbefugte Fabrik*, which he received. At the time, he was operating twenty-six two-man broadlooms and produced about 700 pieces of cloth made of Spanish wool, amounting to about 80,000 fl.

When he died in 1793, Offermann was still operating a middle-sized enterprise, comprising three buildings just outside the inner city of Brno. Only a year before his death he had entered into a partnership with the Viennese firm of Joh. Michael Thomann & Co., for the purpose of enlarging the activities of the Brno woollen mill. Thomann, a native of Switzerland and a member of the association of foreign merchants in Vienna (*Niederleger*) had acted as Offermann's banker in Vienna by discounting the Brno manufacturer's notes. He promised to furnish Offermann immediately with 15,000 fl. cash and an open line of credit for a further 20,000 fl. The Viennese banker agreed to remain a silent partner with the condition

[1] Herzogenrath reportedly settled in Brno in 1756, at which time he was an apprentice of the Nürnberg merchant house of Wolrab (Trautenberger, *Chronik der Landeshauptstadt*, III, 99). Also his son was born in the 1760s in Brno. Nevertheless, in 1780 he was called a 'Nürnberg merchant' (Ibid., IV, 127). In Offermann's inventory at his death in 1793, Herzogenrath was also identified as a creditor from Nürnberg. The younger Herzogenrath married the daughter of Seitter in 1796, thus cementing the social ties of the Brno textile industry even further (Archiv zemského hlavního města Brna Pozůstalosti, no. XLV–79).

[2] Alfred Oberländer, *K. K. Priv. Militär-und Feintuch-Fabrik in Brünn 1786–1911*, (Brünn, 1912), 7.

[3] SAB, M 2047, f. 628, 5 Feb. 1788.

[4] HKA, red no. 882, f. 843–5, 848–57, 27 May 1791.

that he was not responsible for any of the debts of the textile mill for the six-year duration of the contract from January 1792. For his part Offermann had to issue a note to Thomann for this period promising to pay 8 per cent interest per year on it. This provision was not unusual. It was common for investors to receive a specified interest per year on their capital and then, like Thomann, to share in the net profits that remained as a residual. In Offermann's firm the net profit was not calculated until all overheads had been worked out, including the housekeeping costs of the owner's family, as was expressly stated in the contract. Thomann's share of the net profit was to remain in the firm for the contract period, Offermann agreeing to issue a note annually for the required amount.[1]

The partnership agreement is a good demonstration that the private sector of the economy was capable of supporting profitable industrial enterprises. It also testifies to the connexion between the regional industrial centre of Brno and the capital city of Vienna and, in addition, to the presence of private merchant-banking sources in the financing of industrial enterprises. There were a number of other investors who together placed about 34,000 fl. at Offermann's disposal in addition to Thomann's 15,000 fl. and the owner's own equity, which at the beginning of 1793 amounted to over 34,000 fl. Among the outside investors there was only one member of the nobility, a Baron Puchowsky. Two individuals among the investors appear especially interesting. They were the Viennese merchant and writer Weinbrenner, of whose involvement with the Köffiller and the Mundy enterprises mention already has been made, and the Moravian apothecary Vincent Petke, who was also a well-known scientist and promoter of technological progress. While not so formidable an enterprise as Mundy's at the time of the latter's death more than ten years later, Offermann did in 1793 at his own demise leave behind a very respectable business whose assets were in the vicinity of 140,000 fl., with reported liabilities of about 120,000 fl.[2]

Besides his wife, Offermann left two sons, both in their infancy. One of the firm's creditors, Abraham Greisinger, a wholesale merchant in Brno, was the custodian for the heirs until their majority. It may have been through him that the partner in Vienna began to press for the sale of the enterprise, despite the expressed

[1] Archiv zemského hlavního města Brna. Pozůstalosti, no. 533, Litt. 'O'.
[2] Ibid.

wishes of the deceased owner who desired that the woollen enterprise remain in the hands of the family. Greisinger feared that the manager, Mathias Offermann, brother of the founder, and his assistant Gottlieb Schäfer, a brother of Mrs Offermann, were not capable of carrying on the firm successfully. He consequently pressed that one Martin Stählin, a man who was also prepared to marry the widow and who apparently was experienced in the textile industry, be allowed to acquire the mill.[1] Eventually, the Brno magistrate, who had the obligation to safeguard the interests of the minors, agreed that Mathias Offermann was capable of managing the firm without difficulty, especially since he was able to show a substantial profit for the year 1793. Greisinger withdrew his objections pointing out that a recent prohibition of the import of fine woollen cloth from the Austrian Netherlands (by then under the control of the French) had immensely improved the position of the Offermann factory. Moreover, Mrs Offermann had withdrawn her consent to marry the proposed new owner.

In the organization of the firm and in the technology that it employed it was probably little different from its contemporaries. Johann Heinrich Offermann may have been somewhat different in his possibly greater interest in technological innovation. At his death a spinning machine and a carding engine were in existence but unuseable. Offermann had expended over 800 fl., a considerable sum, for this purpose but the attempt was obviously a failure. There is no information concerning the type of machines and it is therefore not possible to state whether it was a spinning jenny, a water frame or a mule, or another type of machine. It does, however, testify to a considerably greater devotion to innovation than his more successful compatriot Baron Mundy displayed. As to the organization of work the entries in the inventory compiled by the management allow the surmise that the looms were standing in the homes of the weavers and that spinning was also carried on in the homes of the workers.[2] The articles that were manufactured were for the most part heavy woollens in the widths of 8/4 and 7/4 ells and their sale was all over the Monarchy with a considerable portion of them going to Hungary.

[1] Stählin became manager and partner in the large woollen mill established in 1795 on the Náměšt estate. The main investors in this mill were the owner of the estate, Count Haugwitz, and Baron von Puthon, a financier in Vienna and owner of a large cotton mill.

[2] Ibid., Lit. 'C', Inventarium.

In 1797 the plant was expanded but in 1813 it still was no more than a middle-sized enterprise with a reported capital of about 50,000 fl. (probably calculated in heavily depreciated currency) and operating only about sixteen hand looms. This represented a considerable decline from the previous year when twenty-five looms were working. It is even possible that in 1811 the productive capacity of the factory was still larger, for, as a government report states, the number of looms in Brno had decreased by 252 compared to the year before.[1] Nevertheless, in 1816 it was clearly still one of the more potent and progressive enterprises. In that year it became one of the early factories in the Monarchy to introduce a steam engine, this being a 10–12 h.p. engine imported from London at a cost of 9,500 fl.[2] The Offermann firm continued to make use of the technological innovations that were emanating especially from England during the nineteenth century. As might be expected, it lagged considerably behind the English in their adoption. Nevertheless by 1834 the woollen mill employed two steam engines, the English one that had been purchased in 1816 and a new one of 25 h.p. constructed in the machine shops of an aristocratic innovator and entrepreneur, Altgraf Hugo Salm-Reifferscheidt at Blansko, somewhat to the north of Brno. At the same time eighty spinning machines with eighty spindles each and a number of other machines were being employed in this factory where about 500 workers produced an average of 3,000 pieces of cloth per year.[3] When the older brother and half-owner of the firm, Johann Heinrich Offermann Jr, died a bachelor in 1837, his half-interest in the firm amounted to nearly 100,000 fl., testifying to a rather prosperous enterprise.[4] While less grandiose in his immediate achievements than Wilhelm Mundy, Johann Heinrich Offermann Sr, the second graduate of the Köffiller firm, created a far more enduring enterprise and his successors as heads of the woollen mill continued into the twentieth century to be outstanding leaders of industry in the Austro-Hungarian Monarchy.

Shortly after Offermann began his enterprise, two other employees of the Köffiller firm, with their employer's blessing, started their own woollen factory. Heinrich Friedrich Hopf, a native of Württemberg and employed in the Köffiller factory for seven years, and

[1] HKA, red no. 1053, f. 149–60.
[2] d'Elvert, *Cultur-Geschichte*, 106, 116.
[3] Wolny, *Mähren*, II, 58 f.
[4] Archív zemského hlaviho města Brna, Pozůstalosti, no. 9025.

Johann Gottfried Bräunlich, a native of Saxony and a Köffiller employee for five years, began their joint enterprise under almost identical terms as Offermann. They ran into opposition from Mundy, who saw in them, as in Offermann, competitors and beneficiaries of foreign capital but also considered them inexperienced scribes who sat in their offices and knew nothing of manufacturing. Inevitably, Mundy felt, the good reputation of Brno cloth would suffer and moreover production costs would go up when so many plants competed for labour.[1]

That Mundy should accuse these men of technical incompetence was ironic in the light of the innovative activity that they unfolded some years later. He may have been correct if he felt that they were less capable businessmen than himself. Hopf and Bräunlich experienced some business problems around 1804[2] and in 1813 dissolved their firm, at which time they were operating only seven large looms.[3] This meant, nevertheless, that they had succeeded in running a respectable business establishment for nearly thirty years, during which they had been in the forefront of technological change. Mundy's interest in technological innovation seems to have been minimal. It spent itself in the discovery of new markets and in his encouragement of improving the supply of the most important raw material. He is held responsible for having got the noble landowners in Moravia to refine the breed of sheep so that the quality of the wool approached more nearly that of the Spanish Merino sheep.[4] Other than that he was a traditionalist. Unlike Hopf and Bräunlich he displayed no interest in the English accomplishments. He may even have instigated his shearers to organize a protest in 1803 against the introduction of a new cloth-shearing machine, which was being developed by a member of the Offermann family.[5] There is little doubt that his competitors were much more open to the new technologies from abroad without whose adoption the further development of Brno's textile industry would have been stunted.

Of the four former employees of the Köffiller firm who became enterepreneurs in the 1780s, Mundy, who displayed all the traits of the rugged individualistic capitalist was the most successful

[1] HKA, red no. 882, f. 553–9, 6 July 1786.
[2] HKA, red no. 883, f. 309–20 (11 ex Jan. 1804 Böhm.).
[3] Archiv zemského hlávniho město Brna, Pozůstalosti, no. 8428. Also, d'Elvert, *Cultur-Geschichte*, 106.
[4] Allgemeines Verwaltungsarchiv, Adelsarchiv, Mundi Diplom, 12 März 1789.
[5] HKA, red no. 837, f. 54, 57–60, 21 Juny 1803.

personally. He died a rich man, having also achieved distinction as a Baron and the husband of a lady of ancient lineage. The other three, whose ambitions may have been frustrated — in one case by an early death and in the other by personal misfortune — provided through their efforts great benefit for the public welfare.

Momentum Achieved

Towards the end of the 1780s before the Köffiller enterprise was forced to close its doors, the fine-woollen industry had been solidly established in Brno and was the largest producer of this type of cloth in the Monarchy. Within a period of about twenty-five years the city had been transformed from a place that could not be identified with any particular industry into a textile centre with a productive capacity of about 240 looms primarily producing fine-woollen cloth. This was all directly or indirectly attributable to the original factory. A momentum had clearly been established. The bankruptcy of the Köffiller firm proved to be only a temporarily retarding interlude. In fact the successor enterprises were probably aided by the demise of the pioneer firm because they were enabled to purchase buildings and equipment cheaply.

In 1790, a year after the Köffiller firm ceased its operations, a new woollen mill was formed by what might be called an offspring-once-removed. Christian Biegmann, a former employee and travelling salesman of the Mundy firm was officially given permission to operate his own business. He purchased some of the buildings of the old Köffiller mill and in the same year had thirty-four looms in operation. He registered a meteoric rise during the 1790s. By the end of the decade he had a manufacturing capacity of 132 looms.[1]

Of the former employees of the firm Heinrich Schmal made the largest purchase of the bankrupt factory's property when he acquired the original building in the Neugasse for 13,150 fl.[2] He had been in the finishing department of the old firm and became independent only after the Köffiller enterprise had crumbled completely. By 1791 he was operating a plant of ten-loom capacity and employing over 500 persons. By the turn of the century he was turning out 900 pieces of woollen cloth per year on thirty-three looms but was employing only some one hundred additional workers than before.[3]

[1] d'Elvert, *Culturfortschritte*, 81, 83.
[2] SAB, M 2110 F, f. 264.
[3] d'Elvert, *Cultur-Geschichte*, 77, 79, 81.

By 1798 a considerable horizontal expansion had taken place. In Brno and its suburbs six fairly sizeable plants were manufacturing woollen cloth, all of them owned by men who had been trained either in the original factory or by one of the persons who had worked in it. The most recent factory to begin operations belonged to Baron Mundy's nephew Mathias Mundy. Besides these plants, several factories had also been established on estates not far from the city. Among these were Baron Mundy's woollen mill in Tišnov, Count Haugwitz's mill in Náměšt (Namiest) (1795), and one that the Brno businessman Johann Herring established in Křižanov (Krzizanau) (1794) in company with the hereditary leaseholder of the estate.[1] Only the Haugwitz factory, which became the largest of its kind in the Monarchy, had no direct connexion with the Brno woollen industry. In the greater Brno area alone 14,000 pieces of cloth were being produced annually and demand continued strong.[2]

All through the 1790s the market for Moravian fine cloth seemed to have been good. Mundy, Offermann and Biegmann were selling goods all over the Monarchy and to distant places like Modena, Cracow, Warsaw, St Petersburg, and Constantinople, places to which in 1792 as much as one-fourth of Mundy's products were going.[3] War conditions benefited the expanding industry, as was specifically asserted in connexion with the creation of the woollen enterprise of Count Haugwitz.[4] Consequently, there was an incentive to create additional productive facilities. And indeed, new manufacturers followed the call of the market. One of them was Johann Gottlieb Schäfer, brother-in-law of J. H. Offermann and an employee in the latter's woollen mill. In 1798 Schäfer combined with Seitter, the son of the former manager of the Köffiller factory to apply for a formal charter for a fine-woollen cloth firm. At first they were turned down by provincial government officials and opposed by the noble owner of the Náměšt textile mill about thirty miles to the west of Brno. In the end they received approval as a result of appealing to the central authorities in Vienna.

The memorandums that accompanied this case reveal clearly various labour and capital problems and different approaches in dealing with them. As far as the provincial officials were concerned

[1] The estate belonged to the *Religious Fond* of the central government. It had been confiscated in the 1780s from a religious order.
[2] HKA, red no. 882, f. 1149–55.
[3] SAB, M 2094, no. 204, 112, 6 Nov. 1792.
[4] HKA, red no. 882, f. 1214.

there was too much industry concentrated in Brno already resulting in an inflation of the prices of wood and food. In addition, a potential labour shortage was just over the horizon. They proposed that new factories should search for locations in the countryside where labour was abundant and cheap and where the price of subsistence would not be inflated by the agglomeration of people in one place. On the other hand, Count Heinrich Haugwitz, lord of the Naměšt estate and part-owner of the large woollen factory there strongly objected to new firms. He feared that his labour, especially workers from abroad, would be lured away. Schäfer, like Mathias Mundy before him, in his appeal to Vienna pointed out that a plant away from the city required greater investment in the form of making available services that in an industrial centre could be purchased on the market. He was thinking specifically of a fullery. There were other benefits of industrial agglomeration in a city, as the approval from Vienna recognized. Mutual aid from the various enterprises resulted, ancillary occupations (*Nebengewerbe*) providing services necessary to the successful operation of such plants sprang up, skilled workers congregated there and could be more easily controlled and a market for the finished product was more easily established.

The attitude of the central government undoubtedly aided the growth of industry in Brno. In addition, Brno industry benefited from the demands of the war raging during this period. By 1802 there were altogether 600 looms operating in woollen-cloth factories with approximately 10,000 workers producing 18,000 to 20,000 pieces of cloth. Not surprisingly, the course of Brno's industry did not move smoothly in one direction. As a result of the adverse effects of the Napoleonic wars, demand for fine cloth receded considerably by 1806 so that the number of looms had to be reduced by about 20 per cent.[1] Once within the Continental System of Napoleonic France, however, the Brno textile industry progressed upward again only to be devastated by the economic difficulties resulting from the so-called state bankruptcies of 1811 and 1816 and the sharply increased competition of English textile manufacturers after the end of the Napoleonic wars. These difficulties seem to have become especially fearsome after 1815, but in that year seven new firms received charters, several of them founded by foreigners.[2]

[1] Vytiska, 'Průmyslová oblast', 21–2.
[2] Trautenberger, *Chronik der Landeshauptstadt*, v, 38.

Except for the Offermann enterprise hardly any of the progeny of the Köffiller firm and its derivatives was able to persist beyond the crisis. Nevertheless, the momentum of Brno's woollen industry was only temporarily interrupted. As in the earlier cases a strong infusion of foreign enterprise was responsible for the renewed vigour of the textile industry. The new era was marked by the transfer of a textile factory to Brno from Düren (Westphalia) by the brothers Johann Peter, Carl Friedrich and Leopold Schoeller in 1819. They made no bones about the fact that they were jumping over the Austrian tariff barrier which had interrupted their trading relationships.[1] In purchasing the building formerly used by the Hopf & Bräunlich firm to house their manufacturing operations, the Schoellers made the tie with the old industry complete.

Johann Herring, Promoter of Innovations

Well before the Westphalian industrialists deliberately jumped the tariff barrier by settling in Brno, Herzogenrath, the merchant from Nürnberg, had been playing the game with the results already alluded to above. His contribution went beyond aiding new manufacturers financially and procuring some of the more scarce material and equipment that they needed. He also provided indirectly some of the entrepreneurial talent when he assigned Johann Herring in 1776 to be his representative in Moravia.[2] Apparently not convinced that Herring was the best man available in 1788 when the government excluded foreign houses from doing business on a permanent basis, Herzogenrath dismissed him and placed Herring's assistant Abraham Greisinger in the position of assisting the young Wolfgang Christoph Herzogenrath in establishing a permanent commercial business in Brno.[3]

Herring seems to have been ubiquitous in Brno during the 1790s. Most of the dyestuffs consumed by the textile industry there went through his hands. When one of the major commission dyers died in 1793, Herring set his successor up in business, a highly important

[1] Benedikt, *Schoeller*, 20: Die Vereinigung des Lombardisch-Venetianischen Königreichs mit den kaiserlich-königlichen Staaten, die Sperrung derselben für unsere Fabricate, . . . hat uns als Eigentümer eine der ansehnlichsten Tuch-und Casimir-Manufactur des Gross-Herzogthums Niederrhein der besten Absatz Quellen beraubt. Diese aufgehobenen Verbindungen wieder anzuknüpfen, sind wir entschlossen unsere Manufactur in Euer Majestät Staaten zu verpflanzen . . . '

[2] Trautenberger, *Chronik der Landeshauptstadt*, IV, 127.

[3] Jindrich Sebanek, Jindrich Mayer and Karl Balbinder, *Blätter aus der Geschichte des Brünner Handels*, translated by Ernst Libich (Brno, 1928), 122. For additional details, see SAB, M 2047, f. 587–622, 718–25.

service facility especially for the smaller manufacturers. In the same year he and two others purchased the Moravian Loan Bank. Although internal evidence is lacking to assert that the Loan Bank still contributed to the industry of the area, Herring and his colleagues were required to set a sum of 200,000 fl. aside for the purpose.[1] In the following year he participated in the founding of a woollen-cloth factory on an estate not far from Brno, an enterprise that by 1795 operated twenty-five looms.[2] All these activities testified to Herring's enterprising spirit but in 1796 he also displayed a strong innovative interest. In that year he acted as co-founder with Count Hugo Salm-Reifferscheidt and the Provincial Apothecary of Moravia, Vincenz Petke, in the establishment of a 'society for the operation of a wool spinning mill using English type spinning machines' (*Verein zur Anlage einer Wollenen-Maschinen-Spinnerei nach Englischer Art*).[3] Since these machines could not be constructed in Brno at the time, Salm-Reifferscheidt and Petke undertook an industrial spying mission to England in 1801.[4] Herring, who acted in other matters as Salm's financial agent, provided part of the financial support for this mission as well.

Vertical Linkages

Vertical linkages began to form even before Herring and his collaborators began their activities. Those that involve technological improvements and especially the introduction of machinery demand our attention. As early as 1769 a local master shearer, Johann Röckl, tried his hand at building a machine that would provide the finished cloth with a better shine (*Glanzmaschine*). The government supported him with a loan of 600 fl. At the time when he began this venture Röckl was a fairly well-to-do master with several presses, some three-dozen shears, a house and a workshop, all of them together valued at nearly 7,500 fl. By 1774, he was reported to be without funds, but he had finished the machine. The evidence however does not disclose what its fate was, except that no one seemed to be working it in 1774.[5]

[1] Trautenberger, *Chronik der Landesauptstadt*, IV, 200.
[2] Slokar, *Geschichte*, 326.
[3] Trautenberger, *Chronik der Landeshauptstadt*, IV, 210.
[4] d'Elvert, *Cultur-feschichte*, 84–6, Being prevented from taking the plans of a new spinning machine out legally, Count Salm secretly purchased a set and calmly folded them around his legs on the voyage across the English Channel. Presumably it was on the basis of these plans, which called for a 66-spindle machine, and a carding engine that Hopf claimed to have invented, that a company was formed in 1806 for the manufacture of textile machines.
[5] HKA, red no. 882, f. 321-49, 31 July 1769; f. 334, 3 Oct. 1774.

Innovation took a firmer hold in Brno in the 1790s. In 1795 Friedrich Wilhelm Offermann, a nephew of the deceased industrialist Johann Heinrich Offermann, arrived with Karl Philipp Eichholz to set up a shop for the manufacture of cloth shears. Eichholz and Offermann stated that they were trying to escape the turmoils of war in western Germany and therefore left Mülheim (Ruhr), the city in which they had resided and where they had been manufacturing shears.[1] The evidence concerning their activities as owners of a factory producing fine cloth shears is somewhat confusing. The nineteenth-century author Christian d'Elvert, who wrote voluminously on numerous details of Brno's history, had them establish their factory as protegees of Biegmann. He furthermore states that it lasted only for three years.[2] The latter assertion is in error; it was not until 1798, or three years after they had arrived in Brno, that they first approached a government office for any purpose. They were successful at that time in having the import duty on fine shears doubled, from one gulden to two gulden.[3]

That Eichholz and Offermann decided to fabricate fine cloth shears in Brno represented as much the forging of an important backward linkage as the introduction of an innovation. All that the two partners claimed was that their shears were as good as the best of those imported. Several years later, however, Offermann requested a privilege for ten years to manufacture shearing machines. The scarcity of labour and the arrogance of the persons employed, he suggested, were major reasons for the introduction of such machines. He promised that the quality of the product would rise and that its cost would decline. One man could operate five machines, and thus would be able to do the work of thirty shearers using the manual method. In this way both the labour costs and the space in a factory for this work would be reduced. Moreover, added the government official in Vienna who passed on this application, it was in finishing that the fine cloth of the Habsburg Monarchy had not reached the standards of quality set in France and England.[4] In approving the privilege, the officials in Vienna specifically

[1] HKA, red no. 845, f. 240–9, 11 Aug. 1798. F. W. Offermann's father was married to Amalia Eichholz. Most likely K. P. Eichholz was therefore related. According to Scheibler, 'Auswanderungen', 64, Offermann's father was from 1797 manager of the Brno woollen-cloth factory bearing his brother's name. Actually, the father, Mathias Offermann, was managing director since 1793 when Johann Heinrich Offermann, the founder died.

[2] d'Elvert, *Cultur-Geschichte*, 83.

[3] HKA, red no. 845, f. 240–9, 11 Aug. 1798.

[4] Unfortunately, the quality of Brno cloth was still inferior to that of foreign competitors in 1812. HKA, red no. 1053, f. 149–60.

rejected the protest of the 650 local journeyman cloth finishers, who maintained that they would be put out of work. Their contention that it was state policy to find remunerative employment for the largest number of persons and that approval for such machines went contrary to long-established policy was easily brushed aside. With the new machine promising so much, the fine-cloth trade would undoubtedly increase, wrote the officials, and would thus provide employment in other areas of the industry for those displaced by the machine.[1] In this way the government officials set aside the welfare implications of Austrian Mercantilism in favour of views more akin to those incorporated in Adam Smith's *Wealth of Nations*.

There being no sketch of the machine in the archives, the nature of the innovation must be derived from the brief description in the forementioned application. The old manual shears were of one piece and during the shearing process had to be oiled frequently, thus smudging the cloth. This problem, the projector claimed, would no longer arise since the machine would have two separate blades, which were probably held in place by fixed frames. With two fingers the blades could be put into operation and consequently a shearer would no longer have to manipulate the sixty-pound-plus, one-piece shears that to an observer today look formidable when merely lying in a museum and seem almost unmanageable when one considers that a man had to hold the one-piece shear and by the force of his arms press the two blades together so that they would cut off only designated tiny strands of the woollen web that stood up. Supposedly, in England most of this work was already done by machine.

While the Offermann factory became in this way one of the important innovators in the Habsburg Monarchy, Hopf and Bräunlich, the other enterprise created in 1786 in Brno, also proved to be a major contributor to industrial progress. Hopf, also known in Brno for his poetry, was partly responsible for the espionage in which the young Count Salm procured drawings of British spinning machines and other preparatory textile machines — a bit of industrial romance, which reminds one of the knightly virtues of great noblemen. Although Salm, as one might expect of rich aristocrats, was soon diverted by other interests, it deserves to be noticed that he continued his innovational industrial activities on his Blansko and Raitz estates, both not far from Brno. He became an important

[1] HKA, red no. 837, f. 8–60.

manufacturer of machinery and in this way contributed greatly to the creation of externalities that aided in the industrial progress of the area.[1]

From the heroic exploit of Salm we must now turn to the more prosaic aspect, that is, the manner in which the English inventions could be made economically useful. In his application for a monopoly for ten years during which no other mechanical spinning establishment would be allowed to operate in the Brno area, Hopf poetically remarked that ten years for an Empire that reached into eternity was not much. Some of his other reasoning was similarly inventive. Probably knowing of the Emperor's fear of a revolutionary industrial proletariat, Hopf maintained that with his set of machines much industrial labour could be saved and workers could therefore return to agricultural pursuits.[2] As further support for this application he pointed to the special difficulties of spinning wool compared to cotton. The officials agreed with him that among the unique problems in spinning wool were the classification of different types of wool and the changing winds of fashion. As Kehrnhofer had also stated several decades before, Hopf noted that orders from customers usually had to precede the manufacture of a piece of coloured cloth. When one realizes that as early as 1761 a manufacturer like Biolley from Verviers went to the annual fair at Frankfurt am Main with sample swatches representing some 130 different colours in one type of cloth alone, one understands the problems presented by Hopf somewhat better. Fashion by this time had a much stronger influence on the market, aided now by numerous printed magazines in a number of different languages. The greater the fineness of the product, the more discriminating would be the clientele. Since Brno was the centre of the fine-woollen cloth industry of the Monarchy, the officials easily agreed that Hopf should have his monopoly. Objections from a local mechanic and from a fine-cloth factory at some distance from Brno were brushed aside. Count Herberstein-Moltke, the official in Vienna who signed the recommendation, also favoured a government loan of 20,000 fl. for the purpose.

[1] See also Freudenberger, 'Progressive Bohemian and Moravian Aristocrats', in S. B. Winters and J. Held eds, *Intellectual and Social Developments in the Habsburg Empire from Maria Theresia to World War I*, (London & New York, 1975), 115–30.

[2] HKA, red no. 837, f. 448–53: 'Bey dieser nun hergestellten Vollkommenheit ihrer Maschinenspinnerey gewinnt zugleich der Staat den grossen Vortheil, dass die durch diese Manufakturwesen dem Ackerbaue entzogenen Hände, und der dadurch erhöhte Taglohn demselben wieder in wohlfeileren Preise zurückfallen.'

In February 1805 Hopf and Company demonstrated the implements manufactured before a group of local officials. For an insight into the technology of the time the detailed report is quite interesting. Twenty-seven pounds of partly white, partly light blue wool was first of all tossed into a willey engine, known as a wolf, where it was loosened and mixed. Specific quantities of the willowed wool were then processed by a second engine, called a *Schrobel Maschine*. A little girl did part of the work. She placed three pounds of wool on the engine and two adult men moved the wheel of the machine. Within one hour they had accomplished the equivalent of twelve persons' work. At the same time the quality of the product was considerably higher than if manually done. During the same time a carding machine was set in motion and the scribbled wool placed on it by a little girl. With a man again supplying the driving power the three pounds of wool were processed within an hour, a feat that eighteen female carders could hardly have accomplished in the same time. Next the finely carded wool was placed on a *Vorspinnmaschine* (slubbing machine) of forty spindles where one man was able to process five pounds within a hour. Finally, the loose, pre-spun yarn was processed on a spinning machine of sixty-six spindles. A female spinner was able to process three-quarters of a pound of pre-spun yarn on this machine within one hour. The result was three hanks (*Strähn*) of yarn, an amount that according to the report would have taken a manual spinner working steadily more than twelve hours to accomplish. The spinning machine, operated by a female spinner and a child, as a piecer, could thus manufacture twenty-four hanks of yarn out of six pounds of pre-spun yarn. Machines with larger numbers of spindles were also to be constructed, the document continued, and one could expect the increasing proficiency of the workers to produce larger quantities soon. Hopf, the officials wrote, was associated in this endeavour with Field Marshal Brady, who was stationed in Brno, Count Salm, Herring, Petke, and, of course, Bräunlich. The firm would be called the 'imperial royal privileged sheep wool-spinning machine works in Brno' (*k.k. privil. Schaafwoll-Spinnmaschinerie in Brünn*).[1]

It turned out that the heroic efforts of Count Salm may have been in vain; similar spinning machines were being introduced elsewhere in the Habsburg Monarchy so that Hopf, Salm, and their fellow projectors were in the end unable to gain a monopoly for themselves

[1] HKA, red no. 837, f. 432–5.

under government protection. Johann Georg Berger & Co. in Liberec, for example, reported that they had one in operation and the woollen-cloth factory of Count Haugwitz at Naměšt was about to receive one from England. Moreover, in Brno itself the Englishman, George Woodward, who had left his native country at the time when John Cockerill did, had already constructed one for the Offermann factory.[1] Although at first Hopf and Company had been accorded a monopoly, it was declared null when it was discovered that others had also introduced spinning machines.

Hopf, of whom Wilhelm Mundy in 1786 had slightingly written that he was no more than a desk man and therefore technologically ignorant, also turned his attention to a shearing and roughing machine. A commission witnessed a demonstration of this machine in 1805 and was duly impressed. With this machine one worker could accomplish a task in six hours, they reported, that previously two men could not have completed in two days. It was a machine that could be constructed by any carpenter and was adapted from the type that was already successfully employed in England and Holland. The Liberec firm of Johann Georg Berger also reported the successful operation of such a machine on its own premises. Nevertheless, Hopf did receive a limited monopoly in 1806 for the construction of the machine in the Brno area for a period of eight years.[2]

The activities of Hopf, Offermann, Herring and others in the first decade of the nineteenth century demonstrate the will to industrialization. This was part of a trend that found its echo elsewhere as for example in the factory of Johann Georg Berger, whose struggle against the clothmakers' guild in Liberec merely to establish a factory had already become legendary.[3] It also became apparent in Lower Austria in the cotton industry when a mechanic from Manchester, John Thornton, was hired by a 'Noble Company . . . [to] make machines to the amount of 50,000 pounds [sterling]', as he wrote back home.[4] This company, which included the Princes Esterhaszy and Schwarzenberg and Count Colloredo-Mansfeld, founded the Pottendorf spinning mill which exists to this day.[5] It was a time when Habsburg industry began to make important

[1] Ibid., f. 713–63, Brünn, 27 April 1808.

[2] Ibid., f. 173–4, 18 July 1805; f. 291, Manetin, 17 July 1805; f. 399, 10 Sept, 1806, on which date the monopoly privilege was approved.

[3] Hermann Hallwich, *Die erste Fabrik in Reichenberg* (Reichenberg, 1869).

[4] University of Manchester, McConnel & Kennedy Papers, Letters 1802.

[5] Cf. Herbert Matis, Die Manufaktur und frühe Fabrik im Viertel unter dem Wiener Wald (Unpublished Ph.D. Dissertation, University of Vienna, 1964).

strides forward in the adoption of the new English inventions. For Brno in particular this decade was merely a preparation for the considerably more innovative one that followed, when despite the fearful monetary crises of 1811 and 1816, new firms were formed for the construction of machinery and as well as for the manufacture of textiles.

One of the new firms founded during this decade was the already mentioned fine-cloth manufacturing enterprise of the Schoeller brothers. With their formal authorization in 1819 they brought into being one of the technologically most progressive textile mills in the entire Monarchy. Among other noteworthy newcomers there were a number of mechanics drawn by the opportunities that the textile industry seemed to represent. Eighteen-fourteen was an especially auspicious year with Daehlen from Eupen, Bonner from Westphalia and Aylardi from Bremen opening a machine shop and the Delhaes brothers from Eupen undertaking to spin wool yarn on a factory basis.[1] In the same year Johann Reiff, a mechanic previously working in Liberec and a native of Württemberg, came to Brno at the request of his relatives, the brothers Schöll, who owned a textile factory. With one of his cousins he established a wool spinning enterprise in one of the town's suburbs. He planned to construct his own machines but for some reason encountered technical difficulties from which another newcomer, Heinrich Alexander Luz, also from Württemberg, was able to extricate him. Following Reiff's death, Luz married the widow and took over the management of the enterprise, which he transformed into a firm manufacturing various textile machines and steam engines. This firm became the most important metal-working manufacturer of the expanding industrial city of Brno in the nineteenth century.[2]

Conclusion

Although the textile industry continued to hold primacy, the manufacture of machines for numerous purposes became an ever more important element in the city's economy. Both the twin leading sectors of industrial revolutions in the eighteenth and nineteenth centuries had come to be settled in Brno. The year 1821 might therefore serve as the fit terminal point for our story. By then

[1] *Die hundertjährige Geschichte der Ersten Brünner Maschinen-Fabriks-Gesellschaft*, (Leipzig, 1921), 10.

[2] Ibid., 8–22.

the textile industry had successfully weathered many crises and the machinery industry was soundly established.

By the middle of the 1820s, Brno's population reached nearly 36,000.[1] It had more than doubled since 1764 when the original fine-cloth factory settled there. The increasing prosperity that we presume to have accompanied Brno's industrialization was to a large extent a function of the Köffiller firm and its direct successors. In the light of this accomplishment the prophetic statement of an Austrian official in 1767 that the sound establishment of the original factory would automatically result in industrial expansion bears repetition.[2] A horizontal expansion did take place in the 1780s and 1790s. Government policies and war demand helped the industry to proliferate at such a swift rate that in the late 1810s bankruptcies hit many of the enterprises that were linked directly with the Köffiller woollen mill. The new enterprises created an even firmer foundation for further industrial progress in Brno.

[1] Vytiska, 'Brnenska průmyslová oblast', 345 n.

[2] HKA, red no. 892, f. 555–61, Degelmann, Referent of a meeting of the Court Commercial Council reported the sense of the meeting in 1767: 'Diese Vermehrung ergibt sich bey dem Forgange der [Fabrik] von selbsten . . . .'

CONCLUSION

The study of Brno's early industrialization should contribute to a further understanding of economic development in the Habsburg Monarchy. Besides serving this purpose, it may also provide a demonstration of industrial growth within a region. It shows one of the methods through which such growth can be induced. Strong government intervention was unquestionably the catalyst. This statement conforms to the standard interpretation of Brno's industrialization. What has been added in this study is an emphasis on the historical preparation that covered the preceding hundred years. According to this hypothesis, a 'gestation' period of about one century preceded the 'vital event', the establishment in Brno of a woollen mill in 1764. The industrial expansion of the region that took place in the nineteenth century can essentially be traced back to this woollen mill. Hence, the bulk of this study has been devoted to a detailed examination of the enterprise.

Since the basis for Brno's regional take-off into modern industrialization was laid during the time of the 'Enlightened Monarch', Joseph II, it is all too easy to jump to the conclusion that this was a case of successful eighteenth-century Rationalism. If Rationalism was practiced under the presumption that man can be manipulated in a skilful manner to provide the means for progress, then the governments of Maria Theresia and Joseph II may be justifiably congratulated on a victory of well-applied Mercantilism. Closer scrutiny and speculative reflection suggest, however, that this ahistorical conclusion is not tenable. Instead, a historical preparation took place, lasting for a century, during which indigenous forces combined with outside influences from the capital of the Monarchy in Vienna to create the conditions in which the massive introduction of government support in the 1760s and 1770s could be successful. It would nevertheless be an unwarranted conclusion that this process of preparation went on in a premeditated or planned fashion. To separate the conscious measures from the unconscious developments we have tried to examine factors that seem to have been instrumental in determining success.

Having speculated on the environment in Brno and the Habsburg Monarchy that permitted Mercantilist government a wide area of action, we turned to a detailed examination of the channel through which success was achieved. Direct linkages between one particular industrial enterprise, the Brno Fine-Cloth Factory, and the proliferation of manufacturing enterprises that followed it, first on a horizontal and then on a vertical basis, have been documented. In the process an attempt was made to outline the 'social learning' process that was required for the industrialization of Brno. Although this study is restricted primarily to the examination of one occurrence in time and place, it is meant at the same time to serve as a useful base for generalization. All regional urban industrializations did not follow the same path as that of Brno; but all went through a social learning process.

Despite the proviso that Brno was subject to a century of preparation, there is little doubt that the city owed the drive to industrialization to Mercantilistic government policies whose aim was the rapid economic development of the Hereditary Lands of the Habsburg Monarchy. It was, moreover, operating under the pressure of having lost through war one of its most flourishing territories, a gap which had to be replaced at least in terms of the revenues of the state. Following a century of haphazard measures and unconscious efforts, Brno became a focus of specific and direct central government policy. While modern sophistication cannot be claimed for this policy, it still can be considered an early effort of conscious central planning.

Part of Habsburg planning had as its goal the use of unemployed resources within the Monarchy in order to induce economic growth. Serf labour and surplus agricultural products were to be used more effectively. The wars in the 1740s and especially the painful loss of Silesia, a province that has been called the wholesaler for other Habsburg lands like Bohemia and Moravia before 1740, resulted in severe economic dislocations. To mend these injuries and to achieve greater economic prowess, the central government took deliberate steps in the direction of achieving autarky. Mercantilistic principles were invoked toward that goal, part of which was to make the country independent of foreign sources of supply. Fine woollens consumed in the Monarchy originated almost totally abroad. To cut off this drain of resources abroad the central authorities had to organize the transfer of techniques from more advanced areas so that the manufacture of fine woollens could find a firm footing in the Monarchy. It proved to be no simple task.

Technologically, fine woollens were manufactured following the same basic processes as coarser cloths. The transfer of woollen technology by means of a cadre of skilled workers from Verviers, a city that served as a major supplier of fine woollens for much of Central and East-Central Europe, became, therefore, more a problem of social adaptation than of a new technology. A first effort for the French-speaking craftsmen to act as teachers-by-demonstration in Jihlava, an ancient woollen centre, met with such hostility that they were moved as a body to the more controlled if less congenial setting of a small village on a large agricultural estate. Numerous factors, including poor communications and transport, distance from markets, conflicts with manorial officials, misdirected efforts to use native wool, managerial and entrepreneurial errors and the destructive influence of the Seven-Years War contributed to the failure of the village factory after more than ten years of trial and error. It became very clear that it was vain to expect the mere transportation of a technology from another place, with the hope that the natural propensities of man abetted and supported by high personages and government officials from afar, would complete the process of adoption and adaptation. More than learning and assimilating merely technology, it was a problem of social change. Man may indeed be motivated by self-interest, but his self-interest is not simply the enhancement of what the disinterested outsider considers sufficient to promote his material welfare. The guildsmen of Jihlava carried their pride and their history with them when they showed apparent preference for their own property over the promise of wealth. Similarly, the Verviers craftsmen, once they were settled in the little Bohemian village of Kladruby, must have felt very isolated, especially faced by the undisguised hostility of the manorial officials and lack of interest of the peasants. They had been torn completely out of their milieu and for over a decade failed to take root in the rural setting.

Was it then the government's purpose to surround them with urban elements in Brno that the woollen enterprise was moved from the Bohemian village? If so, was it a congenial atmosphere in the provincial capital that made adoption of new techniques easier? Or was success in Brno merely a function of coincidence and stubborn persistence? With a massive input of capital, success might as well have occurred elsewhere. Managerial and entrepreneurial problems were not solved without infusion from the outside. Presumably, the town of 15,000 was somewhat more attractive than a tiny village of a few hundred souls. On the other hand, the manager who took over the reins of the enterprise and brought success had lived many years in Monschau, a very small, picturesque town deep in the Eifel mountains of western Germany.

More important than any other locational advantage was the presence in Brno of persons who were deeply interested in having the enterprise prosper. It is therefore with good reason that the entrepreneurial function was discussed in considerable detail in this study. In a modified way, the Schumpeterian entrepreneur served as an excellent heuristic device. Over the forty years during which the enterprise in its various forms existed, many persons were engaged in the entrepreneurial function. They included the Emperor of the Holy Roman Empire and consort of Maria Theresia, the ruler of the Habsburg Monarchy; the Empress herself; Baron Toussaint, the Emperor's chief adviser; von Degelmann, permanent undersecretary of the Court Commercial Council; Kehrnhofer, a government official in Brno and head of the Moravian Loan Bank, which transferred the personnel and equipment of the factory to Brno; and Köffiller, the young heir to a merchant's fortune, who retained control until the firm's bankruptcy. All their decisions weighed heavily in the fate of the woollen mill and the region of Brno. Not surprisingly in the absence of full internal documentation much of the discussion was on a speculative plane. For the persons named, it seems hardly debatable that profit maximization played a subordinate role. Although none spurned increased income, they probably looked more to power and prestige as fulfilling their personal goals. How well they may have achieved such goals need not greatly concern us. Considerably more relevant is the likelihood that they were in this way moved along paths that were uncharted and full of various risks.

Strategic decisions of entrepreneurs had to be complemented by managerial activities, and high purpose had to be implemented on a day-to-day operational basis. In the age of small enterprises and industry spread over the countryside, there were numerous problems of organization and little experience on which to base solutions. It was a time of learning all over Europe. Few persons had experience of managing large bodies of workers in industrial pursuits. Probably even more than with the entrepreneurs, speculation and imaginative guesswork is required to gain insights into management. For over twenty years the enterprise limped along, propped up by numerous outside infusions, because no leader could be found to place the enterprise on a solid footing. All who concerned themselves with the fate of the enterprise pointed to the critical nature of the leadership position. At one of the many crisis points, an outside expert, himself a Belgian woollen manufacturer resident in the Austrian lands, was eventually able to identify the problem succinctly and to outline the type of person who could provide the solution.

This problem was well-documented; the position of other management personnel including book-keepers, purchasing and sales officials and foremen is, however, shrouded in considerable darkness. Yet, when it comes to the detailed organization of modern enterprise, the function of leadership on intermediate levels takes on great importance. One of the chief features of the sophisticated firm is, after all, the ability to internalize operations and to allow the enterpriser to exercise direct control over as many processes as possible. In an enterprise that produces for a specialized high-quality clientele, this control becomes especially important.

Of the functions that fall into the intermediate management category, sales operations proved most susceptible to intensive discussion. The question of sales is not merely a functional problem but the basis of success or failure for the entire venture. Assuming that information from the tariff authorities concerning the importation of fine woollen cloths constituted an accurate indication of the domestic market, it is clear that a large quantity could be sold. In a situation in which a less-developed country tries to replace outside sources of supply for manufactured goods, the quality of the product is often inferior and cost of production high. This means that without support and protection from governments, the developing economy has trouble 'learning by doing'. Since the new native product is unable to compete on equal terms with the import, governments resort to various coercive measures, many of which were applied by the Habsburg government in favour of the woollen mill. Government officials put merchants under pressure to purchase and when convincing proved impossible, force was used. Jewish communities were ordered to buy. The merchant communities of various towns were assigned quotas. Military units were obligated to purchase these goods. And on a more indirect basis, protective tariffs and the prohibition of imports were imposed to aid the infant industry.

Documentary evidence on the buildings and equipment is short. This is of course not unique for the Brno enterprise. As a matter of fact considerably more data are available than for numerous firms in England and elsewhere that in themselves may have been more important. By extracting the pertinent bits of information and examining them in some detail, a framework for a more general study of early industrialization may possibly be formed.

A comparison with other contemporary enterprises aids this goal. Fortunately there is much information available on at least two other Mercantilistic protofactories whose purpose was the manufacture of fine woollen cloths. One of these was located in the western

Bohemian village of Horní Litvinov from 1715 to about 1870.[1] The second was the factory of Jean Thys, whose advice to the authorities has been referred to frequently in the course of this study.

In all three factories there was learning by training as well as learning by demonstration, with workers who had been recruited abroad serving as the instructors. As far as the Waldstein works is concerned, one may be permitted to conclude that the workers did not reach a high level of skill during its first century of operation, but that from about 1819 the introduction of modern machines resulted in the production of a competitive product. Brno had a briefer learning period possibly because of the greater confluence of ideas and the greater exposure to outside influences. Thys died in the 1770s, after having been in the Monarchy only slightly over a decade, during which time he had advised upon the most efficient operation of the three firms. With his death the factory that he had lead stagnated, although it continued to function under his son for several decades more. In all three cases success seems to have been determined by the direct interest of forceful personalities. Although outstanding personalities deserve to be stressed, the fact that no obstinate traditional vested interests were in the way of the learning process helped.

Recruiting labour was at least as much a problem in the Brno factory as in factories all over Europe including England in the late eighteenth century. And as in the English textile industry, spinning was one of the more important problems. Through coercion and forced labour sufficient yarn was to become available. According to a law of 1765 all girls were required to learn to spin. Entire villages were to be placed at the disposal of particular textile firms, and orphanages were established for the purpose. The Brno management insisted at one point that without the subsidized labour of orphans the enterprise was bound to fail. Free labour was not forthcoming in sufficient quantity since the wages were too low for a child, let alone an adult, to subsist on. Higher wages would have increased costs even beyond the level at which sizeable subsidies from government and private owners could sustain the enterprise. From time to time there was talk of introducing spinning machines but even in England there was a long time-lag between invention and application in the woollen industry.

Despite the numerous problems and crises that beset the woollen mill, eventually it proved a public success at the same time that it

[1] This was the Waldstein woollen mill.

became a private disaster. Late in the 1780s it crumbled under the strains of many years of troubles multiplied by the war with Turkey. Nevertheless, Mercantilistic government policy scored a resounding triumph when one after another of the leading persons in the Brno woollen mill made themselves independent manufacturers. In this way they provided serious competition for the enterprise that had spawned them while at the same time they represented the draining of vitality from it. The efforts of the government and the use of the public revenues in supporting this enterprise for numerous years were thus vindicated. For Köffiller, the chief proprietor for over twenty years, the satisfaction of having been a viable tool in the industrializing policies of the state was necessarily made bitter by the sacrifice of much of his wealth. Bankruptcy did not make him a pauper, however, due to his wife's inheritance and his own position as a well-salaried public official, a position that he gained only a few years before the grand debacle.

With the firm's former employees successfully expanding Brno's textile industry there also came vertical linkages. Manufacturers of finisher's shears, of spinning machines and eventually of steam engines and other sophisticated machinery settled in the town. From textile machines they moved to machines for sugar refining and for numerous other purposes.

What this study has attempted is to specify the means by which the soil was for a century prepared to take the acorn from which the great oak of a modern industrial city grew. The Manchester of Austria of the nineteenth century has become the second largest city of Czechoslovakia, and its permanent seat for the country's international industrial fair.

Appendix A

ARCHITECTURE AND LOCATION OF BUILDINGS

Are the problems that prevented the enterprise from being managed successfully the structure of the buildings and their location? The original plant when the enterprise was brought to Brno in 1764 was a small complex of buildings that had formerly served as a starch house (*Stärkehaus*). Purchased by the government for 4,000 fl., it required immediate repairs amounting to 600 fl. by masons, carpenters and other craftsmen. Even then the building was insufficient for the purposes of the new factory.[1] Possibly it was little more than a warehouse separated into a number of rooms around a rectangular courtyard.[2]

Moreover, many of the workers, above all those recruited from abroad as well as some of the supervisory personnel, were living in the factory buildings themselves. For example, the press master had his family quarters in the immediate vicinity of the presses whereas the finishing room in which the cloth had to be processed before it reached the press master was at the other end of the building. This example, it must be added, is taken from a plan of a building prior to its construction and therefore demonstrates a lack of forethought rather than the intractability of a given environment. At the time when plans for the expansion were made, the inclusion of living quarters for some of the personnel was still very much the custom. When Köffiller negotiated with the government officials for the acquisition of the enterprise, workers and their families were still living in the factory buildings without paying rent. In order to expand he requested that these people be moved out to make room for the increasing number of looms that the government was pressing

[1] HKA, red no. 891, f. 396–406, 6 Dec. 1763; red no. 892, f. 444–8, 29 Dec. 1766.

[2] Compare Freudenberger and Redlich, 'The Industrial Development of Europe', 385–92. This was of course not at all unusual even for English factories in the 1790s when the virtues of purpose-built plants were already known. As a matter of fact, it seems very reasonable to suspect that the English word factory is derived from the term warehouse and that the German word *Fabrik* very likely also referred to a large building. When the operators of industrial plants thought of them simply as large, roofed places in which groups that had previously worked in their own homes or in a small workshop would not be concentrated, they did not concern themselves with the benefits of meshing the various processes.

for. He did not, however, suggest an adjustment in wages, rent-free quarters obviously being part of the wages paid at that particular time.[1] Eventually, 44 houses were constructed by the company next to the main factory building. Rent was most probably charged, as was the case in numerous other worker colonies in England and elsewhere. Brno's chronicler gives credit for the construction of these houses to Seitter's background in Augsburg, where the famous Fuggerei provided living quarters for poor persons.[2]

Workers and other personnel living on the premises of the factory was not the only locational factor that inhibited a smooth operation. The fact that the production processes were spread out over four separate locations in the 1780s was harmful and having it in three places early in the 1770s was a point that Thys criticized sharply when he came to examine the enterprise in one of its times of trouble. That the buildings were separated from each other came partly by chance and partly by necessity. The accidental part concerns the acquisition of the plush factory in the Schwabengasse suburb which was meant to be a completely independent enterprise and the house purchased by the company of five Brno cloth merchants in the Kleine Kröna suburb which was also meant to be the site for a separate enterprise. Necessity came in with the construction of a dyehouse and a fullery. In 1767 when Köffiller took over the factory, the government agreed to purchase the so-called *Teichtmühle* in Husovice (Hussowitz), an area in which there was a pond and a gristing mill driven by water power, for 4,500 fl. and erected a water-driven press for making red dye, a mill for wheels used for polishing and sharpening shears, and a dyehouse. For the fullery, however, a memorandum reported that many difficulties arose since all the streams within an Austrian mile (*c.* 6 English miles) of the town were being fully used for various purposes including leather tanning. The problem was apparently solved by a costly digging operation on the mill pond that had been purchased not far from the factory in the Neugasse suburb.[3] Nevertheless, some of the benefits of internalizing the manufacturing processes, one of the chief benefits of the protofactory, were not realized and time and money had to be devoted to these processes, thereby increasing production costs.

We have spoken of the suburbs in which the buildings were located. Actually, these were short streets outside the town walls. The

[1] HKA, red no. 892, f. 565–602, 1 Sept. 1767, 'Pro Memoria'.
[2] Trautenberger, *Die Chronik der Landeshaupstadt*, III, 145.
[3] HKA, red no. 892, f. 533–8, Brünn, 11 April 1767.

original building purchased by Kehrnhofer for the factory was in the Grosse Neugasse. The three other buildings, while they were formally in areas owned by manors, were for all practical purposes under the civil jurisdiction of the city as well.[1] Usually, social status attached to living within the city walls; factories and factory workers were obviously outside the pale of reasonably good society, which included the guild masters. Köffiller, the major owner, was, of course, as the wealthiest burger of the city, resident in the most desirable quarter of the city, living in a house facing the market place. In addition to the undesirability of a factory within the walled town there was also the more economic factor of a shortage of land. Burghers and the provincial nobility had so completely crowded the city with buildings that there was a constant spillover of humans into the suburbs where they were unprotected against the onslaught of foreign armies. The last war in which the walls still provided protection, and in which the neighbouring countryside was devastated, was the Seven Years War (1756–1763) when the Prussian King appeared before Brno's gates.

How did one of these building complexes look? It comprised several buildings surrounding one or more courtyards. The original building seems to have been of one-storey with a basement, separated in the centre by a large entrance way to the street.[2] The first courtyard measured 10 klafter long and 8 klafter wide, i.e., about 19 metres by 15 metres, though an architectural drawing of the factory building suggests a different set of dimensions for the courtyard (see illustration). If the plans accurately showed the building as it appeared before extensive modifications were made, then the courtyard was 25 klafter (about 38 metres) or double as long; moreover it was open at one end or abutted on to a hill or on another structure. The first architectural drawing suggests that the house was originally only one storey high; the second drawing reveals that a second storey was to be added. In the descriptive inventory of 1769, however, there was no mention of the second storey; it had probably not then been constructed. Moreover, a separate drawing in the state archives of Brno (the others are to be found in the *Hofkammerarchiv* in Vienna) shows a front elevation of a one-storey building and the same array of rooms as the drawings presumably

[1] SAB, C/12/45, 'D'. See also, d'Elvert *Landeshaupstadt Brünn*, 334–5; Kleine Kröna. N. 33, k.k. Tuchfabrik und Wollspinnhaus, Radlass (Kameralherrschaft Königsfeld), No. 10 Grosse Neugass (Herrschaft Rzeckowitz, Stadt Brünn and Königsfeld), No. 26, 27, and 28, Schwabengasse (Herrschaft Rzeckowitz), No. 10.

[2] HKA, red no. 893, f. 947–63, ad 18 Jan. 1769 'Inventarium'.

made in 1763 when Kehrnhofer prepared memorandums for the transfer of the factory to Brno. It seems very likely that these plans do not show the factory complex in the Grosse Neugasse in its entirety, since a second courtyard and a field which were mentioned in the inventory of 1769 are not shown. The second courtyard may in fact have been a garden whose dimensions were 46 × 14 klafter (88 × 27 metres). Beyond the garden there was a field, 82 klafter long and 14 klafter wide (155 × 27 metres) in which a forty-ell tentering frame for the stretching and drying of the cloth was located.

In 1766 the government officials who comprised the 'Factory Directorate' proposed a major extension of the factory. They suggested that since the building in the back courtyard was threatening to collapse and inasmuch as the manufacturing capacity of the factory was to be expanded anyhow, a solid construction project costing 2,558 fl. should be undertaken.[1] Unfortunately, the mason's drawing that had accompanied the memorandum is no longer among the documents and no measurements were included in the text. Although it is impossible to specify in detail how this building looked and how the manufacturing processes were arranged, it is certain that substantial revisions were undertaken during the 1760s. In 1767 for example, it was said that it would take 6,068 fl. to make 26 weaving rooms out of the six living quarters (*Wohnungen*) in the back courtyard. This may have been no more than a proposal. Most likely a more modest renovation costing only 2,558 fl. as approved by the Court Accounting Office (*Hofbuchhalterey*) was undertaken. This would mean that a minimum of 6,558 fl. had been invested, though a valuation of only 3,500 fl. was placed on the building in 1780.[2] A master carpenter and a master mason made this assessment and it was accepted as the price for which the firm bought the building from the government.

As mentioned above two other enterprises were merged with the original factory company, each having begun operations in its own building. One of these was located in the Schwabengasse suburb at a distance of about 720 klafter or about 136 metres from the first building. The house in the Schwabengasse was also owned by the government, having been purchased to function as a velvet and serge factory for 2,600 fl. to which should be added 2,265 fl. in renovating costs.[3] The fine-woollen cloth works took it over eventu-

[1] HKA, red no. 892, f. 545–615, 22 Oct. 1767.
[2] SAB, C/12/45, f. 00706, Brünn, 1 May 1780.
[3] HKA, red no. 892, f. 545–615, 22 Oct. 1767.

ally first for housing orphans prior to the formation of a governmental orphanage and later primarily for spinning. This building seems to have been mainly employed for the spinning of yarn.

The Schwabengasse building was considerably closer to the original factory in the Grosse Neugasse than the two other buildings. One of these was located on the opposite side of the town in the Kleine Kröna suburb. It was a building purchased in 1768 for 4,300 fl. by the company of five cloth merchants who for a brief period of time had opened their own factory and then pooled resources with Köffiller.[1] In order to pass from the Grosse Neugasse factory to the building in the Kleine Kröna, one had to pass through the crowded town of Brno. Goods that might have to be transported from one to the other building would have to be taken over a distance of about 1,120 klafter or more than 2 km. by way of two of the town gates. This was particularly inefficient, and the fourth building was even further away. The fullery was located in a area called Hussowitz, 1,600 klafter or over 3 km. from the Grosse Neugasse building and 2,000 klafter or nearly 4 km. from the Kleine Kröna building. It depended of course on the flow of water for its operation and its location was consequently more a function of the availability of a stream of water than of any other decisional factor. As things stood, water rights closer to town were all taken up so that the government found no other means of supplying the woollen mill with the required service than by purchasing and refurbishing this unit that was so far away from the other ones. Quite clearly, the costs of transportation were increased severely by this dispersal and thus one of the main economies entailed in a factory was unharnessed. In addition, as Thys succinctly pointed out in 1771 when he acted as the government's chief adviser, good supervision of the production processes was almost impossible and one of the most important causes of the troubles of the firm.[2] The highly dispersed nature of the productive facilities persisted until the end of the mill's existence and unquestionably contributed to its demise.

When the fateful day came in 1789 that work had to stop in the enterprise, the facilities of the Grosse Neugasse complex had been greatly expanded. In 1783 two houses that adjoined the factory had been purchased for a total of 3,625 fl.[3] When a master mason and a master carpenter estimated the value of this portion of the com-

[1] SAB, M 2110, f. 249, Brünn, 23 Mar. 1789.
[2] HKA, red no. 893, f. 290–335 (61 ex Sept. 771 Böhm).
[3] SAB, M 2110, f. 247, Brünn, 23 Mar. 789.

pany's assets they settled on a sum of 24,350 fl. which according to the detailed description did not include any equipment.[1] One of the former employees, Heinrich Schmal, bought three parts of the complex and two other men purchased each one of the other portions, all paying the sums assigned by the mason and the carpenter.[2] The Schwabengasse building went for only 1,600 fl. indicating that it had deteriorated since the time of its purchase. Similarly, the Kleine Kröna complex brought in only 3,254 fl. — considerably less than the original purchase price. Finally, the fullery was sold for 7,689 fl., a higher price than the original purchase price plus the renovating costs, since it included valuable water rights.[3]

By the time that the firm went bankrupt, all the buildings housed basically productive facilities. In the 1760s, however, this was not the case as the extant plans demonstrate conclusively; workers as well as officials of the firm lived inside the factory, thus permitting a continuation of the paternally orientated family life that had presumably been the case prior to the introduction of the factory. Even after the workers were evicted from the factory buildings themselves about 1780, they could easily have kept to their social family system inasmuch as they were then located in a workers' colony immediately in the vicinity of the Grosse Neugasse complex.

[1] Ibid., f. 39–40, Brünn, 10 Dec. 1793.
[2] SAB, M 2110, f. 239–40.
[3] SAB, M 2110, f. 4, 15 Mar. 1793.

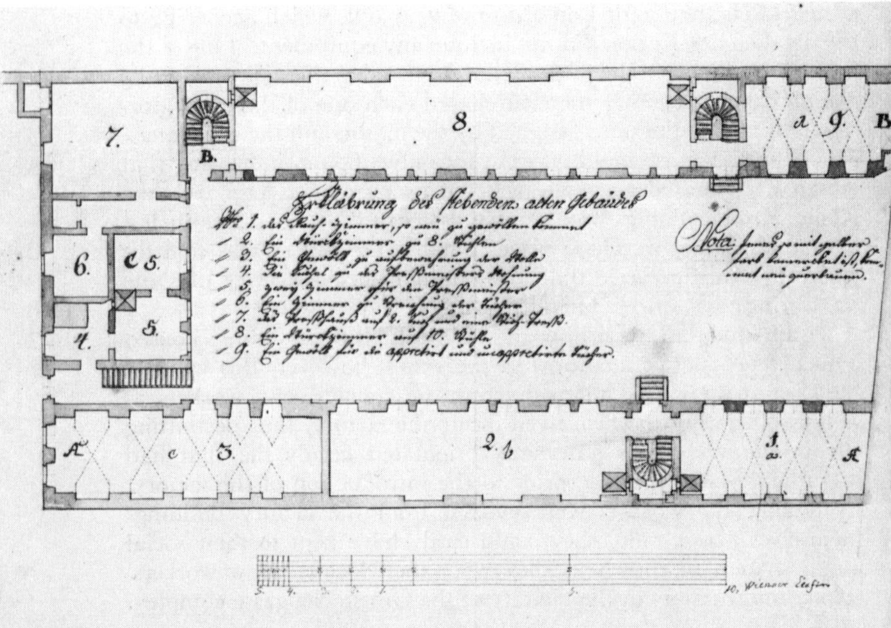

Plan of the fine cloth factory in Grosse Neugasse in 1764: the ground floor (SAB, KKT 1763, 13/207).

Erklährung des stehenden alten Gebaüdes (Explanation of the old building).

No. 1 Das Rauh-Zimmer, so neu zu gewölben kommet (The roughing room in which the ceiling has to be fixed).

No. 2 Ein Würckzimmer zu 8 Stühlen (A weaving room for 8 looms).

No. 3 Ein Gewölb zu Aufbewahrung der Wolle (A storeroom for wool).

No. 4 Die Kuchel zu des Pressmeisters Wohnung (The kitchen adjoining the living quarters of the master presser).

No. 5 Zwey Zimmer für den Pressmeister (Two rooms for the master presser).

No. 6 Ein Zimmer zu Streichung der Tücher (One room for finishing of cloth).

No. 7 Das Presshauss auf 2. Tuch und eine Stich-Press (The Press house for two cloth presses and a small press).

No. 8 Ein Würckzimmer auf 10. Stühle (A weaving room for 10 looms).

No. 9 Ein Gewölb für die appretirt und unapretirte Tücher (A storeroom for finished and unfinished cloths).

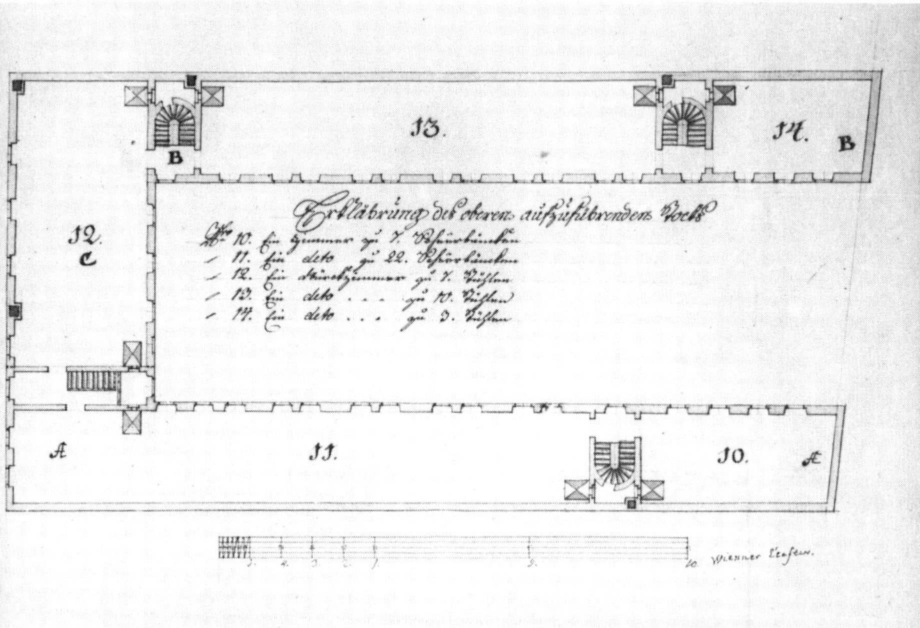

Plan of the fine cloth factory in Grosse Neugasse, in 1764: the proposed second floor (SAB, KKT 1763, 13/207).

Erklährung des oberen aufzuführenden Stocks (Explanation for the second storey, which is to be constructed).

No. 10 Ein Zimmer zu 7. Scheerbäncken (A room with 7 sheering tables).

No. 11 Ein deto zu 22 Scheerbäncken (A room with 22 shearing tables).

No. 12 Ein Würckzimmer zu 7. Stühlen (A weaving room for 7 looms).

No. 13 Ein deto zu 10 Stühlen (A weaving room for 10 looms).

No. 14 Ein deto zu 3 Stühlen (A weaving room for 3 looms).

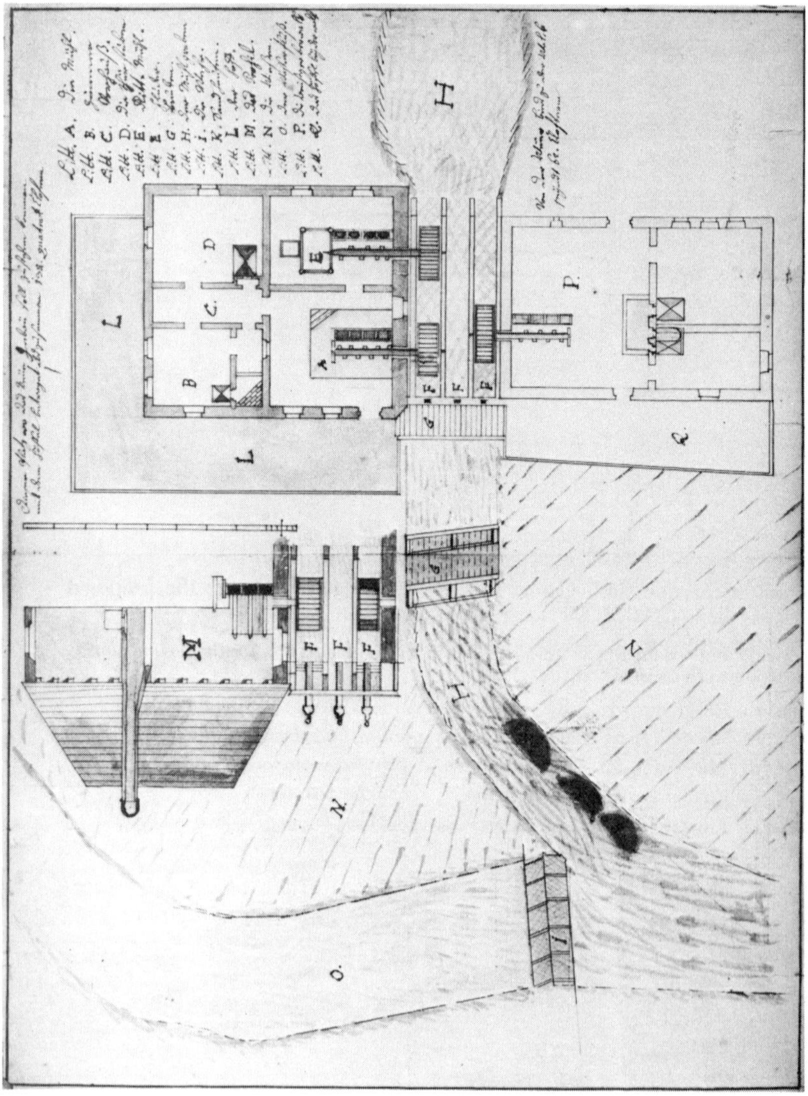

Dieser Platz wo das Neue Gebaü soll zustehen kommen mit dem Höffel betraget als zusammen 133 quatrat Claftern (This place where the new building is to be constructed, with the little courtyard, measures together 133 square Klafter).

Litt. A	Die Muhl (The mill)
Litt. B	Zimmer (Rooms)
Litt. C	Vorhauss (Hallway)
Litt. D	Die Thürstuben (The door room)
Litt. E	Ritt Mühl
Litt. F	Fluder (Float)
Litt. G	Brücken (Bridges)
Litt. H	Der Mühlgraben (The mill run)
Litt. I	Die Wehr (The weir)
Litt. K	Sandhaufen (Sand pile)
Litt. L	Der Hof (The courtyard)
Litt. M	Das Profil (The front elevation)
Litt. N	Die Wiessen (The meadows)
Litt. O	Der Wasserfluss (The stream)
Litt. P	Die Weissgerberwalk (The fullery for the tanner)
Litt. Q	Das Höffel bei der Walk (The yard by the fullery)

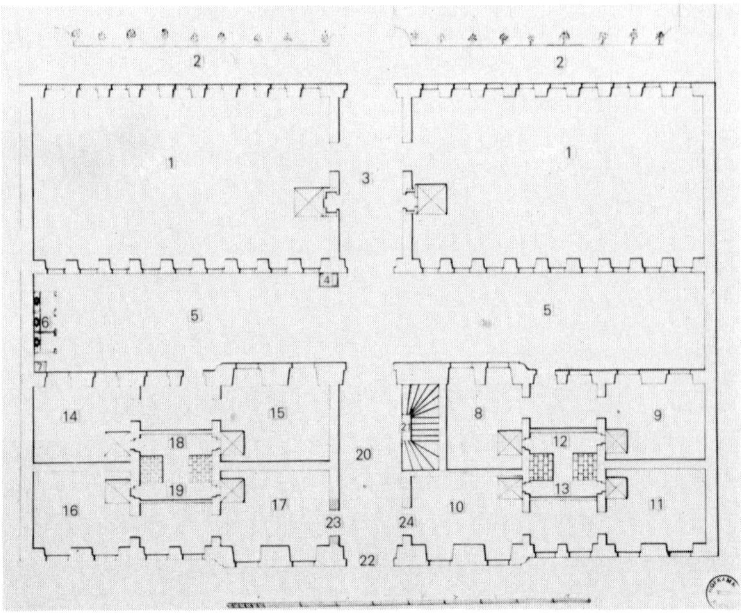

Plan of the Schwabengasse Plush factory in 1767: ground floor (HKA, red. No. 892, f. 437).

Accompanying the plan is the following description:
Beschreibung des gegen über stehenden Grundrisses zum Bau der Pluschfabrik (Description of the accompanying plan for the construction of the plush factory).

No.

1. Die zwey grosse Arbeits Zimmer, in deren jeden von beeden Steiten 10 und also in allem 40 Wurkstühle aufgestellet werden sollen (The two large work rooms in which on both sides each 10 looms are to be placed, i.e., 40 looms altogether).
2. Ist der andere Hof 18 bis 20 Klafter lang und 7 bis 8 Klafter breit gegen den Garten zu (The other yard is 18 to 20 Klafter long and 7 to 8 Klafter wide in the direction of the garden).
3. Der Gang oder Durchfahrt aus dem ersten Hofe in den zweiten (The passageway from the first to the second yard).
4. Platz wo der eigene Brunn angebracht werden soll (Place where the fountain is to be located).
5. Der erste Hof aus den Wohnungs Gebaü (The first yard next to the living quarters building).
6. die S.V. Abtritte (The latrines).
7. Der Canal und Ablauf des Wassers (The canal for the water).

8., 9., 10., 11. } Die Wohnungs Zimmer der beeden Fabriks Meistern (The living rooms of the two factory masters).

12., 13. } beederseitige Kucheln und Einheitzungen (Kitchens and heaters for both).

14.–17. Vier Wohungen für die Arbeits Leute (Four apartments for the working people).
18.–19. Kucheln und Einheitzungen für diesselbe (Kitchens and heaters for the same).
20. Gang oder Durchfahrt nach dem ersten Hof (Passage to the first yard).
21. Die Stiegen in den Obern Stok (Staircase to the upper storey).
22. Das Portal oder Eingang in das Fabrik Haus (Gate or entrance into the factory building).
23.–24. Zwo neu zu erbrechenden Thüren in due Wohnungs Zimmer (Two doors to be constructed in the living rooms).

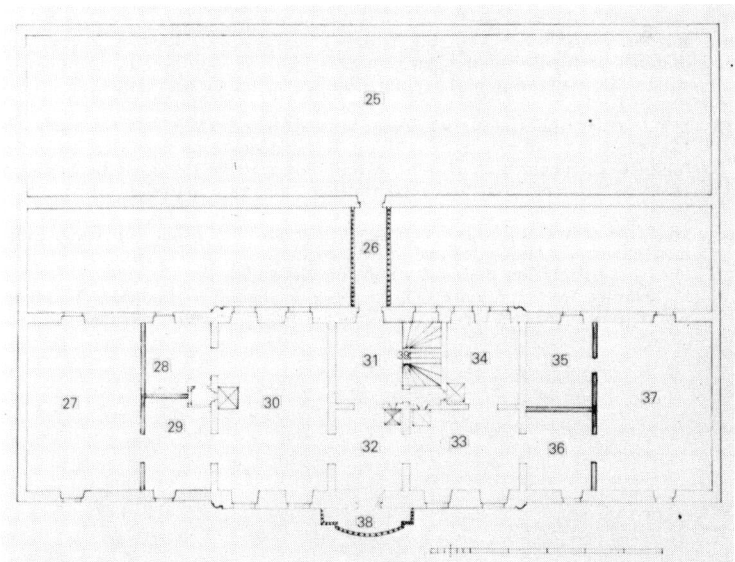

Plan of the Schwabengasse Plush factory in 1767: upper storey (HKA, red No. 892, f. 437).

Accompanying the plan is the following description:
Beschreibung des gegenüber stehenden Grundrisses des obern Stoks der Plusch-fabrik (Description of the sketch for the upper storey of the Plush Factory).

No.
25. Der Boden über die beeden Arbeits Zimmer zum Abtroknen der Wolle un des Gespünstes (The loft above the two working rooms for the drying of wool and yarn).
26. Der Gang nach dem grossen Boden (The passageway to the large loft).
27. Eine Art von Boden, welcher aber gedillt, mit Rohrböden und solchen Wänden versehen, und zu einen Behätnis für Waaren und Wolle tauglich gemacht wird (A type of loft which has fastened-down reed floorboards and has such walls that are useful as a storeroom for merchandise and wool).

28. Ein Platz, wo die Stiegen auf diesen Separirten untern Boden angebracht und zugleich das grosse Zimmer No. 30 geheitzt werden kann (A place where the staircase for the separate lower loft is to be found and where at the same time the large room No. 30 can be heated).
29. Ein Gemach zur Stelle der Corroy und Appretirung der Plüschen (A room for the finishing of the plush fabrics).
30. Das Grosse Zimmer, in welchem die Zwirnmühle und Schweifrahmen wie auch die Blätmühle, getrieben und gebraucht wird (A large room in which the yarn mill is placed; there is also a finishing frame).
31. Das Vorhaus zu dem Zimmer No. 32 (The hallway to the Room No. 32).
32. Ein Spinn Zimmer (A spinning room).
33. Das Schreibzimmer für den Factor (The factor's office).
34. Das Schlaf und Wohnungszimmer des Factors (The bedroom and livingroom of the factor).
35. Die Stiegen auf den tiefern Boden des rechten Flügels (The staircase for the lower loft in the right wing).
36. Ein Vorgemach zur Material Kammer und Verwahrung des gespühlten, doublirt und gezwirnten Kammelhaares (An anteroom for the chamber in which raw material as well as spun, doubled camelhair and camelhair thread is stored).
37. Der zu einer Material Kammer und Verwahrung des Wollen Gespünstes mit Legung eines hölzernen Fuss dann Rohrbodens wie auch Rohrwänden tauglich zu machenden Boden (A loft that is to be prepared by laying a wooden and reed floor and reed walls to store raw materials and woollen yarn).
38. Der über den Haupt Thor befindliche Balcan oder Erker von Eisen (The iron balcony that is located over the main gate).
39. Die Stiege nach den Boden des höheren Gebäudes, wo allenfalls auch dolle aufbehalten werden könnte (The staircase to the loft of the higher building, where wool could be stored).

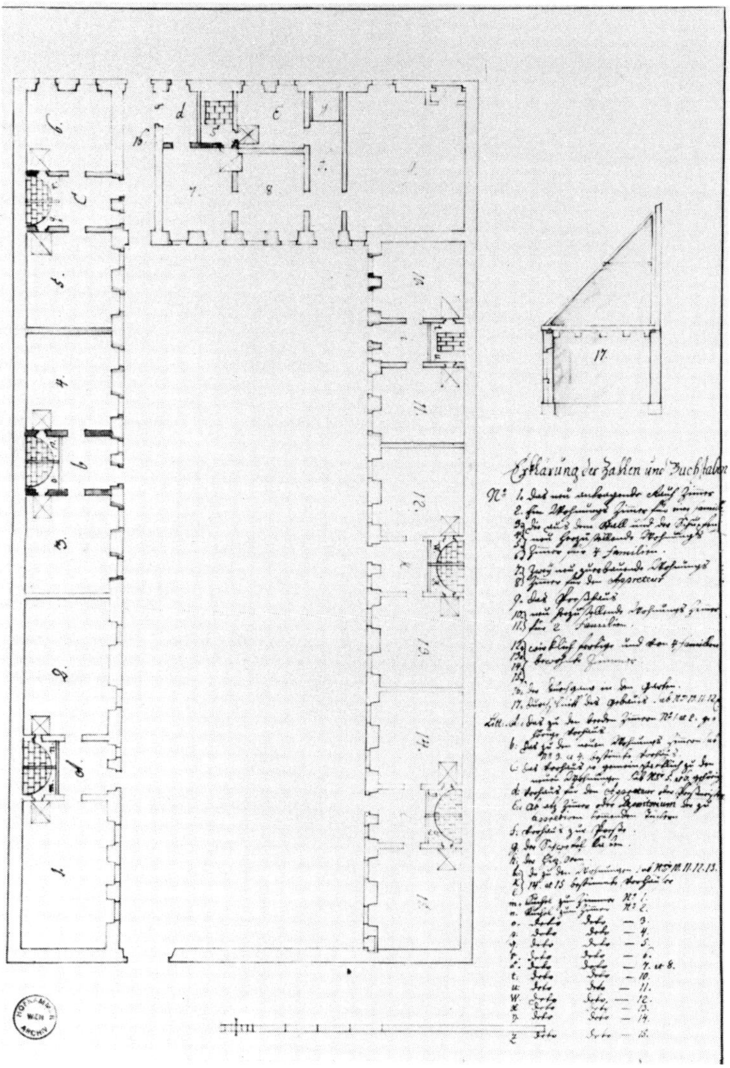

Plan of the Schwabengasse Plush Factory in 1767 (HKA. red. No. 892 f. 437)

		1786						1787						1788						1789					
B	Total	8/4	7/4	S	L	B	Total	8/4	7/4	S	L	B	Total	8/4	7/4	S	L	B	Total	8/4	7/4	S	L	B	Total
		1	12	1	5		19					5	5												
	11	1			13	3	17	2			19		21	3	2		44	10	59	6					6
4	10		2			4	6	1			4		5												
	12					14	14																		
	77				16		16																		
															2		12	10	24						
											10		10			1		4	5						
	50	2	24		135	11	172	8	30		32	6	76	6	3		61	14	84		12		26	22	60
4	14					16	16					54	54					54	54						
1	67	9	19	48	32	107	215																		
	17				4		4								7		5	5	17						
														8		1		2	11	7		8	10	1	26
									10				10												
	25													11	4	5			20						
	6				2		2																		
	38																								
	16	12		5	14		31	13		7	10	8	28	6	2		1	5	14						
	30																								
														3		2	4		9						
								4	2		4	2	12												
1	44																	1	1						
10	10				12		12																		
	47	4		2	52		58	2			117		119												
									12		12		24	10		1	13	15	39				9		9
								8					8												
	50										120		120				4		4						
					15		15				13		13												
									2				2												
	2	8	7		7		22																		
														11			6		17	1					1
		14		4			18							1	3		6	14	24						
	4	1			22		23				1		1												
														2	3			2	17	6			1		7
											2		2												
	12			1	18	6	25	1	4	3	32	4	44	7	5	2	51		65	1		1	1		3
															2		11		13				6		6
														2	8		21	5	36						
												30	30											8	8
		2	4		22		28																		
			6		3		9	2	1		6		9					1	1						

	1777/8						1778/9						1779/80							
	8/4	7/4	S	L	B	Total	8/4	7/4	S	L	B	Total	8/4	7/4	S	L	B	Total	8/4	7/4
Ambassador of Morocco in Vienna																				
Army													5	2				7		
Amstetten																				
Banská Bystrica (Neusohl)																				
Banská Štiavnica (Schemnitz)																				3
Bjelovar (Belowar)																				
Bolzano (Botzen)																30		30		
Bratislava	8	7	2	0	28	45	3	4	0	0	3	10								
Břeclav (Lundenburg)																				
Breschon																				
Brescia (Breschia)																				
Brno (Brünn)	5	4	0	7	11	27	24	40	1	16	32	113	30	60	1	8	27	126	3	21
Brody																				29
Bucharest																				
Budapest (Ofen, Pest, Altofen)		16				16		8				8							10	
Cherson																				
Cluj (Clausenburg)																				
Comorn														1				1		
Cracow (Krakau)																				
Croatia																				
Debreczin																				
Dobromit																				
Egedin																				
Constantinople										20		20							2	
Dachau																				
Eger (Erlau)	7					7														
Frankfurt a/M																				
Florence	4			10	6	20	7			18		25	1	1				2		
Galicia																				
Gelnica (Göllnitz)																				
Graz		14			13	27		2		1	8	11		1			14	15	1	7
Grodzisk (Graetz)																				
Grosenged																				
Guenns	7	7			4	18														
Györ (Raab)																				
Gorizia (Görz)					22	22					18	18					18	18		
Hall														4				4		
Hamburg																				
Hessen-Cassel																				
Jihlava (Iglau)																				
Innsbruck																				
Karlovac (Carlstadt)																				

The abbreviations are as follows: 8/4 = 8/4 ell width (i.e. 2 ells wide) 7/4 = 7/4 ell width. S = Summer cloth. L = *Londrin*

	1777/8						1778/9						1779/80						1780/81					
	8/4	7/4	S	L	B	Total	8/4	7/4	S	L	B	Total	8/4	7/4	S	L	B	Total	8/4	7/4	S	L	B	Total
Klagenfurth	6	20	4		7	37	1				12	13	2	6			56	64					8	8
Košice (Caschau)							3				1	4												
Kroměříž (Kremsier)					5	5	9	21	1	14	8	53	9	9		2	1	21	2	4				6
Leningrad (St Petersburg)																								
Leipzig																								
Levant																								
Levoča (Leutschau)																								
Linz	5	7				12					5	5												
Ljubljana (Laibach)																								
Lublin																								
Lvov (Lemberg)																								
Mahrburg (Hungary)																								
Miasteczko (Georgenberg)																								
Milano																								
Miskolc (Mischolz)	14					14																		
Moscow																								
Novi Sad (Neusatz)																								
Nový Jičín (Neutitschein)													1	3		1		5						
Olomouc (Olmütz)	7	5				12	20	4	2	5	10	41	19		7	26	3	55	13	3	12	21	13	62
Oppava (Troppau)	2					2	1					1	12				2	14	4				9	13
Pecs (Fünfkirchen)																								
Podjone																								
Poland																								
Poznan (Posen)																								
Prague	3					3	7				2	9	10					10						
Prešov (Eperies)																								
Regensburg																								
Salonika																								
St Pölten																								
St Veith		4				4		6				6												
Sibiu (Hermannstadt)																								
Sopron (Ödenburg)																								
Stanislav (Stanislau)																								
Stein b. Krems																								
Šternberk (Sternberg)													3	6			6	15						
Strischof																								
Szekesfehérvár (Stuhlweisenburg)																								
Szetzeschin																								
Szomolnok (Schmolnitz)																								
Tallin (Reval)																								
Tambor																								
Tarnów																								

	1783						1784						1785			
	8/4	7/4	S	L	B	Total	8/4	7/4	S	L	B	Total	8/4	7/4	S	L
Klagenfurth					20	20					30	30				
Košice (Caschau)							8	1		5		14	10	1		
Kroměříž (Kremsier)		3		4	1	8				2		2	2	1		3
Leningrad (St Petersburg)							11			74	66	151	12			
Leipzig					92	92										
Levant										252		252				77
Levoča (Leutschau)																
Linz		1		3	19	23		2		2	11	15				
Ljubljana (Laibach)													13	5		32
Lublin				16	16	32					11	11				
Lvov (Lemberg)		23			83	106			14		114	128	6	14		16
Mahrburg (Hungary)																17
Miasteczko (Georgenberg)																
Milano																
Miskolc (Mischolz)																
Moscow																25
Novi Sad (Neusatz)																6
Nový Jičín (Neutitschein)																38
Olomouc (Olmütz)	3		9	27	2	41	13	4	4	33	13	67	2			14
Oppava (Troppau)	4				3	7	1				25	26		5		22
Pecs (Fünfkirchen)																
Podjone																
Poland		28				28		5		3		8	8	3	2	20
Poznan (Posen)		19				19										
Prague		1		10	12	23	3			65		68				47
Prešov (Eperies)																
Regensburg																
Salonika																50
St Pölten																
St Veith		1	2			3										
Sibiu (Hermannstadt)	2	3		6	14	25	4	1			15	20	2			
Sopron (Ödenburg)																
Stanislav (Stanislau)																
Stein b. Krems			4			4				3		3	1		3	
Šternberk (Sternberg)																
Strischof																
Szekesfehérvár (Stuhlweisenburg)																12
Szetzeschin																
Szomolnok (Schmolnitz)																
Tallin (Reval)																
Tambor																
Tarnów																

Appendix B

SALES BY TYPE AND PLACE, 1777–1789

1780/81			1783						1784						1785						1786						1787						1788						1789					
L	B	Total	8/4	7/4	S	L	B	Total	8/4	7/4	S	L	B	Total	8/4	7/4	S	L	B	Total	8/4	7/4	S	L	B	Total	8/4	7/4	S	L	B	Total	8/4	7/4	S	L	B	Total	8/4	7/4	S	L	B	Total
						17		17										3		3																								
																														7		7												
										3		3	1	7	3			3	1	7														4		18	1	23						
	3	6				4		4										5		5																								
																											12			1		13							2					2
35		35				54		54										14		14																9		9		4		7		11
8		8	5			169	32	206	20			211	18	249		6		65	25	96	8	4		180	6	198	52	17	37	191	3	300	14	25		182	3	224	9			2		11
																												2		18		20		5				5						
																														7	3	10					8	8						
																																		9	2	21	1	33						
10	20	54	21	4	7	22	2	56	3	2			12	17	1					1	8	2		9	16	35	13	1		15	16	45												
	13	42		23	2			25							3	20			15	38		2			12	14	7	2			59	68	2	9		4	67	82						
																		29	1	30			2			2																		
		10				36	8	44	8	12	11	90	14	135	28	18		125	11	192	40	8	1	102	29	160	21	4		84	11	120	33	16	20	161	25	255						
			60		14			74	33				31	64				3		3																								
																																				24	2	26						
						24		24																													5	5						
						6	23	29		7		2	17	26																														
															2	5		20		27																								
																					1	3				4							5					5						
																											1	4		12		17												
										7				7		7				7																								
351		353				583		583				724		724				1192		1192				740		740										24	2	26						
						4		4																																				
															31					31	21		6			27	4		10			14	37	4	6	45		92	6	2		15		23
																									2	2																		
6		6																																										
																		4		4										120		120					4	4						
																																		5				5						
8	16	32		23			15	38	10			14	8	32		3			10	13	9	15		89	40	153	1	18	2	70	17	108	5	12	10	69	7	103				9		9
																10		17	4	31				6		6																		
																																	14	2		6	36	56	11				13	24
																		20		20				4		4							11		1	4	2	18	9			2		11
	18	18					11	11																																				
				9				9		4	3	18	7	32																6		6												
			1		1		6	8					7	7											5	5																		
							2	2					6	6																													2	2
											4	10		14	5	3		19		27	1			1		2	6	1	1	14		22	3	14	16		7	40						
					5		2	7																																				
																						6			8	14	24			6		30		4				4		4				4

Seconds

B = Berg-op-Zoom

Appendix C

CALCULATIONS OF PRODUCTION COSTS

Calculation of Production Costs for 3 Pieces of Fine-Cloth, Fashion-Colour, Manufactured in the Imperial Royal Fine-Cloth Factory in Brno by the Factory Master Delimont.

	No. 3	No. 4	No. 11
width	8/4	8/4	8/4 Ell (Vienna)
length	25	25	25 Ell (Vienna)

Raw Wool per Piece 34 lb. Spanish Wool	fl.	kr.	fl.	kr.	fl.	kr.
	60	38	60	38	49	48½
Wool washing		10		10		10
Dyeing	9	30	2	50	6	—
Picking and Opening	1	12	1	12	1	12
Oil		54		54		54
Warp spinning	4	55½	4	35	4	40½
Weft spinning	5	2½	5	1½	4	39
Spooling warp		24		24		24
Sizing for the warp, 2½#		45½		45½		38¼
Spooling weft		22½		22½		22½
Weaving	6	—	6	—	6	—
Napping of unfinished cloth		37½		37½		37½
Examination and correcting		7		7		7
Fulling		54		54		54
Soap for fulling		50		50		50
Roughing	1	48	1	48	1	48
Shearing	3	—	3	—	3	—
Napping of Cloth		30		30		30
Napping Expenses		12		12		12
Salary Account	6	55	6	55	6	55
Pressing		40		40		40
Total	105	54½	98	53	90	49½
One Ell (Vienna) comes to	4	14⅛	3	57⅓	3	38

Source: HKA, red no. 891, f. 763, ad 35/1765.

Bibliography

I. ARCHIVAL SOURCES

Archiv zemského hlavního města Brna. Pozůstalosti. (Provincial archives of Brno. Inheritances.)

Haus-, Hof-und Staatsarchiv, Familien Archiv, Poschakten, Jüngere Series, 36 Cartons.

Hofkammerarchiv. Altes Commerz, fasc. 1, red no. 1; fasc. 2, red no. 2; fasc. 3, red no. 3; fasc. 38, red no. 26; Böhm. Commerz, fasc. 9, red no. 742; fasc. 49, red no. 789; fasc. 53, red no. 794; fasc. 54, red no. 796; fasc. 61, red no. 816; fasc. 71, red no. 836, 837; fasc. 98/1, red no. 881, 882; fasc. 100, red no. 890; fasc. 101/1, red no. 891; fasc. 101/2, red nos. 892, 893, 894; Handschriften, red no. 130, 'Iglauer Untersuchungs- Commissions Bericht . . .' 13 Aug. 1772; Inner-österreich, fasc. 105/2, red no. 442; Niederösterrich, fasc. 1, red no. 40; fasc. 21, red no. 73; fasc. 54, red no. 116; fasc. 63/1, red no. 134; Kommerz Kommission, fasc. 8, red no. 1053.

Státní archiv v Brně. (State Archives in Brno.) C/12/40; C/12/45; KK P 1764; KK F-5-1769; M 2110, M2047–50, M 2052, M 2053, M 2055, M 2058, M 2060; Zemský soud civiliní Brno. (Provincial civil court of Brno.)

Státní ustředny archiv. (Central State Archives in Prague.) CG, Elenchen; CG, 1731–54; 1755–72; SM C-66-1; ČDKM v Pardubice (also under 'Pardubitzer Akten').

Allgemeines Verwaltungsarchiv, Adelsarchiv; Hofkanzlei IV o 5.

II. SECONDARY SOURCES

Anonymous. *Die hundertjährige Geschichte der Ersten Brünner Maschinen-Fabriks-Gessellschaft.* Leipzig, 1921.

Anonymous. *Bericht der Handels-und Gewerbekammer in Brünn über die gewerbs-und handelsstatistischen Verhältnisse ihres Bezirkes im Jahre 1851.* Brünn, 1854.

Barkhausen, Ernst. *Die Tuchindustrie in Montjoie, Aufstieg und Niedergang.* Aachen, 1925.

Barkhausen, Max. 'Staatliche Wirtschaftslenkung und freies Unternehmertum im westdeutschen und im nord-und südniederländischen Raum bei der Entstehung der neuzeitlichen Industrie im 18. Jahrhundert', *Vierteljahrschrift für Sozial- und Wirtschaftsgeschichte,* XLV (1958), 168–241.

Barkhausen, Max. 'Verviers: Die Entstehung einer neuzeitlichen Industriestadt im 17. und 18. Jahrhundert', *Vierteljahrschrift für Sozial- und Wirtschaftsgeschichte,* XLVIII (1960), 363–75.

Beer, Adolf. 'Die österreichische Handelspolitik unter Maria Theresia und Joseph II', *Archiv für österreichische Geschichte,* LXXXVI (1898), 1–202.

Beer, Adolf. 'Studien zur Geschichte der österreichischen Volkswirtschaft unter Maria Theresia, I. Die österreichische Industriepolitik', *Archiv für österreichische Geschichtsforschung,* LXXXI (1894).

Beer, Adolf. 'Die Zollpolitik und die Schaffung eines einheitlichen Zollgebietes unter Maria Theresia', *Mitteilungen des Instituts für österreichische Geschichtsforschung*, XIV (1893), 237–326.

Benedikt, Heinrich. *Alexander von Schoeller 1805–1886*. Wien, 1958.

Bidermann, H. J. 'Die Wiener Stadtbank', *Archiv für österreichische Geschichte*, XX (1859), 343–443.

Brentano, Lujo. 'Über den grundherrlichen Charakter des hausindustriellen Leinengewerbes in Schlesien', *Zeitschrift für Sozial- und Wirtschaftsgeschichte*, I (1893), 318–40.

Bretholz, Bertold. *Brünn, Geschichte und Kultur*. Brünn, 1938.

Brusatti, Alois. 'Die Stellung der herrschaftlichen Beamten in Österreich in der Zeit von 1780 bis 1848', *Vierteljahrschrift für Sozial- und Wirtshaftsgeschichte*, XLV (1958), 505–16.

Burian, Vladimir, 'První moravský merkantilista Pavel Hynek Morgentaller' (The first Moravian Mercantilist, Pavel Hynek Morgenthaler), *Brno v minulosti a dnes* (Brno in the Past and Today), III (1962), 72–92.

Cameron, Rondo. *Banking in the Early Stages of the Industrial Revolution*. New York, 1967.

Cameron, Rondo., ed. *Banking and Economic Development*. New York, 1972.

Chylík, Jindřich, 'První obchodní banka u nás' (The First Mercantile Bank in Our Area), *Časopis Matice Moravské*, LXIX (1950), 261–82.

Codex Austriacus, Vol. VI. Wien, 1777.

Courtecuisse, Maximilien. *La manufacture de draps fins Vanrobais aux XVIIe et XVIIIe siècles*. Paris, 1920.

Dinklage, Karl. 'Klagenfurts industrielle Entwicklung', in Gotbert Moro, ed., *Die Landeshauptstadt Klagenfurt*. Klagenfurt, 1970.

Dosoudil, J. 'Die Brünner Bürgeraufnahmen 1559–1845', *Zeitschrift des deutschen Vereines für Geschichte Mährens und Schlesiens*, XXXI–XXXIX (1929–37) (rendered in dispersed form).

Dřímal, J. and Václav Peš. *Dějiny města Brna*. (History of the City of Brno.) Brno, 1968.

Dullinger, Josef. 'Die Handelskompagnien Oesterreichs nach dem Oriente und nach Ostindien in der ersten Hälfte des 18. Jahrunderts', *Zeitschrift für Sozial- und Wirtschaftsgeschichte*, VII (1900), 44–83.

Elvert, Christian d'. *Beiträge zur Geschichte der k. Städte Mährens, insbesondere der k. Landeshauptstadt Brünn*. Brünn, 1860.

Elvert, Christian d'. *Geschichte und Beschreibung der (königlichen Kreis- und) Bergstadt Iglau in Mähren*. Brünn, 1850.

Elvert, Christian d'. *Die Culturfortschritte Mährens und Oesterreichisch-Schlesiens, besonders im Landbaue und in der Industrie, während der letzten hundert Jahre*. Brünn, 1854.

Elvert, Christian d'. *Zur Cultur-Geschichte Mährens und österreichisch Schlesiens*. 2 Vols. Brünn, 1868, 1870.

Elvert, Christian d'. *Zur österreichischen Finanzgeschichte mit besonderer Rücksicht auf die böhmischen Länder*. Brünn, 1886.

Endrei, Walter. *L'évolution des techniques du filage et du tissage du moyen age a la revolution industrielle*. Paris, 1968.

English, W. *The Textile Industry*. London and Harlow, 1969.

Erceg, Ivan. 'Der Merkantilismus in Kroatien', *Österreichische Osthefte*, VIII (1966), 300–8.

Fechner, Hermann. *Die handelspolitischen Beziehungen Preussens zu Österreich*. Berlin, 1886.

Fischel, Alfred. 'Zur Finanzgeschichte Mährens. Reformvorschläge unter Kaiser Leopold I', *Zeitschrift des deutschen Vereines für Geschichte Mährens und Schlesiens*, XXV (1923), 44–77.

Fisher, F. J. 'The Development of London as a Centre of Conspicuous Consumption in the 16th and 17th centuries', *Royal Historical Society Transactions*, 4th series, XXX (1948), 37–50.

Fojtík, Karel. 'Tři typy dělnických obydlí v Brně' (Three types of workers' quarters in Brno). *Brno v minulosti a dnes* (Brno in the past and today), I (1959), 23–40.

Fournier, August. 'Eine amtliche Handlungsreise nach Italien im Jahre 1754. Ein neuer Beitrag zur Geschichte der österreichischen Commercialpolitik', *Archiv für österreichische Geschichte*, LXXIII (1888), 223–74.

Fournier, August. 'Handel und Verkehr in Ungarn und Polen um die Mitte des 18. Jahrhunderts', *Archiv für österreichische Geschichte*, LXIX (1-87), 318–481.

Freudenberger, Herman. 'Das Arbeitsjahr' in Ingomar Bog et al. eds., *Wirtschaftliche und soziale Strukturen im säkularen Wandel*. Hanover, 1974. 307–20.

Freudenberger, Herman. 'An Exploration in Entrepreneurial Motivation and Action.' *Explorations in Economic History*, VII (1970), 433–49.

Freudenberger, Herman. 'On the Genesis of Modern Management', *Technology and Culture*, X (1969), 593–602.

Freudenberger, Herman. 'Progressive Bohemian and Moravian Aristocrats', in Stanley B. Winters and Joseph Held, eds, *Intellectual and Social Developments in the Habsburg Empire from Maria Theresia to World War I* (New York and London, 1975), 115–30.

Freudenberger, Herman. 'Three Mercantilistic Proto-Factories', *Business History Review*, XL (1966), 167–89.

Freudenberger, Herman. *The Waldstein Woollen Mill: Noble Entrepreneurship in Eighteenth Century Bohemia*. Boston, 1963.

Freudenberger, Herman and Fritz Redlich. 'The Industrial Development of Europe: Reality, Symbols, Images', *Kyklos*, XVII (1964), 372–403.

Gerstenberg, Heinrich. 'Philipp Wilhelm von Hörnigk', *Jahrbücher für Nationalokonomie und Statistik*, CXXXIII (1930), 813–71.

Gilboy, E. W. 'Demand as a Factor in the Industrial Revolution', in *Facts and Factors in Economic History*. Essays presented to E. F. Gay. Cambridge, Massachusetts, 1932.

Grossmann, Henryk. 'Die Anfänge und geschichtliche Entwicklung der amtlichen Statistik in Österreich', *Statistische Monatschrift*. N.F., XXI (1916), 331–426.

Hainisch, Michael. 'Das österreichische Tabakmonopol im 18. Jahrhundert', *Vierteljahrschrift für Sozial- und Wirtschaftsgeschichte*, VIII (1910), 394–444.

Hallwich, Hermann. *Die erste Fabrik in Reichenberg*. Reichenberg, 1869.

Halm, Hans. *Habsburgischer Osthandel im 18. Jahrhundert*. München, 1954.

Handlungseinverständniss zwischen dem kais. königl. Hofe und der ottomanischen Pforte . . . 24. Hornung 1784. Wien, 1785.

Hassinger, Herbert. 'Die erste Wiener orientalische Handelskompagnie 1667–1683', *Vierteljahrschrift für Sozial- und Wirtschaftsgeschichte*, XXXV (1942), 1–53.

Hassinger, Herbert. *Johann Joachim Becher 1635–1682*. Veröffentlichungen der Kommission für Neuere Geschichte Österreichs, Vol. XXXVIII. Wien, 1951.

Heckscher, Eli. *The Continental System*. Oxford, 1922.

Hermann, Franz Benedikt. *Herrn Johann von Hornek's Bemerkungen über österreichische Staatsökonomie*. St Petersburg, 1784.

Herzfeld, Marianne von. 'Zur Orienthandelspolitik Österreichs unter Maria Theresia', *Archiv für österreichische Geschichte*, CVIII (1917), 216–341.

Hinrichs, Carl. *Die Wollenindustrie unter Friedrich Wilhelm I*. Berlin, 1933.

Hintze, Otto. 'Ein Berliner Kaufmann aus der Zeit Friedrichs des Grossen', *Historische und politische Aufsätze*. Berlin, 1893.

Hintze, Otto. 'Der österreichische und der preussische Beamtenstaat im 17. und 18. Jahrhundert', *Staat und Verfassung*. Göttingen, 1962.

Hinze, Kurt. *Die Arbeiterfrage zu Beginn des modernen Kapitalismus in Brandenberg-Preussen*. Berlin-Dahlem, 1927.

Hoffmann, Alfred. *Wirtschaftsgeschichte des Landes Oberösterreich*. Salzburg, 1952.

Hofmann, Viktor. 'Beiträge zur neueren österreichischen Wirtschaftsgeschichte. Erster Teil. Die Wollenzeugfabrik zu Linz an der Donau', *Archiv für österreichische Geschichte*, CVIII (1920), 345–778.

Hönig, Fritz. 'Schröders Bankprojekt', *Zeitschrift für Volkswirtschaft und Sozialpolitik*, II (1893), 489–533.

Hörnigk, P. W. von. *Österreich über alles, wann es nur will*. Leipzig, 1707.

Hübel, Ignaz. 'Die Einführung der Merinozucht in den Sudetenländern', *Zeitschrift des deutschen Vereines für Geschichte Mährens und Schlesiens*, XL (1938), 105–19.

Huber, Alfons and Alfons Dopsch, *Österreichische Reichsgeschichte*. Wien, 1901.

Jakobovits, Tobias. 'Jüdisches Gemeindeleben in Kolin (1763–1768)', *Jahrbuch der Gesellschaft für Geschichte der Juden in der čechoslov. Republik*, I (1929), 332–68.

Janáček, J. 'Westerholdovská zahrada' (Westerhold's gardens), *Časopis Společnosti Přatel Starožinosti* (Journal of the Society of Friends of Antiquity), LXII (1954).

Joza, Jaroslav. *Z minulosti textilniho prumyslu v libereckem kraji* (From the history of the textile industry in the district of Liberec). Liberec, 1958.

Justi, Johann Heinrich Gottlob von. *Abhandlungen von den Manufakturen und Fabriken*. 2 vols. Berlin, 1780.

Justi, Johann Heinrich Gottlob von. *Staatswirtschaft oder systematische Abhandlung aller Oekonomischen- und Cameralwissenschaften die zur Regierung eines Landes erfordert sind*. 2 vols. Leipzig, 1758.

Justi, Johann Heinrich Gottlob von. *Vollständige Abhandlung von denen Manufacturen und Fabriken*. 2 vols. Koppenhagen, 1758.

Kallbrunner, Josef. *Kaiserin Maria Theresia Politisches Testament*. Wien, 1952.

Keess, Stephan von. *Darstellung des Fabriks- und Gewerbewesens im österreichischen Kaisterstaate*. 3 vols. Wien, 1819.

Kisch, Herbert. 'Das Erbe des Mittelalters, ein Hemniss wirtschaftlicher Entwicklung: Aachens Tuchgewerbe vor 1790', *Rheinische Vierteljahrsblätter*, XXX (1965), 253–308.

Klíma, Arnošt. *Manufakturní období v Čechách* (The Manufactory Period in Bohemia). Praha, 1955.

Kopetz, Gustav W. *Allgemeine österreichische Gewerbs-Gesetz Kunde*. 2 vols. Wien, 1829, 1830.

Král von Dobra Voda, Adalbert Ritter von. *Der Adel von Böhmen, Mähren und Schlesien*. Prag, 1904.

Kraus-Elislago, Anton von. *Autobiographie*. Wien, 1849.

Krüger, Horst. *Zur Geschichte der Manufakturen und Manufakturarbeiter*. Berlin, 1958.

Koulischer, Joseph. 'La grande industrie aux XVIIe et XVIIIe siècles: France Allemagne, Russie', *Annales d'Histoire Economique et Sociale*, III (1931), 11–46.

Landes, David. *The Unbound Prometheus*. Cambridge, 1969.

Lebrun, Pierre. *L'industrie de la laine à Verviers*. Paris, 1948.

Lemon, Hugo. 'The Development of Hand Spinning Wheels', *Textile History*. 1/2 (1968), 83–91.

Licht, Stefan. *Die österreichische Schafwollwaaren-Industrie in Die Grossindustrie Oesterreichs*. Vol. IV. Wien, 1898.

Mann, Julia de L. *The Cloth Industry in the West of England from 1640 to 1880*. London, 1971.

Marek, Ferdinand and Alfred Oberländer. *Festschrift der Handels- und Gewerbekammer in Brünn*. Brünn, 1909.

Mainuš, František. *Vlnařství a bavlnařství na Moravě a ve Slezsku v XVIII. století* (The woollen and cotton industries in Moravia and Silesia in the 18th century). Brno, 1960.

Matis, Herbert. *Die Manufaktur und frühe Fabrik im Viertel unter dem Wiener Wald*. Unpublished Ph.D. Dissertation, University of Vienna, 1964.

Mayer, Franz Martin. *Die Anfänge des Handels und der Industrie in Österreich und die orientalische Companie*. Innsbruck, 1882.

Mayer, Franz Martin. 'Zur Geschichte der österreichischen Handelspolitik unter Kaiser Karl VI', *Mitteilungen des Instituts für österreichische Geschichte*. XVIII (1882), 129–45.

Meister, Oskar. 'Johann Leopold von Köffiller und die Anfäge der Brünner Tuchindustrie', *Zeitschrift des deutschen Vereines für Geschichte Mährens und Schlesiens*. XX (1916), 57–86.

Meister, Oskar. 'Mährische Beiträge zur Geschichte der österreichischen Gewerbepolitik zwischen 1701 und 1833', *Zeitschrift des deutschen Vereines für Geschichte Mährens und Schlesiens*, XVIII (1914), 278–96.

Mensi, Franz v. *Die Finanzen Oesterreichs von 1701 bis 1740*. Wien, 1890.

Migerka, F. *Rückblicke auf die Schafwollwaaren-Industrie Brünns von 1765–1864*. Brünn, 1890.

Mikoletzky, Hanns Leo. 'Franz Stephan von Lothringen als Wirtschaftspolitiker', *Mitteilungen des österreichischen Staatsarchivs*, XIII (1960), 231–57.

Mikoletzky, Hanns Leo. *Franz I Stephan und der Ursprung des Habsburgisch-Lothringischen Familienvermögens*. Wien, 1962.

Mikoletzky, Hanns Leo. 'Holics und Sassin, die beiden Mustergüter des Kaisers Franz I. Stephan', *Mitteilungen des österreichischen Staatsarchivs*, XIV (1961), 190–212.

Mises, Ludwig von. 'Zur Geschichte der österreichischen Fabrikgesetzgebung', *Zeitschrift für Volkswirtschaft, Sozialpolitik und Verwaltung*, XIV (1905), 209–71.

Mitrofanov, Paul von. *Joseph II*. trans. from Russian by V. von Demelic. Wien and Leipzig, 1910.

Nožička, Josef. 'K hospodářske politice Brna koncem 17. stoleti' (On the economic policies of Brno at the end of the 17th century). *Brno v minulosti a dnes* (Brno in the past and today), II (1961), 170–9.
Oberländer, Alfred. *Festschrift des Vereines der Woolindustriellen Mährens in Brünn.* Brünn, 1908.
Oberländer, Alfred. K.K. Priv. *Militär- und Feintuch-Fabrik in Brünn 1786–1911.* Brünn, 1912.
Paudler, A. *Graf Joseph Kinsky.* Leipa, 1885.
Piettre, André. *Économie Dirigée d'Hier et d'Aujourdhui.* Paris, 1947.
Platière, Roland de la. *Encyclopédie Méthodique, Manufactures, Arts et Métiers.* Paris and Liège, 1785.
Pollard, Sidney. *The Genesis of Modern Management.* Cambridge, Massachusetts, 1965.
Pribram, Alfred Francis. *Das böhmische Commerzcollegium und seine Tätigkeit.* Prag, 1898.
Pribram, Alfred Francis. *Urkunden und Akten zur Geschichte der Juden in Wien.* 2 vols. Wien and Leipzig, 1918.
Pribram, Karl. 'Die Einführung der Schutzdekrete unter Karl VI. in Wien', *Schmollers Jahrbuch*, XXX (1906), 883–910.
Pribram, Karl. *Geschichte der österreichischen Gewerbepolitik von 1740 bis 1860.* Leipzig, 1907.
Ranke, Leopold von. 'Aus den Papieren des Grosskanzler Fürst. Maria Theresia, ihr Staat und ihr Hof in Jahre 1755', *Historisch-politische Zeitschrift*, II (1833–6), 677–740.
Redlich, Fritz. *Der Unternehmer.* Göttingen, 1964.
Riegger, Joseph von., ed. *Archiv der Geschichte und Statistik von Böhmen.* Dresden, 1792–4.
Rizzi, Hans. 'Das österreichische Gewerbe im Zeitalter des Merkantilismus', *Zeitschrift für Volkswirtschaft, Socialpolitik und Verwaltung*, XII (1903), 71–101.
Rosenberg, Nathan. *Technology and American Economic Growth.* New York, 1972.
Ruby, Franz. *Das Iglauer Handwerk.* Brünn, 1887.
Schachermayr, August. 'Die Pläne Christian Julius v. Schierendorffs über die Einrichtung des Handels und die Anlage von Handelsstrassen in Schlesien', *Zeitschrift für Geschichte und Kulturgeschichte Österreichisch-Schlesiens*, III, 1–11.
Schaller, Jaroslaus. *Topographie des Königreichs Böhmen.* 16 vols. Prag and Wien, 1785–91.
Scheibler, W. 'Die Auswanderungen aus Monschau nach dem Osten im 19. Jahrhundert', in *Nordrhein-Westfalen und der deutsche Osten.* Dortmund, 1962.
Schneider, Simon. *Brünn und seine Denkwürdigkeiten.* Brünn, 1831.
Schramm, Wilhelm. 'Mähren unter Karl VI', *Oesterreichisch-Ungarische Revue* (1889).
Schumpeter, J. A. *History of Economic Analysis.* New York, 1953.
Schünemann, Konrad. *Österreichische Bevölkerungspolitik unter Maria Theresia.* Berlin, 1935.
Schümann, Konrad. 'Die Wirtschaftspolitik Josephs II. in der Zeit seiner Mitregentenschaft', *Mitteilungen des Instituts für österreichische Geschichtsforschung.* XLVII (1933), 13–56.

Scoville, Warren C. 'Minority Migration and the Diffusion of Technology', *Journal of Economic History*, XI (1951), 347–60.

Šebánek, Jindřich. 'Textilní podniky moravských Kouniců' (The textile enterprises of the Moravian Kaunitzes). *Časopis Matice Moravské*, LX (1931), 95–168, 418–68; LVI (1932), 101–80.

Šindelář, Bedřich. 'K nejstarším pokusům se stroji v brněnskych textilnich manufakturách na přelomu 18. a 19. století' (To the oldest efforts to introduce machinery in the Brno textile industry at the turn of the 18th and 19th centuries). *Časopis Matice Moravské*, LXXVI (1957), 73–93.

Šindelář, Bedřich. 'O západoevropských odbornících v některych textilních manufakturách na Moravě koncem 18. století' (About west European specialists in several textile manufactories in Moravia at the end of the 18th century). *Časopis Matice Moravské*, LXXVII (1958), 54–74.

Slokar, Johann. *Geschichte der österreichischen Industrie und ihrer Förderung unter Kaiser Franz I.* Wien, 1914.

Smelser, Neil S. *Social Change in the Industrial Revolution.* Chicago, 1959.

Šmída, J. 'Brněnske textilní cechy v první třetiné 18. století' (Brno textile guilds in the first third of the 18th century). *Časopis Matice Moravské*, LVIII (1934), 287–94.

Sommer, J. G. *Das Königreich Böhmen.* 14 vols. Prag, 1841–3.

Sommer, Louise. *Die österreichischen Kameralisten.* 2 vols. Wien, 1920, 1925.

Sonnenfels, Joseph von. *Grundsätze der Polizey, Handlung, und Finanzwissenschaft.* 3 vols. Wien, 1770–2.

Sonnenfels, Joseph von. *Von der Theuerung in den grossen Städten und dem Mittel derselben abzuhelfen.* Wien, 1770.

Špiesz, Anton. 'Die Manufaktur im östlichen Europa', *Kölner Vorträge zur Sozial- und Wirtschaftsgeschichte*, Heft 2. Köln, 1969.

Špiesz, Anton. *Manufakturne obdobie na Slovensku 1725–1825* (The Manufactory Period in Slovakia 1725–1825). Bratislava, 1961.

Špiesz, Anton. 'Die orthodoxen Handelsleute aus dem Balkan in der Slowakei', *Balkan Studies*, IX (1968).

Srbik, Heinrich von. 'Abenteurer am Hofe Kaiser Leopold I', *Archiv für Kulturgeschichte*, VIII (1910), 52–72.

Stark, Werner. 'Die Abhänigkeitsverhältnisse der gutsherrlichen Bauern in Böhmen im 17. und 18. Jahrhundert', *Jahrbücher für Nationalökonomie und Statistik*, CLXIV (1952), 270–92, 348–74, 440–53.

Stark, Werner. 'Niedergang und Ende des Landwirtschaftlichen Grossbetriebs in den böhmischen Ländern', *Jahrbücher für Nationalökonomie und Statistik*, CXLVI (1937), 416–49.

Stein, Erwin, ed. *Die Städte Deutschösterreichs* Bd. IV, *Klagenfurt.* Berlin, 1929.

Stoianovich, Trojan. 'The Conquering Balkan Orthodox Merchants', *Journal of Economic History*, XX (1960), 234–313.

Šujan, František. *Dějepis Brna* (History of Brno). Brno, 1902.

Tarle, E. *L'industrie dans les campagnes en France a la fin de l'ancien regime.* Paris, 1910.

Taylor, George V. 'Notes on Commercial Travellers in 18th Century France', *Business History Review*, XXXVIII (1964).

Thienen-Adlerflycht, Christoph. *Graf Leo Thun im Vormärz.* Graz and Köln, 1967.

Trautenberger, Gustav G. *Aus der evangelischen Kirchengemeinde in Brünn.* Brünn, 1866.

Trautenberger, Gustav G. *Die Chronik der Landeshauptstadt Brühn.* 5 vols. Brünn, 1896.
Tschierschky, Siegfried. *Die Wirtschaftspolitik des schlesischen Kommerzkollegs 1716–1740.* Gotha, 1902.
Van Dillen, J. G., ed. *History of the Principal Public Banks.* New York, 1964.
Vauban, *Projet de dime royale*, ed. by E. Ceornaert. Paris, 1933.
Voldán, Vládimír. 'Ceste hofmistra Morgentallera jižní a západní Evropou' (Travels of Hofmeister Morgenthaler in southern and western Europe). *Brno v minulosti a dnes*, IX (1970), 104–15.
Volksbundverlag, *Das Vermögen der Habsburger.* Wien, 1929.
Vytiska, Josef. 'Brněska průmyslová oblast v první podovině 19. století' (The Brno industrial territory in the first half of the 19th century). *Brno v minulosti a dnes* (Brno in the Past and Today), v (1963), 313–89.
Wadsworth, A. P. and Julia de L. Mann. *The Cotton Trade and Industrial Lancashire 1600–1780.* Manchester, 1931.
Walter, Friedrich. 'Die ideellen Grundlagen der österreichischen Staatsreform von 1749', *Zeitschrift für öffentliches Recht*, XVII (1937).
Walter, Friedrich. *Die österreichische Zentralverwaltung.* II. Part, Vol. I, half-vol. I. Wien, 1938.
Wandruszka. 'Maria Theresia und der österreichische Staatsgedanke', *Mitteilungen des Institutes für österreichische Geschichtsforschung*, LXXVI (1968), 174–88.
Weber, Ottocar. 'Der Zolltarif für Böhmen vom Jahre 1737', *Mitteilungen für Geschichte der Deutschen in Böhmen*, XXXI (1892), 358–95.
Weinbrenner, Joseph von. *Patriotische Gedanken und Vorschläge über den gehemmten Ausfuhr-Handel.* Wien, 1792.
Welzl, Hans. 'Zur Geschichte der Juden in Brünn während des XVII. und XVIII. Jahrhunderts', *Zeitschrift des deutschen Vereins für Geschichte Mährens und Schlesiens*, VIII (1904).
Werner, Karl. *Urkundliche Geschichte der Iglauer Tuchmacher-Zunft.* Leipzig 1861.
Wilson, Charles. 'The Other Face of Mercantilism', *Royal Historical Society. Transactions.* Fifth Series. IX (1959), 81–101.
Wolny, Gregor. *Die Markgrafschaft Mähren.* 6 vols. Brünn, 1835–42.

INDEX